D0915706

Revealing Antiquity

· 11 ·

G. W. Bowersock, General Editor

POMPEII

Public and Private Life

PAUL ZANKER

Translated by Deborah Lucas Schneider

Harvard University Press
Cambridge, Massachusetts
London, England
1998

Copyright © 1998 by the President and Fellows of Harvard College
All rights reserved
Printed in the United States of America

Publication of this volume was assisted by a grant from Inter Nationes.

Originally published in German as *Pompeji: Stadtbild und Wohngeschmack* (1995).

Library of Congress Cataloging-in-Publication Data
Zanker, Paul.
[Pompeji. English]
Pompeii : public and private life / Paul Zanker ; translated by
Deborah Lucas Schneider.
p.   cm. – (Revealing antiquity ; 11)
Includes bibliographical references and index.
ISBN 0-674-68966-6 (cloth : alk. paper)
ISBN 0-674-68967-4 (pbk. : alk. paper)
1. Pompeii (Extinct city).
2. Cities and towns, Ancient—Rome.
3. City planning—Rome.
4. Politics and culture—Rome.
5. Pompeii (Extinct city)—Social life and customs.
I. Title.   II. Series.
DG70.P7Z3613   1998
937′.7—dc21
98-24720

Contents

Preface

Every author is pleased to be read, and so I hope readers will understand why I agreed to an English translation, although with some hesitation. My concern arose from the origins of this book—first published in 1993 in Italian, and later in German—as three separate essays written at different times between 1979 and 1993. Since 1979, however, Pompeii studies have undergone an astonishing renaissance, and more books and articles on Pompeii have appeared in the last ten years than in the previous two generations. Few areas of research exist in which international teamwork and cooperation among the various disciplines of classical studies have functioned so well. Thanks to the admirable volumes of the *Enciclopedia Italiana* entitled *Pompei: Pitture e Mosaici* and the series *Häuser in Pompeji* edited by V. M. Strocka, documentation of residential buildings in Pompeii has been substantially improved, although this applies mainly to their pictorial decoration. (At the same time, these houses have been decaying more rapidly since the earthquake of 1980, and valuable cultural artifacts are being lost forever. In view of the highly developed techniques for preservation that now exist, this situation is particularly deplorable.)

Current research at the site has acquired a new focus in contrast to earlier eras: little excavation of new buildings is under way; instead, archeologists are attempting to dig below the levels of A.D. 79, especially in residential buildings, to discover more about the history of these houses. They are looking not only at structural alterations to individual houses, but also to the development of whole architectural complexes or *insulae* (blocks). Their interest is clearly directed toward finding answers to social and economic questions.

New studies of how private and public space was used belong to the same general context. They range from new excavations and the laborious but rewarding reconstruction of the course of earlier digs (using notes and logs) to the development of new theories and analyses concerning the practical use of space and how inhabitants experienced the space in which they lived. Happily, these concerns reflect vital interests of our own time. This is particularly true of questions about different ways of forming living space, about the social and psychological implications of particular uses of space, and—in the larger context—the connections between the way in which a society is ordered and the way it orders space (see especially the works of Wallace-Hadrill, 1988–1994, Laurence, 1994, and Zaccaria Ruggiu, 1995). Researchers' emphasis on private living space as opposed to the public and political sphere also corresponds to a current trend (see Laurence and Wallace-Hadrill, 1997).

My own studies are devoted to only a small section of these larger concerns. It has been gratifying to see the questions I have pursued taken up in later studies and in some cases used as the basis for debate. Naturally, some of the conclusions I reached are in need of revision today. If I have nonetheless left the present essays largely in their original form—apart from the correction of obvious errors—it has been in order not to disrupt the logical coherence of the argument. The notes, however, have been thoroughly revised and brought up to date, so that they contain information on the most recent debates and new insights, as well as improved documentation.

On the whole my concept of four successive townscapes as reflections of a society and its outlook (originally published in 1988) and my reconstruction of certain features of late Pompeian domestic taste (1979) have stood the test of time. Significant revisions are needed, as far as I can determine, in two areas above all: the assessment of the state of the town—particularly the forum—at the time of the eruption that buried it (see chapter 2); and

Preface

my attempt to link domestic taste with shifts within Pompeian society after the earthquake of A.D. 62. I have added notes in the relevant passages to alert the reader to new developments in research on these points. The first chapter, written in 1993, sketches some new ideas on the topics covered in chapters 2 and 3.

In the German edition I expressed my gratitude to a number of people for their support and assistance. In addition to them, I would like to thank Felix Pirson for his help in revising the text and notes for this edition; of course I remain responsible for any errors. J. J. Dobbins, who is currently conducting a large project on the forum in Pompeii that is expected to produce important new results, has kindly kept me informed of his progress and contributed to the success of this book. I am grateful to Deborah Lucas Schneider for her commitment to the translation, and finally, I would like to express my special thanks to Kathleen M. Coleman, who read the English text and contributed valuable suggestions.

Note

Throughout, building locations are specified by region, *insula* (block), and building; thus VII 4.57 cites region VII, *insula* 4, building 57. Figure 2 shows the distribution of the regions and *insulae*.

CIL = *Corpus Inscriptionum Latinarum*

POMPEII

Townscape and
Domestic Taste

The city is a popular topic nowadays, in classical archeology as elsewhere. Nevertheless, it would be virtually impossible for an archeologist to write a history of Greek and Roman cities comprehensive and detailed enough to satisfy modern-day interests and answer the types of questions currently being asked. The reason is simple: we know too little about how ancient cities actually looked. This may seem an odd claim given the vast numbers of surviving ruins and excavations, but it is nonetheless true.

Of course we know of countless temples, theaters, baths, amphitheaters, basilicas, circuses, and squares; sometimes we can even recognize large parts of a city's network of streets. We can describe the development of certain architectural forms (an approach that has been followed almost to excess), and even say a little about their function in the lives of the people who used them (a subject of interest mostly to specialists).[1] Only in rare cases, however, are we able to analyze the overall organization of space in a city and see it in relation to the society that inhabited it, drawing connections between the use of space and residents' particular lives, habits, and needs.

The reasons for the rarity of such instances are connected with the history of archeology and the shifting interests of excavators and their public over time. As long as excavators were primarily searching for works of art and displayed little interest in anything other than particularly impressive and well-preserved examples of ancient architecture, it rarely occurred to them to ask the types of questions that interest us today. Systematic investigations of a town as a whole, or even selected precincts, were the exception even during the heyday of large-scale digs in the nineteenth and early twentieth centuries. And in those days archeology was not yet burdened by the caution and scrupulous methods that make excavation of such vast areas all but impossible today. Over the last several decades techniques have been refined to the point where teams of specialists are necessary if a project is to appear competent in the eyes of professional archeologists. Furthermore, exhaustive documentation is demanded, in publications that require time-consuming preparations and entail high costs. The lamentable result is that even important excavations go unreported for decades.

Classical archeology, a field not noted for its progressive techniques, has taken these standards so to heart that even limited projects involving excavation of small residential neighborhoods—such as the houses on the acropolis hill at Pergamum or the terrace houses at Ephesus—consume the energies of a whole generation. These difficulties are further increased by the enormous costs connected not only with the actual excavation work, but also with designing and laying out the sites as outdoor museums afterwards. Any site that could conceivably arouse the interest of the general public must nowadays be reconstructed and presented attractively to visitors. Artificial ruins are going up on all sides as a result.

Improving the woeful state of the sources—especially with regard to our knowledge of cities as a whole and residential neighborhoods in particular—will be a very slow process, even though excavators themselves have begun to give high priority to this task. Thus for the time being there is no alternative but to revisit familiar sites and ask new questions. Because the cities around Vesuvius were virtually sealed up when the volcano erupted, they are of central importance for this type of work. The two chapters that follow, one focusing on public buildings and the townscape, the other on Pompeians' tastes as they created their domestic environments, take this approach.

Townscapes

The next chapter is devoted to the "townscapes" of Pompeii, with emphasis on the public buildings. I use this concept to describe the outward appearance of a city in the most comprehensive sense, meaning not so much the architecture of single buildings as their function within the total context of public space.[2] The focus of the inquiry is thus not the relatively narrow field of architectural history, but rather the town as a concrete instance of inhabited space. Public buildings and their setting are then viewed as a kind of performance space, a stage created by a society to meet its own needs. The public buildings, squares, streets, and monuments, together with dwellings, cemeteries, and their decorative art, represent one key way in which the inhabitants could express who they were: the city as a combination of public stage and private living space.

Seen from this point of view, a townscape also represents the framework within which urban life takes place. It not only shapes the inhabitants but is shaped by them, for the buildings and spaces, having been constructed to embody certain messages and values, continue to communicate these same messages to succeeding generations.

Pompeii

At the time of its destruction in A.D. 79 Pompeii was already an old city and had been inhabited by many generations of people from different origins, each with its own uniquely structured society. If, as is usually the case, we look only at the townscape as it happened to be preserved in A.D. 79, then what meets the eye is just the last of a series of successive townscapes. In fact for the period between the early second century B.C., when wealthy Oscan patricians built their expensive houses in the cosmopolitan Hellenistic taste of the day, and the date Pompeii was buried by Mount Vesuvius, it is possible to identify four different concepts of urban organization that left their mark on the town. I believe these different townscapes can be reconstructed, at least in outline. I will do this by investigating the interests that lay behind each construction project and promoted its realization, and then analyzing how these interests interacted as political and social changes affected the city. From the conglomeration of the city preserved by chance in A.D. 79, the outlines of four distinct townscapes emerge, each corresponding to the larger world in which its inhabitants lived.

Pompeii was by no means an important urban center; it was only one of many medium-sized country towns in Italy. But fortunately the structures of its public space and the changes observable in them are characteristic of Italian cities and the western provinces of the late Roman Republic and early Empire. This has been demonstrated by comparison with archeological evidence from other cities, many of which also expanded beyond their walls in the first century B.C. Everywhere we find imposing funerary monuments lining the main roads outside city gates; we find the rich building sumptuous villas outside the city walls, and the cultural traditions of local peoples giving way to a new and unified Roman culture. Because Pompeii lies close to the cities of Campania that came under Hellenistic influence quite early, the elementary processes of acculturation, which so thoroughly altered Roman culture after the invasion of the Greek East by the Roman armies, can be followed even more closely in Pompeii than elsewhere. The reshaping of Pompeii's public spaces in the Augustan age has parallels in many other places as well. The cult of the emperor and homage paid to him left their stamp on its forum as they did in virtually all Roman cities in the western half of the Empire. In addition, theaters were renovated and enlarged in most towns, and urban elites everywhere made similar efforts to make their city more beautiful and improve its infrastructure.

It is their very typicality that makes the various stages of these developments in Pompeii deserving of careful attention and study. Despite the fact that Pompeii is by no means entirely excavated, no other ancient city furnishes us with a picture even remotely comparable in scope and detail. And, unlike most of the excavated Roman sites in North Africa and Asia Minor, Pompeii is particularly interesting because it spans the two periods that probably saw the most profound and sweeping changes in urban structures: the last years of the Republic, when cities were growing more uniform, and the early years of the Empire, when the establishment of the monarchy embedded new values in the townscape.

The developments discussed here using the specific example of Pompeii would thus be central to any broader discussion of how the Roman cityscape evolved. They would emerge with greater clarity if considerations of space allowed for comparison with the typical Greek city of the classical or Hellenistic era on the one hand, and the cities of the middle and late Roman Empire on the other. Although my focus here is much narrower, I would like to provide at least a rough outline of the larger historical framework surrounding the townscape as it will be reconstructed for Pompeii.

Public Space in the "Democratic" Greek City

If we compare the Greek townscapes of the classical era with their Roman counterparts, it is evident how much the former were shaped by the ideals of active citizenship and political equality (of full citizens). Nowhere in Greek cities—be it in the agora, the theater (where the assembly met), or the *bouleuterion* (where the council met)—do we find the markedly hierarchical structures so prevalent in the Romans' ordering of space. In Greek cities, the sites where citizens gathered to discuss and vote on political matters, to meet one another, and to worship local divinities were integrated into a single compact public space, which also included the educational institution, the gymnasium. The only important exceptions are the temples of the various religious mysteries (and later the Oriental gods), instances governed by the concerns and needs of certain private groups.

In the fourth century B.C. the idea of democratic equality carried over even into the design of the houses. When new cities were founded such as the small country town of Priene near Miletus, citizens were assigned plots of equal size, on which they built surprisingly similar houses. This did not correspond to actual equality of wealth by any means; it was a symbolic use of space, in which the private sphere was designed to reflect the public sphere and thus politicized in a certain sense. (The fact that such idealized designs were quickly undermined by the existing unequal distribution of wealth—meaning that the rich soon bought out their poorer neighbors to enlarge their dwellings—is a different matter.) The decision to create such a democratic appearance or symbolic use of space might even run counter to the actual political organization of the city in question: the political ideals of civic equality were transferred to other spheres of life as aesthetic forms, which continued to spread in the areas of taste and outlook even when the politics did not. But even apart from the specific considerations that gave rise to these democratic cityscapes, it remains significant for the citizens' view of themselves that for centuries, well into the days of the Empire, they continued to inhabit public spaces shaped by democratic ideals. Citizens held onto the traditional design of their cities in the same way that they preserved the old political rituals embodying their ancestors' ideals (out of nostalgia, of course). This did not change until the government of Rome became a monarchy, and, in accordance with the new norms emanating from the West, political power came to be expressed in the cult of the emperor in the East as well.[3]

The Structure of Roman Cities

Roman and romanized Italic cities reflect a political structure entirely different from that of the Greek cities, even during the Republican period. Here the great noble Roman families inhabited opulent houses near or directly abutting the Forum Romanum (as in Pompeii). The people dependent on their patronage, whose numbers directly reflected the family's prestige and power, assembled in their spacious atria. Influence spread from the residences of powerful families into the public sphere and not vice versa, as was the case in Greek cities. And in the forums, too, the scene was dominated to a much greater extent than in a Greek agora by impressive public buildings often commissioned and paid for by one of the same great families. One need only think of the basilicas in the Roman forum, which were without exception named after their builders, or of the close proximity of the main temples of the state cults to certain private residences.

The forums of Roman and Italic cities were dominated by these temples to political divinities. This was not the case in Greek cities. There the chief city gods were worshiped in their own sacred precincts, whereas the agora belonged to the body of citizens as a whole. In the temples of the Roman forum, by contrast, the union of religion and the state was celebrated early on. The Dioscuri were honored as helpers in battle; Saturn watched over the sowing of crops; and Concordia was supposed to guarantee harmony within the state. The fact that the Senate frequently met in these temples was also significant. The most striking instance of the Romans' need to celebrate the unity of religion and the state, however, occurs in the *capitolia* (religious centers) of their citizen colonies. These were laid out on the axis of each forum so that overland traffic had to pass in front of them, a principle that made them very visible as symbols of the colonies' association with Rome and submission to Roman sovereignty.[4]

Whereas the compact political space used daily by citizens of Greek cities contained fully integrated educational and sports facilities as well as theaters, Roman cities initially possessed hardly any comparable structures. And when increasing Hellenization gradually led to their creation, at first they constituted a separate form of public space distinct from the political center. This circumstance reflected the fact that education and culture were not integral parts of communal life, but instead luxuries borrowed from the Greeks. The theater quarter of Pompeii demonstrates this in exemplary fashion. Indeed, even in Rome itself all the important "cultural" buildings of the late Republic were erected on the Campus Martius outside the walls of the city.

From the early days Roman cities were more open to the outside than a Greek *polis* for, unlike the latter, they belonged to an empire. This resulted in a very different relationship to space, as is evident from the way Romans built their overland roads through the centers of cities, and through the forums if possible. The extravagant funerary monuments built by rival families along these roads were intended to be seen by passing strangers, and amphitheaters were usually built at the edge of cities for the same reason. The shaping of public space (or lack of it) in the second and first centuries B.C. must be seen in this context.

The fact that in Pompeii, just as elsewhere in the West, Augustan ideology influenced the outward appearance of public space needs no additional commentary and, as noted, is reflected in no old Roman or Italic city more clearly than in Pompeii itself. Glorification of the emperor in the form of temples dedicated to him in the forum occurs in even more demonstrative fashion only in new cities such as Nîmes, Aosta, or Mérida. Here, too, we find theaters in central positions, corresponding to their significance in Augustus' program of cultural renewal, and fortified walls with elaborate gates as highly visible symbols of Roman preparedness for war.[5]

Urban Public Space in the Empire

Changes occurred in this ideologically determined townscape over the next few generations. These changes, so important in the context of cultural history, are connected with new forms of "public" space that developed gradually under the altered conditions of the monarchy. Perhaps the most significant among them are the large baths. (Pompeii is no exception in this respect, for after the major earthquake of A.D. 62 construction of a new bath complex added a striking new feature to the town's appearance.) Citizens spent many hours together at the baths, enjoying the warm water, heated air, and swimming pools. The baths offered an opportunity to spend leisure time, exercise, and care for one's appearance, activities that in the larger cities could be indulged in amid luxurious surroundings and in combination with the most varied kinds of entertainment. Those who frequented the baths were usually from the same district. The distribution of baths in various residential quarters can be documented again and again in larger towns. The sites where this type of social encounter took place thus tended to shift from the center of the city to various neighborhoods.

Subdivision by neighborhood and/or social class is a feature of public space at the height of the Roman Empire.[6] In the townscapes of the second century A.D. this development occurred not only in baths but in other types of buildings as well, principally the clubhouses of private associations, shrines to Oriental divinities, and shrines of other religious sects. As communal life shifted increasingly to these subdivided spaces and became associated with activities and pleasures previously relegated in large part to the private sphere (such as shared meals in clubhouses), the forum lost its old importance as a center of social activity. By the time it had become the site for monuments honoring the emperor and ceremonies for his worship, citizens ceased to pass through it on their daily errands, and most unscheduled activity there appears to have died out. This is certainly true for the cities of Italy and the western provinces of the Empire, where there is little sign of new construction in forums after this time. Worship of the emperor and his administration continued to be carried on there, of course, and honorary statues were erected in great numbers, but there seems to have been little spontaneous participation by citizens in these ritual demonstrations of loyalty. Indeed, the space could hardly have been filled with so many statues if large numbers of people had still been using it regularly.

As we have seen, certain functions of forums were shifted to new and geographically scattered public places like baths, clubhouses, the shrines of exclusive religious associations, and also certain particularly busy streets. The most popular meeting spots in the townscape can be identified by various features including porticos over the sidewalks, squares with pleasant fountains, and—occasionally—splendid public latrines. Strange as it may seem to us, the last-named actually became significant centers of urban communication![7]

From this time on the population could experience gatherings of the entire civic community in a new way: as spectators in the arena or at the circus. These two places thus also became the only sites where citizens could express themselves politically, either through applause or—protected by the anonymity of the crowd—through vocal protests. And in both places the emperor or other representatives of political power sat in their reserved boxes, visible to all, but inaccessible: another significant characteristic of townscapes in the imperial age!

All these developments were clearly under way in Pompeii when the city was buried: they provide striking proof of the sensitivity of townscapes to social change.

Domestic Taste and Cultural Self-Definition

Dwellings represent another fundamental component of townscapes. They mark the transition from public to private space, and they offer to their owners manifold possibilities for expressing their own personalities and identities. In speaking of the effects created by these dwellings, however, we must distinguish between the glances of casual passers-by and the impressions of people who lived there or came as invited guests. Although inhabiting a particular space is a fundamental part of daily life in every historical era, one can scarcely imagine a cultural sphere where the differences between what is familiar to us and what a Roman experienced are greater than here. Yet our ingrained assumptions make it difficult to approach the topic of houses as "inhabited space" without bias; almost inevitably we are inclined to ask the wrong questions and draw mistaken conclusions.

Residents and Visitors

Our homes are private spaces, in which we live for the most part in nuclear families, screened from the public gaze in every sense. We place great value on undisturbed privacy there; indeed, it is a right protected by law. For all but a few, little space is available to receive large numbers of guests or present an image of ourselves to the rest of society. As a rule, family dwellings are entered only by friends and relatives; hospitality has ceased to be a means of demonstrating a family's official or social position to the community at large. We tend to select home furnishings and decor to satisfy personal preferences and desires for self-expression rather than to convey to strangers a sense of who we are (Bourdieu's "distinctions" notwithstanding). Even the very wealthy, who may still open their houses for semipublic occasions in the traditional manner, are inclined to avoid ostentatious display at least on the exterior. In our society distinctions are expressed more indirectly and discreetly, for example, in choosing the location of a home or the size of a lot.

The Roman house, by contrast, was a center of social communication and pointed demonstration of the occupants' standing. As such it was located in the center of town. Even the façade and entrance offered clues to the owner's status. During the day, when the front door stood open, the lines of sight were purposely designed to allow glimpses deep into the interior of the house from the entrance. If we take the houses in Pompeii as a guide, even "middle-class" homes provided luxurious amounts of space—at least by modern standards. Much of this space, as well as all the furnishings in it, however, served to declare the owner's identity to the world.

The most important principle dictating the organization of space required clear distinction between the parts of the house devoted to socializing and display, and the purely functional areas of the infrastructure (from the kitchens to the servants' quarters). In our "servantless" households the exact opposite is the case; we have "eat-in" kitchens, and bathrooms designed to be attractive as well as utilitarian. The occupants of a Roman house "lived" only in the social space, and it alone was furnished and equipped accordingly. Pliny the Younger thus limits his detailed descriptions of villas to this area.[8] The boundaries between the two areas were open as a rule, but clearly demarcated symbolically and through visual signals. Guests could easily recognize where the service area began, for instance, from the sudden cessation of all elaborate decoration.

Modern middle-class domestic conventions are based on matching particular rooms with particular functions; our rooms tend to be dominated by specific items of furniture that make them identifiable as adults' or children's bedrooms, dining or living rooms, and so on. In Roman houses, by contrast, the elaborately decorated rooms were used for a variety of purposes. Here, where family life took place during the day—where children played, clients and visitors were received, slaves and freedmen were given their instructions—formal dinners were served to guests toward evening.

Romans had far less furniture than we do, and what they had was lighter and more portable.[9] Even the couches on which guests reclined at dinner could be carried from one room to another if necessary. Another great difference was the absence of cabinets and shelves, those symbols of our modern desire to collect objects and fill our homes with them. As a result the rooms themselves became effective as spaces and could be decorated from floor to ceiling. Pictures dominated Roman interiors in a way familiar to present-day Europeans only from baroque churches and palaces. Even ceilings and floors were treated as large surfaces to be covered systematically with bands and fields of decoration, very much in contrast to our homes, where furniture blocks most of the walls and empty spaces tend to be "filled in" with pictures more or less randomly.

The area open to visitors in a Roman house offered no privacy, and there were clearly no separate rooms for the women or children of the household, for instance, or for guests. In the central "access" spaces, the atrium and peristyle (a colonnaded courtyard), any of the people in the house might encounter one another. Their awareness of these comings and goings, the large number of adjacent rooms, and the varied tasks performed throughout the day inevitably turned the house of a large family into a site of intense social activity, which cannot be adequately described with our terms "public" and "private." It remains unclear even now whether in addition to these multifunctional rooms on the ground floor for socializing and display there were also truly private spaces such as bedrooms and children's rooms above them, since for the most part the upper stories of the houses in Pompeii were destroyed and cannot be reconstructed in detail. This uncertainty throws into sharp focus the gaps in our knowledge of the most ordinary daily activities and the specific places associated with them in Roman houses.

Houses as Indicators of Identity and Social Status

In recent years Andrew Wallace-Hadrill has offered a convincing description of the social structure of Roman houses, demonstrating the extent to which the entire space was arranged to present the identity and status of the owner to the surrounding community.[10] This is anything but a trivial observation, for the social function of a house determined both the layout of the rooms and the choice of decorative elements. Two aspects of this social function are especially characteristic, namely, the different use made of space depending on the type of visitor, and the significance of extravagant dimensions and "wasted" space as an example of what Veblen called "conspicuous consumption."[11]

The image of clients waiting in the atrium for a morning audience was used by ancient authors as a yardstick for the social status of the *patronus*. He received the more important visitors in the smaller rooms that were usually situated in the interior of the house. Confidential discussions were conducted in private, in even more secluded chambers that might also serve as bedrooms. Friends *(amici)* came to dinner in dining areas that were often located at the rear of the garden peristyle. Thus a social pecking-order was created, corresponding in spatial terms to ever-increasing access to the interior parts of the house. In the last few years it has been shown that architects took great pains when designing the peristyles of Pompeian houses of the first century B.C. to ensure that a guest would receive the most comprehensive impression of the dwelling's size and expensive decor on his way to meet his host. One way of achieving this was to place the most impressive reception rooms around the peristyle courts, so that visitors would glimpse them all, along with the garden, before reaching their goal.[12]

The number of available reception rooms played a major role in determining the rank of a house in the social hierarchy. A wealthy homeowner could choose among several settings to receive visitors, depending on their type and number as well as on the time of day or season of the year. This possibility for choice was a key status symbol. Decor also varied accordingly. Thus both architecture and interior design were employed in the competition for social status, and naturally this had an effect on stylistic developments in the various arts and crafts employed in interior decor, especially painting.

Naturally, the preceding remarks apply only to the houses of the wealthy and socially prominent. They were the only ones who needed large atria to receive clients and large dining rooms for entertaining friends (Vitruvius VI.5). But in a competitive society with relatively extensive upward mobility, the powerful create models for less wealthy and powerful contemporaries through their habits and the style in which they live, at least when they place themselves on display as ostentatiously as Roman aristocrats did. Yet creating and decorating a special part of one's house for purposes of social display was not a specifically Roman phenomenon. In Greek cities of the classical era the houses of the rich were more elaborately constructed and better furnished than those of the less affluent. A guest invited to the house of a wealthy Athenian in the fourth century no doubt expected to find a peristyle or colonnade and a pleasant room for the men's "symposium." In the houses of the Hellenistic era on Delos and elsewhere we find a separate "display" area with several reception rooms, not infrequently adorned with elaborate architectural details, floor mosaics, and walls with plaster decoration, paintings, or more mosaics. The decorative style of corresponding areas in Roman houses drew its inspiration from these Hellenistic sources, but soon acquired entirely new dimensions in the highly competitive climate of the late Republic.[13]

Living Space and Values

This discussion of the way in which the layout and decoration of rooms in Roman houses were used to communicate the owners' status and identity addresses only one aspect of these dwellings' social function. A second, no less interesting question concerns the values that received symbolic expression in such ostentatious spatial displays, and the underlying self-image of the owners. This question seems even more apposite for Roman domestic environments. Why did Romans feel a special affinity for particular architectural forms, images, and mythological figures? What thoughts, memories, wishes, and hopes were supposed to be inspired by the symbolic forms in the decor? I am referring here to everything that made up the *content* of the "discourse" in which Romans expressed their identity, for whatever a homeowner chooses to present to visitors confronts his own eyes as well. In addition to the neighbor, who looks at the home as a competitor, and the visitor who comes to compare, there are the house's occupants, who spend every day in its rooms and live with its images. The owner of a house did not see his home solely in relation to visitors on whom he wished to make an impression; he also wanted to enjoy it himself! For this to be possible, he had to be able to identify himself with it.

We have an easier time understanding this aspect of Roman houses on the basis of our own experience. Creating the environments in which we live has become a subject of enormous interest to people with disposable income, a topic of dinner-party conversation as popular as the constant talk about food. A flood of magazines, books, and catalogues offers us every conceivable model to suit our pocketbooks and our tastes, from country cottages to the last word in modern design. There is also no lack of articles by psychologists and sociologists analyzing the connections between taste in interior design on the one hand and a canon of shared values, self-definition, and social or cultural aspirations on the other. Merely by studying the floor displays of different department and furniture stores, a future historian could glean a great deal about our values and the ways we dream of spending our leisure time.

An Archeological Task

If we were to look in ancient literary sources for answers to the questions posed above, we might easily gain the impression that Romans did not give much thought to this subject. Even in the days of the Empire, when one might expect otherwise, detailed discussion of the appearance and decoration of rooms in fine houses is rare.[14] This implies not that conversation in those days excluded the subject of living conditions, but only that literature was not the primary medium for such discussions. (Because of their strong orientation toward the golden age of Greece, Roman authors only rarely occupied themselves with any aspect of contemporary life.) An intensive dialogue did, however, take place in the form of developing symbolic shapes and patterns for use within the houses themselves, for Roman householders and artisans' constant attempts to imitate, combine, and outdo previous designs are simply an ongoing discourse on the subject of refined living in a different medium.

An investigation of Pompeian tastes in domestic environments therefore presents us with a genuine archeological task, but one that has only recently been articulated. To perform this task properly new strategies must be invented, for current research tends to be limited either to the typology and dating of individual genres such as painting, terracottas, bronzes, and tools, or to the ground plans of houses and their chronological development. Once the question of taste in creating these environments has been raised, however, it is crucial to be able to reconstruct overall contexts. The ground-breaking studies of Roman houses and their interiors date from the second half of the nineteenth century. In that era Johann Friedrich Over-beck and August Mau produced their admirable books on Pompeii, in which they painstakingly assembled the knowledge then available about ancient architecture, painting, and artifacts of all kinds to give us a first impression of "the Roman house."[15] Despite their normative orientation, these books still offer a good introduction to the question of domestic environments. Nevertheless, simply recording the appearance of a house and providing an inventory of its contents from a positivist standpoint are no longer sufficient to answer the questions of interest today.[16] Domestic environments need to be studied as part of an epoch, as we study town-scapes, and we need to make the same kind of attempt to create models that reflect the particular characteristics of "Roman houses as inhabited space" and combine them with insights about the processes of social and cultural change occurring at the time. This brings me to the narrower focus of the subject addressed here.

The third chapter of this book, on the villa as a model for late Pompeian taste in domestic environments, can cover no more than a small part of the history of domestic environments in the Roman Empire, for most of it still remains to be written. I have therefore concentrated on a single phenome-non, but one that is, in my view, essential if we are to understand how Romans lived at home. I take as my starting point the obvious connections between the architectural forms and decorative elements of many Pom-peian houses on the one hand and those of luxury villas dating from the late Republic on the other.

The Villa: A New Way of Living

Beginning in the middle of the second century B.C., the Roman aristocracy developed an entirely new concept of "domestic environment," the *villa urbana*.[17] It was so successful that it was later adopted throughout the Ro-man Empire as a general style transcending class divisions. In this new concept the main rooms acquired a function above and beyond the practi-cal needs of daily life, namely, to express a single idea in as many different ways as possible. Every element was intended to evoke the idea of Greece and its model civilization, and to symbolize the presence of Greek culture—as a kind of higher sphere—within the house.

A variety of decorative elements, both visual and atmospheric, went into realizing this aim. Courtyards, gardens, rooms, fountains, and watercourses echoed the forms of Greek architecture and were occasionally even given Greek names. Wherever one looked in a richly decorated villa, references to Greek themes met the eye. Copies of Greek sculptures in varying sizes, sometimes whole series of them, were placed around the rooms; wall paintings and floor mosaics reproduced scenes from Greek mythology, and even the furniture and tableware contained pictorial allusions to classical art and culture. Gardens recalled Greek sanctuaries. Views of the landscape were designed to correspond to the new Hellenistic experience of nature. Creating a three-dimensional enclosed representation of Greek culture was a way of claiming symbolic possession of it. Domestic environments thus became a new form of cultural memory.

Although the rich pictorial fabric of the Roman villa is in many respects comparable to the systematic pictorial decoration of Renaissance and Baroque palaces, it differs in that its elements were not chosen to complement one another or to contribute to a single thematic whole; rather, they appear to be connected loosely or not at all. What mattered was that they be artistically executed and have some association with Greece. An educated man such as Cicero, of course, attached importance to decorating a room with images that were not *inappropriate;* Dionysiac scenes would not suit a peristyle used as a study, whereas they would be fitting for dining rooms, where they are in fact often found in Pompeian houses. The same is true for the many erotic scenes with which bedrooms were decorated. Only in this very general sense can the images be related to the functions of specific rooms and houses described "topographically" as sites devoted to the pleasures of life (a description that also applies to earlier Hellenistic houses).

This fascinating new development of using domestic spaces to evoke a cultural memory had its origins in the enthusiastic adoption of Greek civilization by a portion of the Roman aristocracy beginning in the late third century B.C. The trend extended beyond classical Greek models of education and the arts to include the cultivation of *tryphe,* the luxurious and hedonistic lifestyle characteristic of the courts of Hellenistic rulers. Throughout the Greek-speaking world *tryphe* was symbolized by the figure of Dionysus. In Rome the new friends of Greek culture could not display the results of their conversion to Dionysiac values in public, for they ran counter to austere Roman traditional values and customs, and therefore came under political attack as *luxuria.* Devotees were forced to create a private world of *tryphe* at their country villas, where they could indulge in their pastimes unhampered by political considerations.

Villas became the stage sets for a new lifestyle of leisure *(otium).* Certain rituals associated with this style were sometimes enacted in reality and sometimes only in the imaginations of the villa inhabitants and their guests. They would meet and talk in the gymnasium, which they mentally transported to Athens, although in fact it was in the peristyle. Or they would stroll up and down beside an artificial watercourse *(euripus),* which had associations with the hedonistic life of Alexandria, and carry on learned discussions with friends or even with real Greek philosophers who belonged to the household and lived with the family. Or, inspired by works of sculpture in the garden, a host and his guests might converse about Greek literature, history, and art, or retire to a more secluded room for philosophical meditations.

No matter that all of this amounted to a Roman construct of Greek life, and that no such part-time, make-believe Greek intellectuals ever existed in classical Greece. Naturally, reality in Roman villas and townhouses often differed considerably from the role-players' imagined ideal as conjured up by the symbolic reminiscences of Greece in these spaces. Nonetheless, for the first time in history a distinct domestic setting had been created for cultural life, to which devotees could withdraw in their leisure time. The world of the villa and leisure was a private retreat, an antithesis to the world of business, politics, and law courts in the city.

The word "private," however, should not suggest a total withdrawal from society; the opposite was the case. The new private sphere of life was used with great frequency for social contacts. Villa owners met with friends, other members of their social class or political party, business associates, and clients. Banquets in particular—imitating Greek models—offered a new form of social communication. Here architecture, decor, and furnishings all contributed to the villa owners' efforts to display their status, becoming important tools in the competition for power, influence, and money. Possession of a luxuriously equipped villa in one of the prestigious country districts (such as on the Bay of Naples, or near Tusculum or Terracina) was indispensable for any aspirant to the highest political circles in the late Republic. From the very start, therefore, the new cultural self-definition of the Roman aristocracy became one means of display in the general competition for status. In the architecture and leisurely style of villa life two elementary needs were fused into a cultural unity.

The Romans had no desire to become Greeks, however, despite the ubiquity of Greek images and cultural rituals in their villas. They were merely expanding and revising their cultural self-definition (and, incidentally, also laying the foundations for their claims to be a great world power). The forms of their new domestic architecture gave symbolic expression to their conviction that they had absorbed the Greeks' cultural heritage, and understood how to "live" as well as how to conquer and rule, for they had adopted in equal measure the refined culture of the classical *polis* and the hedonistic, Dionysiac lifestyle of Hellenistic monarchs. The fact that in the beginning this was possible only in two separate spheres, that of public affairs in Rome and that of private leisure in country villas, reveals some of the tensions inherent in this extraordinarily fruitful process of acculturation. It is no exaggeration to say that only with the achievement of the ambitious new self-definition represented by the villa did the Romans acquire the authority in the eyes of the Greek East that military might alone would never have won for them.

The Villa and Domestic Taste in the Empire

The aristocrats' new style in domestic architecture gradually became a model for all of Roman society. The lifestyle of an elite gave rise to a general taste to which wider circles could aspire. Presumably elements of the architecture and decoration of aristocrats' townhouses in Rome were adopted first; the new style spread to the houses of the ruling class in smaller cities *(domi nobiles),* and had probably become widespread by the second half of the first century B.C.

In the third chapter we will see how various elements of the new domestic architecture and decor were imitated particularly in medium-sized and smaller residences in Pompeii in the early years of the Empire. Clearly the owners of these houses were not bothered by the fact that limitations of space permitted them to recreate these settings only in miniature, or that social life on the scale of villa owners was out of the question. Pompeians no doubt continued to lead the same modest and relatively educated or uneducated life as before. But why, in that case, did these owners expend so much money and imaginative effort to give their homes something of the flair of the great villas? What made the citizens of Pompeii want to participate in the luxurious world of their wealthy contemporaries, at least in their daydreams and imaginations?

The villas of the Roman aristocracy lay just outside the walls of Pompeii. One might easily conclude that the impetus was an urge to imitate their immediate neighbors. Whether this was actually the case, however, or whether villa imitation spread from Rome like the models for wall decoration in the second, third, and fourth styles and garden statuettes, is impossible to determine today.[18] The latter is very likely. We can say for certain only that the spread of the new style of domestic architecture and decor was a general phenomenon that prevailed throughout the entire Roman Empire until late antiquity. Or, to be more precise, we can say that the values underlying the symbolic forms associated with their style remained in force. The actual expressions these then took varied considerably over the course of generations. Nonetheless, the symbolic expression of a unified vision of culture, luxury, and pleasure, as first realized in the Roman villa, predominated throughout the era.

This form of domestic environment thus involves more than just an especially blatant case of status imitation.[19] The new taste in domestic settings became both a symbol of a concept of culture and a statement that the owner identified himself with a particular way of life.

Social Identification and Cultural Self-Definition

The individual phases of the spread of the new taste in domestic decorating have not yet been described as such. The spread of wall paintings from the second to the fourth styles, however, could be used as a paradigm. In a statistical investigation Andrew Wallace-Hadrill found that the presence and quality of wall paintings in Pompeian houses are directly related to the size and number of rooms.[20] In the early Empire the fashion of having rooms painted in the fourth style spread throughout the middle classes. As a rule, only very small houses with a total of approximately 1,000 square feet or less (small by the standards of the time!) have few wall paintings or none at all. The villa elements I have described date from the same period and are expressions of the same taste in domestic decoration. Merely by having his walls painted, a homeowner could achieve a minimum of the new look. Wallace-Hadrill observes correctly that the most rudimentary paintings, frequently of inferior quality, are intended more as demonstrations that the owners possess a certain level of culture (for the upwardly mobile, above all, in the form of "rebirth through imitation") than as displays of luxury and wealth. Given the actual conditions in the humbler houses, the latter would of course have appeared absurd. Yet simply applying terms such as "kitsch" or "lack of refinement" to the phenomenon fails to do it justice, for this approaches it too narrowly from the perspectives of imitation and cultural deficit.

A demonstration that one "belongs" in fact means more. The process by which the new style spread and was altered to fit modest dwellings was at the same time a process of its adoption and internalization by those who could afford neither luxury nor an expensive education. It was a process of abstraction or even of sublimation, in a manner of speaking, and one can see it in operation in the wall paintings themselves.

On the more ambitious or elaborate walls in the second or third style, for example, the central mythological images occasionally still refer to real picture galleries *(pinacothecae)* of wealthy collectors, which included original Greek works (as in the case of a copy of a well-known painting in the Villa Farnesina). Obviously, however, the wall paintings were not a "substitute" for a real *pinacotheca,* since they are found in even the most expensive houses. Rather, they create a symbolic system in which luxury articles actually present in many villas are combined with imagined spaces and objects. Like the villas themselves, the mural paintings in the second style evoke spaces reminiscent of Greek culture, but as abstractions, a transformation that makes them available to anyone who can afford to hire a painter, in contrast to real rooms. The process of abstraction thus set in motion rendered the images increasingly independent of the objects depicted. This process is clearly reflected in the formal changes occurring between the walls in the second style and those in the fourth (from about 80 B.C. to A.D. 79). In place of the almost palpable architecture and luxury goods in paintings from the late Republican period, we find that the architecture, objects, and people of the later paintings have become manneristic, and have been transported into an oddly unreal sphere. As we shall see, this formal removal corresponds to a process of abstraction in the underlying values. Precisely because the aim of wall paintings was to depict symbols of general values rather than concrete luxuries, even the most modest wall paintings could fulfill their intended function: namely, to give the room in which they were located a certain aura of elevated taste, and thus to express the owner's membership within a cultural circle. The message could be conveyed independent of all competition for status.

The example of mythological images shows that this need to belong was more than just pretty decor, and now had little to do with imitating wealthy villa owners' art collections. Through constant repetition (which we find occurring in other areas of contemporary cultural life as well, such as theaters, schools, and recitations) some of the myths had become so familiar that people began to associate them more and more directly with their own lives, seeing them as metaphors for situations in which they found themselves. The extent to which myths were associated with the present by a broad spectrum of the population is evident in the countless reliefs of mythological scenes on sarcophagi. For the Romans of that era, the use of myths to allude to the present seems to have been as natural as biblical references were in our own society not long ago. Ordinary people could use this relatively educated and "international" language of allusion to express their claims to membership in dominant social and cultural circles, just as they did with wall paintings. At the same time, however, the myths appear to have supplied them with models for conducting their own lives; otherwise they would not have used mythical images to express their personal sorrows and joys, hopes, and need for solace. This is what I meant earlier when I referred to the diffusion of the new taste in domestic interiors as being accompanied by a process of adoption and internalization.

The case is similar for the paradigm "luxury and the hedonistic life," which had been inseparably linked with the notions of the villa and refined domestic environments since the time of Lucullus. One could say that these "values," too, were simultaneously reflected by the symbolic forms of room decor. The most obvious trappings of luxury—such as expensive marbles and precious metals, costly fabrics and dyes, rare gems and shells, but also culinary delicacies—were present in a house, either in reality or in painted form, depending on the wealth and extravagance of the owner. At the same time the topoi of *luxuria* in the rooms' decoration were so intimately connected with scenes from myths and other highly prized emblems of classical culture that these two pillars of Hellenistic tradition always appeared together, at least in the world of symbolic forms. What had once been decried as corrupting *luxuria* was now obviously perceived, in the context of domestic space and its associated symbolic forms, as an important value, in some sense embodying abundance and enjoyment. The allusions to luxury in the decor, like the many Dionysiac images, assured beholders that they inhabited a happy world; they also corresponded perfectly to the ideological stereotypes of the *felicitas temporum* or "golden age" *(aurea aetas)* in imperial art.

In the context of the domestic environment such representational programs also contained an invitation to bring to life the allusions and reminiscences depicted in art. This occurred in the rituals of the banquet, for instance, which had as its aim the combination of pleasure with edifying conversation.

It seems likely that a connection exists between the neutralization and re-evaluation of luxury in the context of symbolic forms and its reduction in the actual lives of Roman aristocrats as social competition decreased

(Tacitus, *Annals* III, 55). In any event both the walls painted in the fourth style and the imitation of villas in Pompeian houses testify to altered perceptions of the phenomenon.

The Cult of Culture in the Empire

The fact that the new style of domestic architecture and decor gained such ground, and even advanced to become the general standard of taste in the Empire, is without doubt linked to the kinds of social change inevitably brought about by the establishment of the monarchy. One striking phenomenon in Roman art is the subordinate role that the political themes associated with the myth of the emperor played in the imagery of private homes and graves; indeed, in most houses these themes, which so dominated public monuments, do not occur at all. This suggests that, within the overall cultural framework, the Roman concept of the domestic environment functioned as a counterweight to the world of the state and politics, even after its diffusion throughout most levels of society.

The political stage was occupied by the imperial dynasty, and the awarding of public honors was controlled by the official bureaucracy. In this situation cultural activities of all kinds that had previously belonged to the private sphere acquired new significance. As the upper classes came to regard educational and cultural activities as opportunities for self-promotion and furtherance of their careers, participation in them increasingly formed a part of public life. The reason for this is simple: the fields of learning and culture were politically neutral, and therefore safe. By the time of Pliny the Younger, attendance at public or semipublic gatherings where friends and acquaintances recited their latest literary productions consumed a good part of a Roman senator's working day, as Pliny himself grumbled.[21] The huge success of the "second school" of sophists and their oratorical "performances" shows how cultural activities could lead to political office, or in any case to great prestige. In the logical culmination of this trend, ultimately even the emperor himself had to demonstrate possession of the relevant skills: not only the philosophical reflections of Marcus

Aurelius, but also Nero's aspirations as a singer should probably be seen in this context.

Through the introduction of cultural activities in the public sphere, homes designed to evoke cultural memories and the pleasures of life acquired a further significance. They became a symbol of the high level of culture afforded by the Roman Empire. Under the emperors the symbolic forms of domestic decor spread increasingly to the public sphere; one need only think of the lavish ornamentation of the main rooms in public baths, or the fountains, plantings, and sculptures in public parks. These public amenities made particularly important elements of the elite's luxury villas accessible to broader classes of people, and erased the dividing line between *privata luxuria* (private luxury) and *publica magnificentia* (public magnificence) previously demanded by the ideology of the late Republic. The alteration in the Roman definition of the public sphere mentioned above meant that the same values could be celebrated there as in private domestic settings. With this step the lengthy process of acculturation reached a kind of conclusion.

Urban Space as a
Reflection of Society

Experiences of our own "inhospitable" cities have made us more aware of the appearance of urban environments and their effect upon the people who inhabit them.★ The city as living space has become the focus of intense discussion in the past two decades, and the debate has revealed how close the connections are between a given community's economy, social conditions, health, and culture on the one hand, and the appearance of its cities on the other. In the course of only one generation the prevailing views and values have swung from one extreme to the other in Europe, from the modernization of inner cities to accommodate ever more automobiles to the creation of large car-free zones; from the heyday of commuter zones, suburbs, and city centers depopulated in the evening to their revival through construction of downtown entertainment complexes, shopping centers, and luxury apartments.

Discussion of these pressing contemporary issues has had a highly stimulating effect on historical studies. The topic of the city has been very popular for some time now, and among the many new approaches one of the most fruitful and appealing has proved to be the attempt to provide as

★ This refers to the book by the German psychoanalyst and social critic Alexander Mitscherlich entitled *Die Unwirtlichkeit unserer Städte* [The Inhospitality of Our Cities], which was published in Germany in 1965 and fostered a great deal of discussion on urban planning and modern architecture. —*Translator's note*.

complete a description as possible of a city's total appearance in a particular historical period. This approach seeks to interpret the entire physical and aesthetic configuration of a city as a reflection of the condition and mentality of the society that inhabited it. The aim is to understand how its layout, architecture, and visual imagery of all kinds work in conjunction with citizens' rituals and everyday activities to make up a single coherent structure expressive of a society's needs, values, expectations, and hopes.[1]

In cases where a substantial amount of evidence has survived, townscapes have a great deal to tell us. This is especially true where growth was organic and the city's face not created through the will of a single ruler or ideological program, for then the city represents the realization of many anonymous and in part contradictory interests. In a largely self-regulating process—as these interests interact and the participants make decisions based on specific needs, pressures, or personal preferences—inhabitants produce a configuration that becomes a self-portrait of their society, although this was by no means the intent.

Once a cityscape has been established, no historian will underestimate its effect on the mental outlook of its inhabitants. Repeated daily experience of one urban environment can be socially integrative, stabilizing, or even stimulating, while another may arouse feelings of irritation or insecurity, or undermine the citizens' general sense of well-being. In the case of ancient societies, one need only think of the antithetical vistas of late Republican and Augustan Rome, or the effect of the public monuments erected on the Athenian Acropolis in the age of Pericles, or the crumbling public edifices in the city centers of the late Empire. At the very least cityscapes understood in these terms certainly constitute an integral part of the culture of each period.

Pompeii, the best preserved Greco-Roman city, presents great difficulties to archeologists wanting to approach it in this manner, for in fact we can see only the city that was buried on August 24, A.D. 79. Since it was more than six hundred years old at the time, we are forced to imagine what the earlier buildings looked like in their original state and ask what purpose they served at the time of their construction. Many elements of former cityscapes were no longer visible in A.D. 79, yet the sheer numbers of

Figure 1 The forum, as it appeared after the earthquake of A.D. 62. The current state of the ruins is confusing, since most of the structures in the forum had not yet been re-built at the time of the eruption that buried the city. The Pompeians had cleared away the rubble and removed valuable materials such as marble slabs and decorative statuary, some of which was re-used in private houses. The fact that this public quarter with the town's most important temple and the basilica had not been rebuilt seventeen years after the quake, although construction had begun on a large new bath complex, gives an indication of the priorities set by the town council *(ordo)* at the time. Some of the valuable materials appear to have been "excavated" by the former inhabitants of Pompeii after the eruption.

buildings preserved by the eruption, both those already uncovered and those still buried, have (with a few exceptions) prevented the type of stratigraphical excavation normally undertaken at other sites.

We must also take into consideration the fact that Pompeii was not a typical ancient city. The majority of its structures, especially the public buildings, had been devastated by a severe earthquake on May 2, A.D. 62, and perhaps another in the seventies, and still lay in ruins.[2] This explains why present-day visitors find a number of buildings, particularly around the forum, so lacking in vividness and immediacy, especially in contrast to the houses that have been reconstructed (fig. 1). Not only have the forum buildings been stripped of all the carved marble decorations they displayed before the first earthquake; their present state also gives no impression of the full height of the walls or the effect of the structures as a whole.

Traditional approaches to studying Pompeii have also tended to ignore questions about historical contexts and the city's architectural evolution. From the time when excavations began in 1740, researchers' work was dominated first by aesthetic interests and later largely by the school of historical positivism. Pompeii and Herculaneum became the chief sources of our knowledge of ancient material culture, and investigators concentrated on classifying the materials they found according to genre and function.

When the remote past becomes palpable in the immediate present, the effect is fascinating, and every day thousands of visitors to the ruins gain the impression that, all in all, human beings remain basically the same throughout the ages. Pompeii is more conducive to such feelings than other sites, yet to experience the past as essentially familiar rather than as alien is a fatal error for historians.

Beginning with the standard works by Overbeck and Mau, most published studies treat Pompeii topographically, and they provide admirable examples of this approach. As a result, however, virtually no attempts have been made up to now to acquire an overview of the whole city and to distinguish the various historical layers in its fabric. The history of Pompeii continues to be written as a history of individual structures, providing little or no sense of larger connections.

In what follows, at least as far as public buildings are concerned, I shall seek to identify and differentiate three historical aggregates: the Hellenized Samnite city of the second century B.C., the period of rapid change following the founding of the Roman colony in 80 B.C., and the new townscape of the early Empire. I am grateful for a wealth of specialized archeological and epigraphical studies that have appeared in the past two decades; it is owing to their many new findings that such an attempt has become possible. The results—mainly pertaining to genres in the field of archeology and to social and economic history in epigraphy—will be evaluated for their relevance to the approach here, which is to seek a historical synchronicity of culture and mental outlook. Such an approach necessarily gives less priority to the examination of individual monuments, as the aim is rather to demonstrate that particular features common to quite different monuments can be interpreted as indicators of specific historical situations and cultural trends. I have striven to be as precise as possible, although space constraints may have led to some occasional simplification in presenting the material.

We still know very little about the first four hundred years of Pompeii's history. The most recent studies by Stefano de Caro indicate that a first wall of tufa and lava, surrounding all 157 acres of the lava plateau on which the town is situated, dates from the sixth century B.C.[3] In the early fifth century it was followed by a limestone wall, which lay outside the Samnite ramparts (end of the fourth century B.C.). The first wall might reflect an Etruscan attempt to link a number of villages and protect the strategically and economically important site at the mouth of the River Sarno from encroachment by the Greek settlers in Campania. In the course of only a few decades a small town center with the temple of Apollo (the "old city") sprang up on the site that later became the forum, and a Doric temple was built on the Triangular Forum. But by far the greatest part of the area enclosed by the walls appears to have been used for agricultural purposes.

On the basis of pottery finds scholars have inferred that a period of relative prosperity and lively trade occurred in the second half of the sixth and in the early fifth century B.C., followed by a definite decline until the end of the century. The small settlement on the arid lava spur must have languished until the Samnites emerged from their mountainous inland territories in the late fourth and third centuries and settled in the towns of the coastal plain. A portion of the surviving walls, the oldest limestone houses, and the layout of the street grid in the northern and eastern sectors of Pompeii date from this time and reflect a renewed upsurge of prosperity. No public buildings from this period have survived, however. After the Second Punic War there appears to have been a large influx of new settlers; this is suggested by the numerous simple houses without atria in region I that have been studied in recent years.

From the time of the Samnite Wars, Pompeii was an ally of Rome and required to participate in Roman military campaigns, although the town was left to manage its own internal affairs. The language spoken in Pompeii was Oscan. Not until the late second century B.C. do we have a clear enough picture of the city to gain a sense of its specific cultural identity.

The Hellenistic City of the Oscans

The Oscan city of the second century B.C. is marked by great private wealth and efforts by the upper class to acquire the Hellenistic culture that would link them to the larger Mediterranean world. Although the Romans had expanded their overseas empire into the western and eastern Mediterranean, their Italic confederates remained excluded from Roman citizenship and thus from full participation in power. These circumstances allowed the more affluent residents of the towns in central Italy and Campania to concentrate their energies on increasing their wealth. They did so mainly by increasing agricultural production and exports.[4]

From about 150 B.C. the leading families of Pompeii were clearly able to amass large fortunes, chiefly owing to the wine trade, but perhaps also to some extent to the production of oil. Amphorae and seals characteristic of the region document the export of wine by Campanian families to places as far away as Gaul and Spain. Production on this scale could be achieved on medium-sized estates by employing slave labor and using the improved methods of cultivation described by Cato. A further important factor was Campanian participation in trade with the East. Inscriptions with the names of traders from Campanian towns have been found throughout the eastern Mediterranean region and are particularly common on Delos, which was a free port from 166 B.C. and the site of auctions in which, at their peak, up to 10,000 slaves are said to have been sold in a single day.[5]

By such means members of leading circles in these towns came into direct contact with the Hellenistic world and, like their counterparts in the Roman aristocracy, were swept up in a powerful current of acculturation. Unlike the Romans and colonial aristocrats, however, the inhabitants of Pompeii encountered no political or ideological obstacles in their cult of *luxuria* and could indulge themselves to their hearts' content.[6]

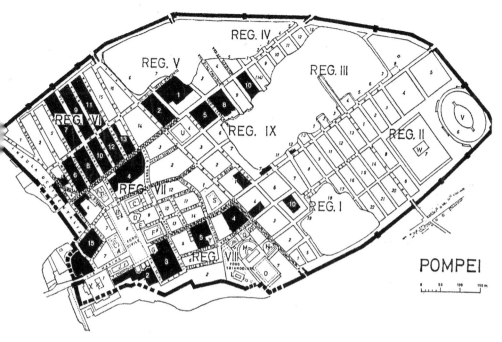

Figure 2 Distribution of elaborate residences in the second century B.C. (following H. Lauter). In this period the largest and most expensive houses were built mainly in the northern part of town (region VI), where large, regularly shaped *insulae* made construction on a grander scale possible. In the crooked lanes east of the forum (region VII) stood modest wooden structures used mostly by tradesmen and artisans.

The Old Families and Their "Palaces"

The situation described above is clearly reflected in the townscape of Oscan Pompeii, which around 100 B.C. boasted opulent private homes and impressive public buildings for both cultural and commercial purposes. By contrast, the structures with more narrowly political functions in the forum reflect only a slow advance of Hellenization with many interruptions. The leading families of this era apparently did not seek to display their status in the arena of civic affairs.

If we take the foregoing as our hypothesis, then it is appropriate to begin sketching the profile of the Hellenized town with the grand townhouses in region VI (fig. 2). They are still easily recognizable today by their façades of

Figure 3 Façades of upper-class houses in region VI. The façades of these houses from the second century B.C. can still be easily recognized today by their walls of neatly hewn tufa blocks. The entrances often have carved door frames, sometimes with elaborately sculpted capitals (compare figs. 6 and 7).

carefully hewn tufa blocks (fig. 3) and elaborate door frames, often with decorated capitals (fig. 4). The best known of these houses, the House of the Faun (fig. 5), occupies one entire *insula* of typically elongated shape, about 2,940 square meters or 31,000 square feet.[7]

A look at the floor plan of this house immediately reveals that only a small part of the enclosed area provided actual living space; two-thirds of it are taken up by two peristyle courtyards that could easily compete with the colonnades of public buildings and offer impressive proof of the family's desire for luxury and conspicuous display. As preserved today, the house shows signs of expansion and renovation in the late second century B.C. Yet even in the first half of this century it and some other houses in the town were designed as virtual palaces, boasting two atria, large rooms with high ceilings, and elaborately decorated entrances.

34

The new concept of luxury dictated use of space on a truly princely scale. Similar dimensions in private homes are unknown in the Italian and Greek cities of earlier times. The dwellings in newly planned Greek towns of the fourth century occupy on average only about one-tenth as much space as the House of the Faun, and the more lavish houses in the theater quarter on Delos from the second century B.C. measure about 4,300 square feet.[8] Lauter observed correctly that the only comparable structures are royal residences, such as the Palazzo delle Colonne in Ptolemais in Roman Cyrenaica (32,000 square feet) and the palaces in Pella (such as I.1, which measures approximately 56,000 square feet).[9]

This suggests that Samnite landed proprietors and exporters adopted the luxury of the Hellenistic world with the same excesses as the Roman aristocrats in their roughly contemporary villas on the Bay of Naples.[10] But unlike the Roman senators, who forced one another to show some restraint in the face of Greek *luxuria* in Rome itself, the richest citizens of

Figure 4 Reconstruction of a street in the Hellenized Oscan town of Pompeii (after F. Krischen).

Urban Space as a Reflection of Society

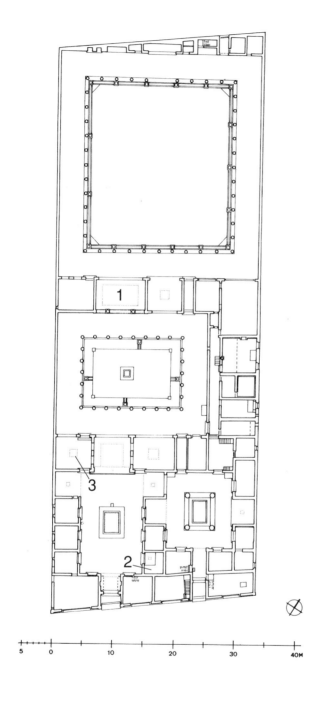

POMPEII

Pompeii apparently knew no limits—on the contrary, they proudly exhibited their newly acquired Greek cultivation. The carefully executed ornamentation of the house portals and the mosaics reveals the extent of their aspirations. This is particularly striking in the figured capitals, usually Dionysiac in theme, which some ambitious homeowners commissioned.

The capitals flanking the entrance to the House of the Figured Capitals (VII 4.57; figs. 6 and 7), directly opposite the House of the Faun, comprise virtually a full program devoted to Dionysus.[11] On the side facing the street each capital displayed a satyr and a maenad. The older satyr to the right leans drunkenly away from the maenad, whereas his counterpart on the left is clasping his partner to him. On the side of each capital facing the entrance there is displayed, in clear counterpoint to the Dionysiac couples, a decorous pair, apparently at a symposium. The men are naked to the waist, the women swathed in the usual modest robes, but their expressions and embrace make it clear that here, too, they are enjoying wine and an amorous encounter. Through this juxtaposition the owner announces in the most explicit manner his identification with the Dionysiac, hedonistic lifestyle celebrated by Oriental monarchs and characteristic of contemporary Greek cities. The portal thus proclaims his adoption of a specific form of Greek culture.

The adoption of Greek images in these and similar forms deserves careful study in conjunction with the other decorative elements of second-century Pompeian houses. Such an investigation would reveal how clearly the entire ambience was conceived as a demonstration of the Greek cult of luxury and an espousal of its values. A few examples must suffice here.

The owner of the House of the Faun increased the grandeur of his imposing atrium in the old Tuscan style by the addition of a blind second-story wall with painted Ionic columns (fig. 8).[12] In addition he tried to make an immediate impression on his visitors with elaborate architectural

Figure 5 House of the Faun, region VI 12. Ground plan (after A. Hoffmann). The house occupies an entire *insula* (approximately 31,000 square feet). The rooms are arranged around two atria and two peristyles. Such lavish use of space was unknown in townhouses of the Greek east; it is found only in palaces, like those excavated in the Macedonian royal capital of Pella.

Figures 6 and 7 Two capitals with figures that once flanked the entrance of the house named after them, the House of the Figured Capitals, across the street from the House of the Faun (now in the Pompeii Museum). On the capital to the right of the entrance the master of the

decor in the front entryway (*fauces;* fig. 9). However, the decoration about eight feet above the floor that imitates the stucco façades of two little temples is oversized for the relatively narrow passage, creating an effect that must have been more menacing than impressive. The almost forced extravagance of taste, combined with a rather haphazard placement of the various decorative elements, appears typical of upper-class outlook in Oscan Pompeii during this phase of acculturation. This mind-set called for everything to be Greek and, if possible, of first-rate quality. The plaster simulated costly marble veneer; furniture and household utensils were imported from the East; bronze statuettes from Greece and the most expensive mosaics adorned the rooms visitors were likely to see. The repertoire of the mosaics shows that the craftsmen had access to the cartoons popular throughout the Hellenistic world. One could interpret the iconography of these mosaics as the sum of everything worth striving for in the hedonistic culture of late Hellenism.[13] The immediate connection with the lives of the

house, naked to the waist, is shown at a banquet, together with his wife. Across from them are a drunken satyr and a maenad. With this type of self-depiction the owner identified himself with the cult of Dionysus and the notion of pleasure as a central value in life.

occupants of these houses becomes evident in such instances as the erotic embrace depicted in a bedroom (the *cubiculum,* in fig. 5, no. 2; plate 1) or the still life with delectable-looking fish in one of the dining rooms (fig. 5, no. 3; plate 2).

The owners of these grand houses felt entirely at home in the Greek culture of their day, which played a role even in their daily lives. This familiarity was a matter of pride and was announced to all and sundry: On the threshold to the atrium in the House of the Faun visitors crossed a broad strip of floor mosaic depicting two masks of the tragic muse and Dionysiac drums framed by an opulent garland of fruit. Classical learning constituted one element of this hedonistic lifestyle.

The most striking example of the owner's identification with Hellenistic culture, however, is the famous Alexander mosaic (fig. 10). Placed along the axis of the house so as to be visible from both peristyles, it was laid in an exedra especially designed to hold it, flanked by two Corinthian pillars on

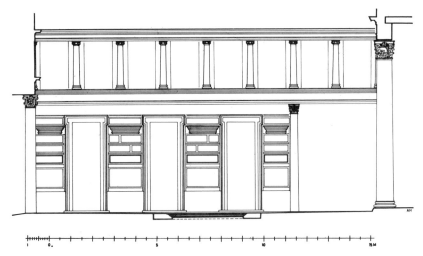

Figure 8 House of the Faun (region VI 12). Reconstruction of the west wall of the Tuscan atrium (after A. Hoffmann). The large atrium in the "Tuscan" style was the grand reception room of the house. Although the form of the room itself remained in the Italian tradition (an atrium without columns around the impluvium), the treatment of the walls used the rich vocabulary of Hellenistic architecture, including tall, carved door frames, columns, and engaged columns. The same combination of Italian and Hellenistic room forms can be found in the inclusion of two peristyle courtyards in the ground plan.

tall plinths. It is a copy, made by highly accomplished artisans, of a famous work painted about 300 B.C. by the Greek artist Philoxenos of Eretria, depicting in all likelihood the Battle of Gaugamela.[14] The mosaic dates from the same period in which the king of Pergamum had copies of famous paintings from the classical era made in Delphi. The Alexander mosaic in the House of the Faun is exhibited like a large painting in its own special room, except that the owner had it executed in the more durable form of mosaic. Perhaps his enjoyment was heightened by the technical perfection with which the craftsmen recreated the painting in the more cumbersome medium. It would be interesting to know if the exedra was used at all, or whether the extraordinary floor was only to be looked at rather than walked on. Probably the showpiece of the owner's art collection, the mosaic can be interpreted at the same time as an almost painfully blatant claim to education and a tribute to the greatest leader of the Hellenistic world. In any event one should not imagine the owner as a great connois-

POMPEII

Figure 9 House of the Faun (region VI 12). View from the atrium into the two peristyle courtyards. From the entryway and the atrium the two courtyards were visible one behind the other, so that on arrival the visitor received an immediate impression of the grand spaces in this palatial house.

seur of art, for directly in front of the Alexander mosaic lay another mosaic in a rather primitive style depicting the Nile with an amusing crocodile, a hippopotamus, and other exotic creatures.

The affluent residents with a taste for Hellenistic culture must have represented a sizable segment of the population, even though Pompeii was not a large town, and their wealth must have varied considerably.[15] This is indicated by the differing sizes of the houses in the northern quarter, which were constructed of tufa by the same painstaking method as the House of the Faun. These occupy areas ranging from one-half or one-quarter down to one-eighth of an *insula* (fig. 11). Despite the variation in their dimensions, they match the quality of the House of the Faun in construction, decorative architectural elements, and other decoration (to the extent that it has survived).

The grandest houses lay in the most important commercial thoroughfares. Rich families exploited the advantages of these sites by including

Figure 10 The Alexander mosaic from the House of the Faun, now in the Museo Nazionale, Naples (after F. Mazois). The mosaic is a copy of a famous Hellenistic painting of a battle from about 300 B.C. and was in a large exedra between the two peristyle courtyards (fig. 5, no. 1) so that it could be viewed from both sides. The owner turned his possession of a work of art into an insistent display of Hellenistic culture. By celebrating the legend of Alexander the Great, the owner of the house established his own connection with the Greek world; the transformation of the celebrated painting into a lasting floor mosaic represents a unique feat of acculturation.

space for shops on the street side of their new houses from at least the early second century B.C. Such premises often had access to a bedroom on a mezzanine floor above the shop, called a *pergula* in Latin. The phrase *natus in pergula* was used to refer to someone of humble origins. These shops were run by dependents of the wealthy owners, in most cases probably slaves or freedmen. Here the floor plans of the houses reflect the old patriarchal structures of Pompeian society.[16]

The less affluent residents must have lived in the "old town," especially in the part to the east of the forum. If we assume that their dwellings were simple wood-frame structures, it would explain the fact that no tufa houses have been found here.

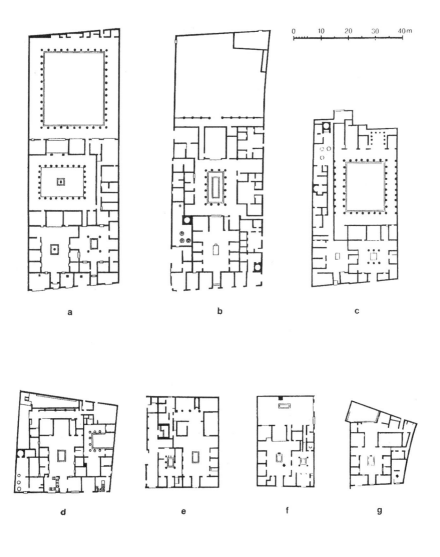

Figure 11 Comparative sizes of well-built tufa houses of the second century B.C.: (a) House of the Faun (VI 12); (b) House of Pansa with surrounding units (VI 6.1); (c) House of the Labyrinth (VI 11.10); (d) House of Sallust (VI 2.4); (e) House VI 8.20–22; (f) House VI 7.20–21; (g) House of the Surgeon (VI 1.10). The range of sizes of these houses with the same high standard of construction and decor points to a relatively large number of affluent families in the Oscan period.

Urban Space as a Reflection of Society 43

The Theater Quarter

Like the private dwellings, most public buildings from the late Samnite period reflect the Pompeians' desire to adopt Greek culture and the Greek way of life. In Pompeii it is striking, however, that the corresponding structures do not dominate the entire townscape as in comparable Greek cities of the same era, but are instead clustered away from the center, in what has come to be known as the "theater quarter" (fig. 12). In choosing a site for the theater the planners probably found the most favorable location to be the natural slope at the southern end of town, near the old Doric temple (fig. 13). Yet it is significant that within only a few decades they erected several other buildings devoted to Greek culture in the immediate vicinity of the theater.

Following the southern Italian and Sicilian practice, the builders of this first theater designed it with tiered seating facing a free-standing structure containing the stage. Campania became Hellenized earlier and more thoroughly than regions farther to the north; thus in contrast to the custom at "Latin" theaters of northern cities, the actors performed simultaneously in the orchestra pit and on the high narrow stage.[17] The reconstructed theaters in Priene and Oropus probably convey a good idea of how the original theater looked in Pompeii.[18]

Unfortunately, we do not know which plays the itinerant actors of the day presented. Undoubtedly the favorites included the type of burlesque named after the neighboring town of Atella. Performed in the local Oscan dialect, these were coarse farces with four stock characters: Maccus, the jester or fool; Bucco, a pot-bellied simpleton; Pappus, the gray-bearded cuckold; and Dossenus, the trickster. Whether Greek comedies or even tragedies were performed in Oscan translations, whether upper-class audiences knew enough Greek to attend performances of classical plays in the original language, and whether the works of Plautus and Terence were presented in Latin—these are all questions to which we would like to know the answers.[19] Later additions to the auditorium *(cavea)* also make it impossible to say how many spectators the theater originally held. For the expanded structure of the Augustan period the number has been estimated

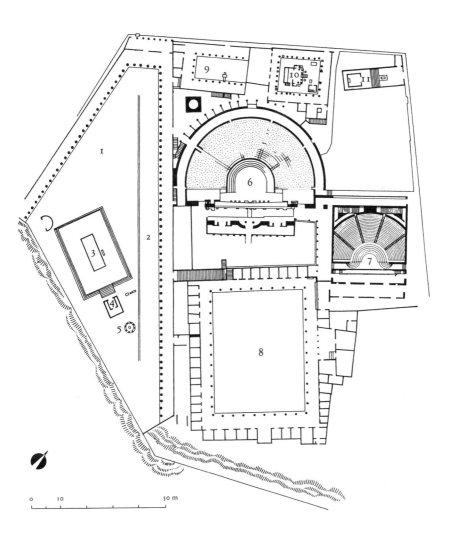

Figure 12 Plan of the theater quarter. Triangular Forum (1) with the old Doric temple (3) and (?) stadium (2); Theater (6); *Theatrum tectum* (7); Gymnasium (?) (8); palaestra (9); Temple of Isis (10); Temple of Zeus Meilichios (11). It is characteristic of the acculturation process that the new buildings associated with Hellenistic culture are not integrated into the urban fabric, but instead clustered together in a kind of cultural center on the perimeter, like an "addition" to the old town.

Figure 13 Theater, looking toward the stage (lithograph of 1884). The excavated theater is the result of several renovations. The original building from the second century B.C. followed the model of southern Italian and Sicilian theaters and had a tall free-standing stage. After renovations in the Augustan period it could hold about 5,000 spectators (compare fig. 56).

at 5,000 (see the section "Seating by Rank in the New Marble Theater," p. 107).

In Egypt and elsewhere in the diaspora the Greeks were called "the men from the gymnasium."[20] Foreigners rightly considered education in a gymnasium, where emphasis was placed on physical fitness along with philosophy and the arts (and the atmosphere was strongly competitive), the hallmark of Greek life and culture. Extremely beautiful gymnasia were constructed of marble in the Greek cities of Asia Minor in the second century B.C. Grave stele of young men from the same period proudly record their training and achievements in the gymnasium. Given these cities' lack of political power, cultural traditions played an increasingly important role, and the gymnasium became the cornerstone of these societies' Greek identity.

The Pompeians could not have felt they truly belonged to the Greek cultural world without such an institution. In his book *Juventus* (1924), Matteo della Corte suggested that the great peristyle behind the theater

Figure 14 Large peristyle building south of the theater, perhaps originally built as a gymnasium and later used as barracks for gladiators (from an old photograph). A comparison with the plans of Greek *gymnasia* supports the hypothesis that it was constructed in the second century B.C. as a gymnasium for the boys and young men of Pompeii. There is no clear indication that it was originally planned to be used in conjunction with the theater, and its size suggests an important function in the public life of the town.

(fig. 14)[21] with its seventy-four Doric columns from the second century B.C. originally served not as a courtyard for spectators to stroll in during the intermission, but as the gymnasium of Hellenistic Pompeii. Although the study reflects a number of problematic attitudes, this particular suggestion is of interest.[22] In the period following the earthquake two stories of cells were added above the colonnade; the wall paintings and discovery of the famous helmets make it clear that the structure was used in that period as the gladiators' barracks. Della Corte's proposal has been largely ignored, probably because of the author's fascist ideology and lackluster scholarship. A comparison of the building's ground plan with Greek gymnasia suggests, however, that the hypothesis has considerable merit after all. Good parallels can be found for the peristyle's general proportions, the propylon (see fig. 18), and the exedra on the eastern side. Furthermore, the structure was clearly not designed at the same time as the theater. At no point do its outer

Figure 15 Reconstruction of the Triangular Forum with the archaic temple (after C. Weichardt, 1896). This idealized view gives an inaccurate impression of the Doric temple, which was actually a simple structure with terracotta decoration. The temple was renovated several times.

walls run parallel to the back wall of the stage building, which is separated from the presumed gymnasium by an irregularly shaped courtyard. The axis of the peristyle complex is even shifted slightly to the east relative to the theater.

By contrast a stairway, originally roofed, connects the complex with the considerably more elevated terrace of the old temple (fig. 15). This could have been the site of the gymnasium's running track and stadium, as della Corte proposed. A strip of ground corresponding to a possible track lies just in front of the eastern portico of the temple precinct, demarcated by a low wall. The track itself would have been only about half the usual length, but this does not necessarily invalidate della Corte's hypothesis. Given the fact that the Pompeians were in the process of absorbing another culture, the main point may have been to have a stadium attached to the gymnasium, its dimensions being of secondary importance. The terrain demanded some concessions, it would seem, but a widely traveled citizen might well have regarded a reduced stadium as something of an embarrassment. In this

POMPEII

connection it would be interesting to know whether the boys and young men of Oscan Pompeii participated in any serious athletic training. For the time being all these conclusions remain speculative, although stratigraphic soundings could easily provide some answers.

The "Samnite palaestra" northwest of the theater (fig. 12, no. 9) does not contradict such an interpretation of the evidence.[23] The structure's modest dimensions would have limited the amount of activity that could take place inside. It may have been a gymnasium for younger boys—cases in which the pupils were divided into two or more age groups using different facilities are documented in several Hellenistic cities—or perhaps, as has recently been suggested, it served as a clubhouse for young people from elite families *(vereiia)*.[24]

The Stabian baths (fig. 16) should also be mentioned in this context, as

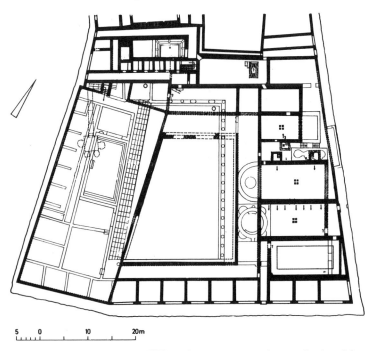

5   0   10   20m

Figure 16 Plan of the Stabian baths (after Eschebach). Roman thermae developed from the simpler baths of Greek *gymnasia*. However, the plan of these baths, the oldest in Pompeii, shows that they were designed with hardly any space for athletic exercise.

Figure 17 Marble sundial from the Stabian baths, a characteristic feature of Hellenistic *gymnasia*. The inscription in Oscan indicates that it dates from the period in which the Roman colony was founded.

they were situated immediately next to the theater quarter.[25] Originally designed to provide basic hygiene in a plain setting, they were remodeled in the second century B.C. and transformed into a more luxurious establishment with separate facilities for men and women and an up-to-date heating system with hypocausts. The old courtyard was converted into a peristyle similar to those in the great tufa houses, and a more elaborate façade on the Via dell'Abbondanza advertised the new comfort and luxury of the complex. Evidence that the courtyard had superior installations at this date is provided by a sundial (fig. 17) with an Oscan inscription. (The first functioning sundial in Rome was erected in 164 B.C.) Unfortunately, we do not know much about Hellenistic baths, but there can be little doubt that this complex represents another element of Hellenistic culture. In the third century B.C., for example, the women of a Fayum village were already permitted to use the public bathhouse.[26]

The development of heated baths presumably evolved in Greek gym-

POMPEII

nasia and palaestrae. It would be interesting to know when and where baths lost their immediate association with physical exercise and athletic facilities, and became part of the cult of luxury. This process was well advanced by the time the Stabian baths were converted, in any event, for the peristyle court hardly offered enough space for serious exercise, and all the additions of this period to the main building served various stages of the bathing ritual, at least in Eschebach's reconstruction.

Returning to the theater quarter, we find that the sacred precinct containing the archaic temple also underwent renovation as part of the large-scale construction program of buildings associated with Hellenistic culture (see fig. 15).[27] Doric colonnades were added bordering the terraces on the eastern and northern sides, to a total length of about 650 feet, and the whole area was opened up toward the town by the addition of a formal propylon with six tall Ionic columns and two flanking three-quarter columns. Now partially restored, this structure is of particularly fine quality (fig. 18). It provided access not only to the newly embellished temple precinct, but also to the theater and—if della Corte's hypothesis is correct—to the new gymnasium. Thus it served as a ceremonial gateway into the world of Hellenism. In all likelihood the wall of the propylon with its

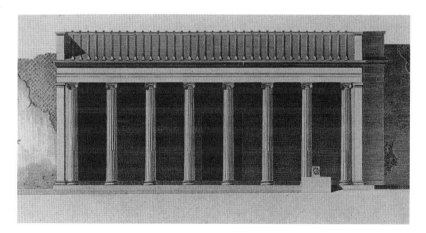

Figure 18 Propylon at the entrance to the theater quarter (after Mazois). The old temple precinct was lined with porticos when the Hellenistic cultural quarter was constructed, and fronted by a formal propylon with tall pillars on the side toward the town.

two wide openings was rebuilt after the earthquake; nevertheless, the thresholds of these passageways give an indication of their original use. The smaller entrance in the middle was intended for everyday traffic and, it is interesting to note, was angled to the left, toward the theater and what was probably the gymnasium. Presumably the wide entrance in the axis of the eastern colonnade was opened only on holidays and at performances, for processions and visitors to the theater.

The terracotta roof tiles of the old temple indicate that it was rebuilt during the second century B.C. as well.[28] The outer parts of the structure, however, were left as they were and only the *cella,* the heart of the shrine, was restored. Given the large expenditure on the colonnades at the same time, this decision seems highly significant. It reveals that the primary aim was by no means to revive the old cult; rather, the town planners were making a grand gesture in imitation of "modern" Greek cities and their aesthetically impressive architecture. This is further indicated by the fact that close parallels for the panoramic opening of the terrace toward the plain—to make the view appear like a "painted" stage backdrop—can be found in the layout of contemporary towns in Asia Minor.[29]

The archaic temple also offered the Pompeians an excellent opportunity to call attention to their city's old Greek traditions. When an elegant *tempietto* (fig. 12, no. 5) was built over the well of the old temple by the highest-ranking official of Oscan Pompeii, a *meddix* (and one from an old family that continued to be important), we may assume that he, too, was motivated more by aesthetic considerations than by a real desire to revive the old religion.

As is demonstrated by the Dionysiac images in the houses discussed above, the religious interests of the town's inhabitants in that era pointed in a different direction. It can hardly be a coincidence that among the many large building projects of the second century B.C. there is not a single major new temple for a civic cult (if we discount the renovation of the Temple of Apollo, which reduced its size), whereas a shrine to Dionysus has been found on the outskirts of town.[30] The two small religious structures in the theater quarter also deserve mention in this connection. Both the Temple of Isis (fig. 12, no. 10)[31] and the small precinct of Zeus Meilichios—or

Asclepius, as has recently been suggested (fig. 12, no. 11)[32]—date from the second century B.C. These were private shrines open only to cult members. It is highly significant that they were erected in the theater quarter, for once again they represent cultural imports, and the men who commissioned them obviously wanted them located near the town's other Greek monuments. The layout of the little shrine to Zeus Meilichios or Asclepius makes it clear that it originated from a private initiative; in the case of the Temple of Isis (see figs. 67 and 68), by contrast, we must assume some degree of public approval, for its construction rendered the theater considerably less accessible. The size of both structures indicates a relatively small number of devotees; indeed, the temple to Zeus or Asclepius strongly resembles a domestic shrine in character. Both these shrines stand in stark contrast to the imposing impression made by the public buildings reached through the propylon: the theater, presumed gymnasium, Samnite palaestra, and temple complex. The ensemble was intended to demonstrate to visitors as well as to residents the town's claims to importance, and the opening of the temple terrace toward the plain "framed" this new Greek quarter, setting it off to even greater advantage.

Extending the Forum

Whereas the construction program for public buildings for cultural purposes apparently proceeded without significant interruptions, the political zone in the center of town presents a different picture (fig. 19), although it, too, began some time around the middle of the second century B.C. with a plan for an imposing square dominated by a central temple. The inhabitants of Pompeii could take as their model the typical forum of earlier Roman colonies, over which the *capitolium* loomed as a striking and monumental symbol of allegiance to Rome. The later form of the forum in Pompeii must also have been planned in conjunction with the new temple (thought to be to Jupiter), since it lies directly along the forum's central axis, parallel to the façade of the basilica and the new wall surrounding the Temple of Apollo. This appears to be the extent of any overall architectural conception, however, for, as Lauter has shown, all other edifices from the

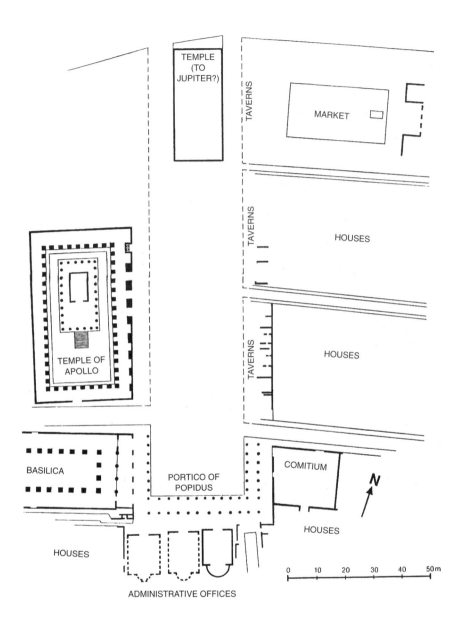

Figure 19 A sketch of the forum as it is thought to have looked before the founding of the Roman colony in 80 B.C. The Oscan elite did not promote the embellishment of the forum with the same energy they expended on the cultural quarter and their own lavish homes. The only significant building finished in a single phase was the basilica.

Oscan period that border the forum were separate undertakings, built virtually without reference to one another over the course of two or three generations.[33]

Of the first temple (to Jupiter?) only the podium with its heavy profile has survived. We do not know whether construction had even been completed when the building was pulled down again early in the first century B.C., to be replaced by a *capitolium* on an even grander scale. The original podium was retained in this modification, however.[34] This meant that the Hellenistic market *(macellum)*, like the building that later replaced it, stood at an angle to the forum owing to the street running along its south side. It occupied roughly the same area as the structure dating from the early Empire, although it was built on a simpler plan without a tholos, and was probably constructed at about the same time as the basilica, around 130–120 B.C.[35]

The basilica, occupying a little over 16,000 square feet, was by far the most elaborate structure in the forum (fig. 20).[36] Designed with three naves, it was constructed from start to finish by an experienced master builder and first-rate stonemasons, and served primarily as the city's commercial center, exchange, and auction house. The elaborately decorated tribunal (fig. 21) no doubt served some special function in this context, perhaps as a podium at auctions. As in the case of the cultural buildings, the leading citizens had a common interest in providing such a facility in Pompeii. With its river harbor, the town was the natural distribution point for goods from the Samnite territories inland. The site of the basilica on the west side of the forum near the harbor was dictated by its function.

Originally the portico of the basilica opened directly onto the forum. The earlier administrative offices, housed in the three small structures at the south end of the forum, also predate the colonial era; or at least the middle one and its neighbor to the east do, as Maiuri's soundings demonstrated. This includes the apse of the structure farthest to the east, so that we may imagine the highest official or officials of the Oscan town carrying out their duties from a suitably prominent position, seated in the apse.[37]

Once again it is striking, however, that these administrative buildings were clearly erected not simultaneously but one after another. As Maiuri

Figure 20 View of the basilica at the entrance from the forum, as shown in a late-nineteenth-century photograph.

noted, their northern façades facing the forum are staggered rather than aligned.[38] Only after the basilica and the small administrative buildings had been finished and work on the *comitium* (assembly) had begun (presumably in Pompeii's last years as an "independent" town) did the collection of individual structures around the forum come to seem awkward; it was then decided to hide their irregularity with a three-sided portico. The inscription commonly associated with this portico, which names a "V. Popidius q(uaestor?)" as sponsor, is in Latin, but we also know that the office of quaestor ceased to exist after Pompeii became a Roman colony. These facts could point to a construction date some time between 89 B.C. and the founding of the colony. The finished portico was not exactly a showpiece. As Lauter has shown, it was a free-standing structure that could not be integrated with the hodgepodge of buildings behind it because of their irregular alignment and varying façades. The remaining space between the colonnade and other buildings became asymmetrical "courtyards," which

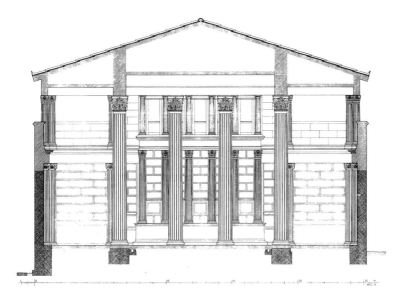

Figure 21 Elevation of the basilica as reconstructed by K. F. Ohr. This enormous roofed hall (ca. 16,000 square feet) with three naves served as a center for commerce and trade. Its position on a street leading straight to the river port opened up vast new trade opportunities for growers in the Campanian hinterland and Pompeian merchants. No wonder that strong support for construction of *this* building existed, in contrast to the forum.

must have been distinctly unpleasant to cross in wet weather and also considerably reduced the overall effect of the ambitious architecture. Furthermore, the colonnade enclosed only the southern end of the rectangle, and presumably the long side on the east had no grand public buildings at all; here two very narrow streets provided access to the forum, on either side of a motley assortment of *tabernae* (chambers; see fig. 19).

As a result the forum remained aesthetically problematic in the last phase of the Oscan city, despite the flurry of building activity, in contrast to other areas of town, such as the ensemble of cultural buildings near the archaic temple, the residential quarter in the north with its harmonious tufa façades and elaborate doorways, and even the northern city wall, punctuated by strong towers for defense. Apparently a common political will was lacking to extend the forum to comparable effect. Only in the beginning stage and during construction of the two commercial structures, the basilica and the market, do civic leaders seem to have been united by a common purpose.

Figure 22 Priene (Ionia): Model of the center of this Hellenistic city as reconstructed by H. Schleif. In contrast to the organization of Oscan Pompeii, the theater and two *gymnasia* lay in the heart of town. The agora, as the center of civic life and site of festivals, was entirely enclosed by colonnades and embellished with numerous monuments.

Creation of a worthy frame for the center of the town's political life and the daily encounters of its residents commanded less interest than construction of cultural showpieces and sites for the private indulgence of luxury.

This anomaly becomes especially apparent when Pompeii is compared with other small Hellenistic towns of the same era. In Priene, for example, the most important public buildings lie directly on or near the agora (fig. 22).[39] The agora itself was framed on all sides by fine marble colonnades, which provided a congenial setting for citizens to meet, and was filled with statues honoring civic leaders. (In Pompeii, by contrast, no such monuments from pre-Roman times have been found.) The Priene council met in a well-designed *bouleuterion;* directly behind it lay the old gymnasium, and not far up the slope stood the theater, where assembly sessions took place. The Temple of Athena, the town's tutelary goddess, looked down on the agora from a dominant position, and was connected with it

POMPEII

by a set of steps. This ensemble gave fitting expression to the self-image of Priene's citizens as a democratic community that took pride in its institutions.

The peripheral location of the main cultural buildings in Pompeii, the stop-and-start construction of the forum, and the inadequacies of its final pre-Roman appearance add up to a very different picture, reflecting other social structures and the particular circumstances of an acculturation process. Here traditional patriarchal patterns prevailed, in which a few families and their clientele dominated local politics. "The people" presumably played only a small role in civic affairs. The cultural interests of the elite were relatively new, and first made their mark on private domestic space. This shared preoccupation then led to the major community projects of the theater quarter. The same holds for the elite's interest in trade and the admirable large-scale basilica.

Lauter has spoken of symbols of "self-Romanization" in connection with the construction or renovation of the temple, administrative buildings, and *comitium* in the forum; he interprets these activities as signs that the inhabitants of Pompeii expected to receive Roman citizenship shortly, the prize so long sought by the great families of Italic cities, but which the Roman Senate had stubbornly withheld. It has also been cited as further evidence of this expectation that even in Oscan times a man like the owner of the House of the Faun greeted his visitors with an inscription in the mosaic floor of his vestibule in Latin, "have," rather than in Oscan—his own language—or Greek.

Proceeding on this hypothesis, one could interpret the repeated interruptions in renovating and extending the forum, the central site of Roman political life, as a sign of disunity among the elite regarding the "self-Romanization" process. Recall that the conception of the new forum with its central temple (to Jupiter?) considerably reduced the size of the old shrine to the town's patron god, Apollo.[40] Strong interest must have been present for the Pompeians to make such a break with tradition.

It would be informative to compare the effects of Hellenization on the appearance of Pompeii with other towns in Campania and central Italy. We would probably find that the acculturation process took very different forms, depending on the location, importance, and cultural traditions of the town in question. The massive building program carried out by L. Betilienus Vaarus in the old mountain town of Aletrium in the territory of the Hernici around 100 B.C. shows tendencies similar to Pompeii.[41] Here, too, buildings with cultural or economic functions dominated the picture: *campus ubei ludunt* (palaestra?), *horologium, seedes* (theater?), *lacus balinearius* (baths?), *macelum* (market), *basilica calecanda.* The streets *(semitae in oppido omnes)* and a *porticus qua in arcem eitur* represent measures to improve the town's appearance aesthetically, most likely in ways similar to the eastern quarter of Pompeii.

By contrast Cosa, founded as a Roman colony with Latin rights in 280 B.C., could not yet boast a single ambitious cultural building by the end of the second century B.C.[42] The well-developed forum was dominated by political buildings, a category that included the temples, the curia, and the *comitium,* as well as a basilica added later. Here hardly any signs of Hellenization are to be found, apart from a few private residences.

The great terrace sanctuaries, particularly in the old towns of Latium, represent an entirely different dimension of public building.[43] In Palestrina and Tivoli the leading families were clearly interested in proclaiming the importance of their cities within the new entity of the Roman state. The case of Palestrina shows that splendid religious buildings could be connected with an ambitious renovation of the political center. In these cases the improvement and embellishment of the town's main buildings in the Hellenistic mode are designed to make an impression on the outside world. We have no reason to doubt that the aristocracy of these towns built and furnished their homes in a correspondingly modern style, but unfortunately virtually no houses comparable to the palatial House of the Faun have been found in other Italian cities.

Even this brief account should make it clear that the townscape of Oscan Pompeii as we have reconstructed it—and presumably the other old towns of Campania—had their own characteristic structure, marked by demand for a well-developed cultural quarter, an ambivalent attitude with regard to political space, and little interest in parading the town's status as an independent political entity or participating in the "rivalry" between towns that was then beginning to emerge in central Italy.

The Roman Colonists' City

Unfortunately Pompeii, in contrast to its neighbor Nuceria, was induced by the early successes of the rebels to join the Social War against the Romans. The town was besieged in 89 B.C.—the damage done by Roman artillery is still visible today in the limestone blocks of the northern city wall (fig. 23)—and probably fell to the attackers. In the war's aftermath the residents of Pompeii, like all the inhabitants of southern Italy, received Roman citizenship, in expectation of which they had built the *comitium* before the war. As participants in the uprising, however, they could not escape punishment altogether. After an interval of almost ten years Pompeii had to accept a contingent of Sullan veterans, as did other cities in Campania, and was thus turned into a Roman colony. Responsibility for planting the colony was entrusted to Publius Sulla, a nephew of the dictator

Figure 23 City wall of Pompeii, with damage caused by Roman artillery during the attack of 89 B.C. still clearly visible.

who later achieved influence in Rome. Estimates of the number of colonists vary, but it seems likely there must have been at least 2,000 veterans, to which must be added their family members and other dependents.

The redistribution of land, existing houses, and building sites in the city must have been preceded by proscription of some of the original inhabitants and confiscation of their property. The colonists were assigned their new holdings *secundum gradum militiae,* so that centurions received double and *equites* triple the portion of an ordinary soldier. The size of the basic share of a colonist in Pompeii is unknown. Thirty years later Caesar gave each man 10 *iugera* of land (about 6.2 acres) in fertile Campania. Nothing is known about the actual procedure by which property was seized in Pompeii or how rigorously it was implemented. Nonetheless, it is certain that the measure, although far-reaching, left the city's economic and social structures relatively unchanged; however, the resettlement did affect the cultural climate.

While, as Henrik Mouritsen has shown, the wealthy old families were able to preserve their influence in the long term, in the early years of the colony political life was dominated by the leaders of the new settlers. But since the older inhabitants had also become Roman citizens, they were certainly able to vote and enjoyed equal status under the law. Latin became the official language and gradually replaced Oscan as the language of daily life as well. Naturally, tensions and conflicts arose between the Oscan Pompeians and the veterans. Indeed, it should be kept in mind that after twenty years' service in the Roman army the majority of the newcomers undoubtedly had different leisure-time interests—and exhibited different social behavior generally—than their affluent, refined neighbors, who prided themselves on their Hellenistic culture.[44]

The Capitolium *and the Amphitheater*

The building activity of the next several decades shows that even though Pompeii was by no means unattractive when the colonists arrived, they made profound changes in its appearance (fig. 24). In the forum, on which the Pompeians had expended considerable effort in the preceding decades,

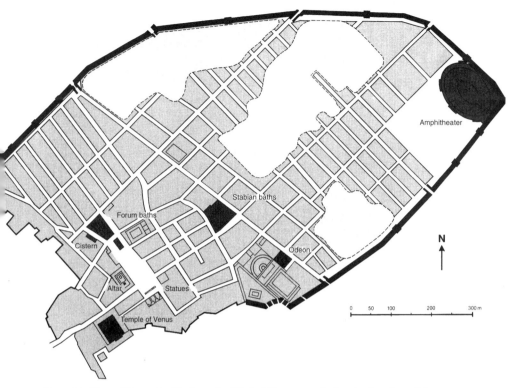

Amphitheater

Stabian baths

Forum baths

Cistern

Odeon

N

Altar

Statues

Temple of Venus

0   50   100   200   300 m

Figure 24   Plan of Pompeii with sites of public buildings erected after the founding of the Roman colony in 80 B.C. On their arrival the colonists found a town already equipped with the most important facilities. Their new construction reflects new requirements, most spectacularly a giant amphitheater far surpassing the needs of the town itself, which was financed by two rich partisans of Sulla. The location on the extreme edge of town shows that large numbers of visitors from the hinterland were expected. Some of the colonists were presumably settled in the surrounding countryside, where numerous farmyards have been discovered.

the veterans found little in need of improvement. Naturally, they completed construction of the *comitium* and began using it. Presumably the forum then began to play a larger role in public life. It seems highly likely that the two matching plinths in front of the magistrates' buildings held statues honoring leading civic officials, of the type that became customary in the course of the following decades.

The most significant alteration to the forum, however, was the conversion of the temple into a *capitolium,* an event I would place in the early

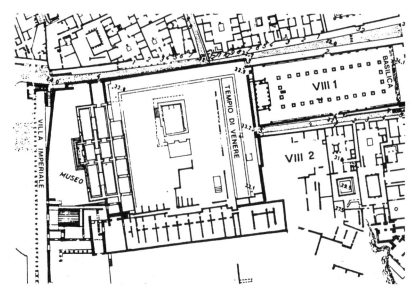

Figure 25   Western sector of Pompeii with the Temple of Venus and the town villa of M. Fabius Rufus. The temple was erected as a symbol of the *Colonia Cornelia Veneria Pompeianorum* in honor of the town's new patron goddess. Venus was also the deity who protected the general and dictator P. Cornelius Sulla, whose veterans were settled in Pompeii. The land sloped sharply downward from the city wall, making the temple visible from a great distance on the plain to the south.

years of the colony (in contrast to Lauter; see above). In the new construction on the old podium, the temple cella was fronted by immense two-story columns, and the interior was decorated with mosaic floors and wall paintings in the second style. Images of the three divinities Jupiter, Juno, and Minerva stood on top of a high podium, each in its own aedicula.[45] The aim here was to celebrate the city's status as a *colonia* in a suitably elaborate display, although from an aesthetic point of view it does give the impression that the Pompeians went a bit overboard. The city's presentation of itself as a new *colonia* was served further by the construction of a temple to Venus on the southern slope between the Marine Gate and the basilica (fig. 25).[46] The veterans had formally renamed the city *Colonia Cornelia Veneria Pompeianorum* in honor of their commander Sulla and his patron deity. Dominating the river valley from its hillside, the temple of the city's new tutelary goddess greeted passers-by and visitors on their arrival,

POMPEII

and should be seen in the context of the large new terrace sanctuaries of central Italy, whose extravagant character has already been mentioned. But with the building of this temple to its patroness the new *Colonia Cornelia Veneria* also stated its own aspirations, announcing—albeit in the context of its modest resources—its entry into the competition for prestige among Italian cities.

It is also possible, however, to view the Temple of Venus as a companion piece to the archaic temple near the theater, which has a similar geographical orientation. In a self-confident gesture, the settlers now set the new identity of the city as a Roman *colonia* against the Greek traditions of old Pompeii. Hardly any of this Sullan edifice has survived apart from the foundations and parts of the portico, so that very little impression of the original structure can be gained on site nowadays. But the one published ground plan shows a precinct laid out on a different axis from that of its successors, with a three-sided colonnade and an outer wall fronting the street in line with the north wall of the basilica (compare fig. 20).

The *capitolium* and the Temple of Venus were of course built to compete with the Temple of Apollo, the old patron deity of the city. It is therefore noteworthy that in one of the first years after the colony was founded the two duumviri and two aediles donated a new altar to the Temple of Apollo. One of the duumviri was the same M. Porcius who was soon to become a dominant figure in the new colony. Since this temple had been completely renovated only shortly before, in 100 B.C., and was certainly not lacking an altar, the dedication of a new altar and removal of the old one had symbolic significance (fig. 26). The Latin inscription of the new altar names the donors and the city council's decree authorizing its construction, thereby underlining the intention of the city's new masters to appropriate the religious traditions of the old inhabitants for their own use, or—viewed from the latter's perspective—to eradicate important emblems of their previous identity.[47]

Construction of the roofed theater *(theatrum tectum)* next to the large theater was also begun in the early years of the colony (fig. 27).[48] Strangely enough, no one has yet asked why the colonists should have chosen to erect an odeon, as this type of building came to be known during the

Figure 26 Dedicatory inscription on the new altar in the sanctuary of Apollo. As soon as the new political structure had been instated after the colony's founding, the four highest officials *(quattuorviri)* dedicated a new altar in the old Temple of Apollo next to the forum. The dedication in Latin represents a symbolic act of appropriation of the old civic cult by the colonists.

Empire, so soon after their arrival. One must assume that it served some necessary function. Yet, given the veterans' probable cultural interests, they are scarcely likely to have been in urgent need of a lecture hall for small-scale recitations and musical performances (as is occasionally claimed). Since the structure's architecture and size recall the *bouleuteria* of Hellenistic cities, might the building, which would have accommodated between 1,500 and 2,000 people, not perhaps have served as a meeting place for the veterans? They were living as a minority among "fellow citizens" who must have regarded them with some suspicion, at least at the beginning. Their need for contact with one another and a sense of community must have been very great, and the new settlers are also likely to have faced certain practical problems in common during the early years.[49]

Construction of the roofed theater was directed (and probably paid for as well) by Quinctius Valgus and Marcus Porcius, the duumviri who a few years later also sponsored construction of the large amphitheater (plate 3.1). These two men, who had amassed fortunes from Sulla's campaigns, were familiar with the veterans' needs.[50] They hired a firm of experienced local stone cutters to do the work, and the similarity between the supporting figures at the roofed theater (plate 4) and those on the *analemmata* (enclosing walls) of the slightly earlier theater in Pietrabbondante has rightly been pointed out. Because this type of building had long been known in the Hellenistic world, and because the combination of a large theater with a small roofed assembly room is known to have existed in Sicily and even in the neighboring city of Neapolis (Statius, *Silvae,* III 5.91), scholars have

Figure 27 The Odeon *(theatrum tectum).* Able to hold 1,500 to 2,000 people, this small "theater" is reminiscent of Greek *bouleuteria,* where city councils met, and was presumably built as a meeting place for the colonists.

conjectured that the colonists merely carried out a previously conceived plan.[51] The way in which the roofed theater is joined to the large theater and its location on the street make this seem improbable, but that the colonists should have turned to the superior cultural traditions of Campania in choosing a type of architecture for their building is not surprising.

The same holds true for the public baths, which were already common in Campania, although still rare in central and northern Italian cities at that time. A further project undertaken by the settlers in the early days of the *colonia* was a second public bath complex with a huge cistern, erected in the immediate vicinity of the forum.[52] The residents of the adjacent quarter of town were thereby spared the rather long trip to the older Stabian baths. The new role the forum was intended to play may also have influenced the choice of site. The forum baths presumably filled a pressing need of the new settlers, some of whom, as Zevi has suggested, may have lived in the countryside to the north of the town. Significantly, the dedicatory inscription of this structure mentions explicitly that it was financed *ex pequnia publica,* in contrast to all the other public buildings with surviving inscriptions that date from the early period of the *colonia*.[53] At about the same time the Stabian baths appear to have been renovated and equipped with a *laconicum* (sauna) and *destrictarium*. Clearly the renovations had the aim of offering visitors to both establishments the same amenities.[54]

But by far the largest public building of the early colonial period was the amphitheater. At the time it did not yet go by this rather high-sounding Greek name, and was instead appropriately known as *spectacula* (the term used in its dedicatory inscription). Its two sponsors, Quinctius Valgus and Marcus Porcius, made it known in the inscription that the funds for it had come *de sua pequnia*. The amphitheater was erected during their term as *quinquennales,* that is, when they had reached the summit of their careers in local government, in about 70 B.C.[55]

It was a very sizable gift, out of proportion in every respect for a medium-sized country town. But then the donors' money had not been earned there either, at least not Quinctius Valgus' fortune: he had profited from Sulla's proscriptions and may be considered one of the dictator's followers.[56] Valgus' main activities were concentrated in Hirpinian territory to the north of Pompeii, where he held the highest municipal office in several towns and endowed large public works in all of them. In one town (not yet identified) where he was made *duumvir quinquennalis,* he donated money for the walls and their gates, a forum with porticos, the curia, and a cistern (presumably for the baths), that is to say, for every edifice contributing to the settlement's new identity as a city, apart from the sacred buildings. In Aeclanum he served as a *patronus municipii* and counted among the sponsors of the "walls with towers and gates."[57] M. Porcius may be identical with a large wine producer of the same name whose amphorae have been found in Gaul and Hispania Tarraconensis. In any event he must have had a similarly large fortune at his disposal. M. Porcius remained loyal to the *Colonia Cornelia Veneria.* His monumental tomb occupying the best site outside the Herculaneum Gate is evidence that he was honored by the community almost like a founding hero.[58] The aim of these huge endowments in various cities was to acquire the largest possible following for a political career in Rome.

As a site for the amphitheater (*spectacula;* fig. 28, plate 3.2) the two donors chose the southeastern corner of town, a particularly suitable location for two reasons: first of all, the wall surrounding the city could be used to support part of the huge structure (approximately 455 by 340 feet), reducing the need for a massive foundation and other retaining walls. And second, a site on the edge of town with few other buildings nearby could more easily accommodate the arrival and departure of large crowds on days when shows were presented. The plan for seating for 20,000 spectators shows that visitors from the surrounding communities were expected. Originally, perhaps, the planners reckoned first and foremost with other Sullan veterans from nearby settlements such as Abellinum or Nola.[59]

This type of structure was new at the time. Presumably few other cities in Campania possessed such an arena, and in any event the amphitheater in Pompeii is the oldest of its kind. It is evident from the construction that, unlike the case of the roofed theater, the architect had no previously tested models to follow. To avoid having to build an elaborate foundation he set

Figure 28 Aerial view of the amphitheater, known as *spectacula*. Donated by the town's two highest officials around 70 B.C., it could hold some 20,000 spectators and was the setting for gladiatorial combat and *venationes* (combat between men and beasts). Clearly many spectators from neighboring towns were expected. The thirty-five rows of seats are divided into three raised sectors by tall podia. Did the veterans perhaps originally take their seats according to the military rank they had achieved? The Pompeii arena is one of the oldest known amphitheaters. It points to a radical change in the cultural climate of the city.

the floor of the arena and part of the building below ground level. In addition the entrances and logistics of the circulation system are quite primitive in comparison with later amphitheaters (fig. 29).

All the same the Pompeians could pride themselves on being among the first to be presented with such a splendid structure: it is no accident that the sponsors included in the inscription the fact that they had erected it *coloniai honoris caussa*.[60] They also dedicated the building expressly to the colonists: *coloneis . . . in perpetuom*. Understood in a legal sense this phrase certainly refers to all the citizens of Pompeii, although repeated use of the terms *colonia* and *colonei* as beneficiaries gives one pause. As late as 62 B.C. representatives of the "townsfolk" *(municipes)* and "colonists" *(colonei)* appeared separately in court in Rome to testify on P. Sulla's behalf at his trial (Cicero, *Pro Sulla* 21, 60–62). At any rate the inscription lays great stress on what a blessing the founding of the colony had been and con-

Figure 29 Amphitheater: staircase to the *summa cavea*. The plan and execution of the Pompeii arena (unlike those of later amphitheaters) reveal that the architect had no tested models to follow. This is particularly apparent in the location of entrances and access to seats, and the awkward position of the staircases.

tinued to be for the city, a sentiment that is unlikely to have sat well with the older inhabitants.

Such an amphitheater must have primarily served the needs of the veterans, although this does not mean that the precolonial residents necessarily turned up their noses at the gladiators and wild animals, for all their pretensions to Hellenistic culture. The old soldiers could sit with their former comrades from nearby towns, probably divided by military rank, as the thirty-five rows of seats are divided into three sections by high retaining walls *(pulpita)*. One cannot help wondering whether the townsfolk really had any chance of obtaining good seats in the early days. It is probably no accident that one of the earliest amphitheaters was built for a veterans' colony: the soldiers may have needed this type of spectacle as an outlet for their aggressions more than other people. At any rate it is certain that their preferences played a decisive role in determining the kind of spectacle that became firmly established in the arena at Pompeii. The enormous popularity of the gladiators' contests can still be deduced from the numerous graffiti on walls throughout the city. More than any other of the colonists' innovations, the amphitheater altered the cultural climate in the town.

Display and Self-Promotion in Houses and Tombs

Unfortunately, no attempt has ever been made to identify which houses in Pompeii were owned by colonists. Since we may assume that at least those members of the elite with friendly feelings toward Rome retained their elegant homes in the northern part of town, and that the established inhabitants—who had become Roman citizens, after all—could not simply be driven out, it was necessary to build many new houses and remodel many others. In this connection I at first considered the one-family dwellings studied by A. Hoffmann as a possible "colonists' quarter,"[61] but in the meantime several scholars have advanced convincing arguments for dating them to a considerably earlier period.[62] Future studies might take as starting points the consolidation of several houses to make a lavish complex in I 4.5 and 25 and the façade of IX 1.20, both described by H. Lauter.[63] Without more thorough investigation, however, these scattered observations remain too hypothetical. In our particular context it is more important to note that despite the influx of new residents the overall appearance of the existing residential quarters did not undergo marked alteration. The tufa façades of the second-century houses continued to set the tone in the grander neighborhoods. New construction was limited largely to the eastern end of town, but even there builders followed the established style. Fausto Zevi has recently advanced plausible arguments for the view that the veterans lived on the estates and in the villas to the northwest along the Via dei Sepolcri outside the Herculaneum Gate, while the old inhabitants remained in their houses in town. He regards the wall decorations in the late Hellenistic first style as evidence that these dwellings belonged to the old Oscan families.

In any event, however, entirely new "townscapes" arose over the course of the first century B.C. on the hillsides to the west and south and outside the gates (fig. 30). Previously, the families constituting the old Pompeii

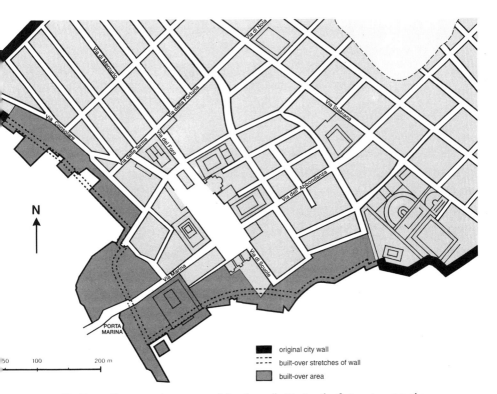

Figure 30 Pompeii, construction on top of the city walls. During the first century B.C. the city walls were built over with large terrace villas on the sites with the best views. The luxurious villas built around the Bay of Naples by Romans beginning in the preceding century had clearly influenced the taste of wealthy Pompeian families.

elite had lived in the middle of town and were fully integrated in day-to-day life there through their dependents and clients; one need only recall the number of houses containing shops facing the street. But in the ensuing period more and more affluent residents took their cue from the new taste established by the owners of Roman villas.[64] In the mid–second century B.C. Roman aristocrats began building such country retreats overlooking the most beautiful spots on the Bay of Naples—within view of Pompeii, whose inhabitants soon took to imitating them. Some Pompeians built small villas just outside the Herculaneum Gate, while others tried to combine the comfort and sea view of the Romans' houses with the convenience of a townhouse. The preferences of this second group led to construction of terrace houses on the site of the southwestern portion of the city wall, now clearly no longer required for purposes of defense. They altered the town's appearance spectacularly.[65] The largest of these complexes, the House of Fabius Rufus in the Insula Occidentalis (fig. 31), compares in square footage with the House of the Faun, but differs in that it is entirely closed off from the street.[66] This residence has turned its back on the town. Of course, one must keep in mind the possibility that old entryways may have disappeared as the complex grew. Yet the smaller houses in the theater quarter reveal essentially the same structure, with closed fronts on the street side and terraces opening out onto the landscape; inside, the rooms are arranged not around the atrium in a strict pattern, but rather to conform to the sloping terrain.

The new situation is characterized by the make-up of the affluent class interested in building in the "new taste": it is broader and culturally far less homogeneous than the Hellenized elite of Oscan Pompeii. A study of the distribution of wall paintings in the second style around the city might be highly revealing; in the process it would be important to note the occurrence of room forms used in villa architecture and the relationship of such villa elements to the rest of the house. The House of the Cryptoporticus, joined with the House of the Trojan Shrine as a single dwelling (I 6.2 and 4), seems representative: in the mid–first century B.C. the owner had a large *cryptoporticus* (underground portico) with baths built in his garden and painted with literary motifs at enormous expense. Although the quality of

Figure 31 House of Fabius Rufus (Insula Occidentalis), view from the south, compare fig. 30. This house, excavated only in the past two decades, is comparable in size to the grandest townhouse of the second century B.C., the House of the Faun (see fig. 5). But, by contrast, this house is closed off on the side facing the town and possesses neither shops nor a large atrium. These are all indications that the owner's social behavior was also different.

the painting is superb, the owner's showy gesture and cultural aspirations stand in striking contrast to his modest dwelling and social status.[67] When the house was later divided in two, the contrast became even more striking.

In the case of the palatial tufa houses of the second century B.C., by contrast, the proportions had been correct. The Oscan landowners and merchants who built them were newcomers to Hellenistic culture, but nonetheless full participants in it, indistinguishable from the Greeks of the mother country and Asia Minor except perhaps for a slight degree of excess. When their successors began taking the great Roman aristocrats' villas as their point of orientation, however, Pompeii lapsed into cultural provincialism.

The role played by extravagant display in the altered cultural climate can be particularly well observed in the tombs of this epoch flanking the roads out of town.[68] Large funerary monuments were unknown to the inhabitants of Oscan Pompeii. Even the great families buried their dead in the enclosed cemeteries situated away from the road. It was the colonists who first erected grand tombs along the main roads, a custom they had observed in Rome and other cities of the Roman world. Soon various types of ostentatious monuments were ranged next to one another, for the most part altar tombs and aediculae on tall plinths. The intent was to give prominent display to the achievements and wealth of the deceased, but above all to their political and social rank.

The community gave a political leader like M. Porcius a place of honor outside the Herculaneum Gate in the *pomerium* (sacred zone), which extended a hundred feet out from the town walls. His tomb in the form of an enormous altar with a Doric frieze resembles a monument to a hero. With the passage of time these graves came to reflect the competition for—and nuances of—rank and status within the town more and more clearly. An important element of this competition was that it was open to anyone with the requisite funds: if the town did not vote you an honorary statue in the forum, your relatives could simply commission one and place it in an aedicula on your tomb. And if they could not afford that, they could join forces with others in the same position and share the cost of a monument. The freed slaves of the Flavii, for example, erected a tomb for themselves at the crossroads by the Nucerian Gate that resembled a kind of apartment house—and in an exclusive neighborhood, too, next to the monuments of several citizens of vastly higher rank, from the colony's first families.[69]

Such "streets of tombs" (plate 5) were created all over Italy during the first century B.C. These displays by urban dwellers of their own wealth and importance were placed outside the gates of their towns in order to impress passers-by as well as fellow citizens. Travelers through Italy could now make comparisons and assess the consequence of a city even before they entered it; they could also learn the identity of the most prominent local households, the *domi nobiles*. Here again the point of orientation was Rome, the capital that politically ambitious men from every town aspired to reach.[70] Although this alteration of the townscape was not specific to Pompeii, it acquired a unique dimension by departing so radically from previous burial customs. At least in the early days of the colony, every time the older inhabitants of the town took a stroll out past the gates, the sight of the new ostentatious tombs would have reminded them who now ran the town. The shift of language from Oscan to Latin was not the only change Pompeii witnessed.

If we try to sum up the total effect of these separate and quite heterogeneous phenomena, we cannot help concluding that the half-century from 80 to 30 B.C. represented a period of significant transformation.[71] Although the Hellenistic appearance of the town was preserved on the whole, the major new buildings shifted the accents. No coherent construction program developed similar to the one that had taken place in the previous century, for in Pompeii the colonists had encountered a town with excellent modern facilities, in contrast to most of the cities in central and northern Italy. They erected a number of public buildings in the first decade after their arrival, but these structures were separate projects; they served less as a response to the new inhabitants' basic needs than as a means of cementing Pompeii's new identity as a colony and adding to its attractions. But the political and ideological motives behind them were new. From then on sponsors and donors had more in mind than simply the effect of their gifts on their fellow citizens; their gaze was fixed on places farther afield, especially Rome. The resulting spirit of competition then spread from the elite to all strata of society. On all sides we see the need for exhibition and self-promotion growing, reflected in public statues and private tombs, and by a new taste in domestic decor visible in more modest houses as well as in those of the rich.

The perspective opened up by the new orientation toward Rome and other Roman towns altered the cultural climate and townscapes profoundly in the first century B.C. The catchphrase according to which every citizen had two *patriae*, his own city and the Roman state as a whole, found direct and material expression in the extravagant outward display observable everywhere in urban vistas and funerary monuments.

Townscape and Ideology in the Age of Augustus

Another set of major alterations to the townscape of Pompeii occurred in the early years of the Empire. Almost all public building from about 20 B.C. was undertaken, either directly or indirectly, as a result of Augustus Caesar's establishment of a monarchy and his policies of religious and cultural renewal. Like the urban elite throughout Italy and the western provinces, the most influential families in Pompeii identified themselves with the cultural aims of the *princeps* and the cult developing around his person. It was these families, the *domi nobiles,* who interpreted the signs of the new era for their fellow citizens and attempted to imitate the exemplary actions of the ruler in their own cities. After the chaos of the Republic's final years, marked by civil wars, proscriptions, and expropriations of property, the elite class found itself able to arrive at a new self-definition by adopting his prescribed code of conduct. The prerequisite for this step was the return of peace and personal security, followed by a significant economic upswing in the first half of Augustus' reign.[72]

The most important leitmotif of Augustus' new policy was *pietas* (piety). The return to the old faith in the gods would, he hoped, lead to a renewed flowering of virtue and morality, and halt the decline in cultural activity. From 28 B.C. Augustus had taken the lead in reviving piety in Rome. He had renovated all the crumbling temples and built magnificent new shrines for his special protectors Venus, Apollo, and Mars.

Renovating the Temples, Reviving the Cults

All the great donors and benefactors of early Augustan Pompeii held priestly offices. Like their ruler, they both restored and embellished the old temples, and also built new ones. (Not all these temples date from Augustus' reign, however; presumably some of them required decades for their completion.) The city's two patron divinities, Apollo and Venus, gave the Pompeians a special connection with the new era and a particular reason to welcome it, for the emperor was descended from Venus, and he ascribed his success at Actium to Apollo's intervention. Enormous temples to both had been erected in Rome, and in Pompeii the old Sullan temple to Venus was no longer regarded as sufficiently grand. Perhaps, too, its negative associations with the dictator Sulla and the unhappy period of the colony's founding were considered serious disadvantages. In any event the council ordered work begun on a new temple—at an unknown date, unfortunately, since the structure still awaits detailed investigation—which was presumably not yet completed when the earthquake struck in A.D. 62. In order to enlarge the site for the new Temple of Venus, substructures were built on the southern side; they were so extensive that a part of the "Villa Imperiale" had to be sacrificed to make room for them. A stairway that led from the substructures directly up to the temple forecourt is reminiscent of the link between the house of Augustus and the Temple of Apollo on the Palatine in Rome. Possibly the owners of the Villa Imperiale wished to imitate Augustus in this respect as well, or perhaps the priestess of one of the civic cults *(sacerdos publica)* actually lived there. The latter possibility is no more than speculation, of course. But several details show that the enlargement of the sanctuary of Venus represented a symbolically charged and highly important act; moving the northern wall of the sacred precinct one yard farther north required that the entire sidewalk along the street running from the Marine Gate to the forum be sacrificed to the goddess, yet it was done! The aim was to transform the old shrine into a lavish marble temple with double colonnades on the eastern and western sides and a broad terrace with a view toward the sea to the south. A decision to make such sweeping changes is most easily comprehensible in the context of the grand innovations of the Augustan age.

Apollo received renewed attention as well (figs. 32 and 33, plate 6). Sometime shortly before 3/2 B.C. the town council granted the two duumviri the right to construct a new wall on the western side of the god's shrine, which obstructed an existing window of the house next door (VII 7.2; *CIL* X 787). One of them was M. Holconius Rufus, the man later awarded the honorary title "benefactor of the colony" *(patronus coloniae)* for undertaking the costs of renovating the theater. Two other duumviri erected a sundial in front of the Temple of Apollo (*CIL* X 802). The wall and the sundial were of course relatively modest tributes to the town's

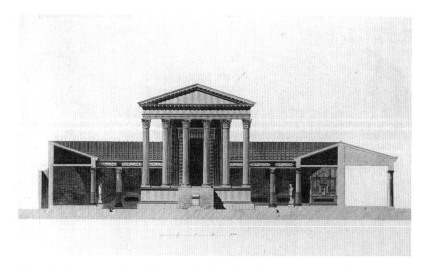

Figure 32 Reconstruction of the Temple of Apollo (after Mazois). As in Rome and many other Roman cities, the sanctuaries and temples of Pompeii were renovated and richly embellished during the reign of Augustus. The emperor's program of encouraging religion included revival and lavish observance of the temple festivals. Some parts of the Games of Apollo *(ludi Apollinares)* were celebrated in the forum, which had a direct connection to the temple.

traditional patron deity. An inscription from the Augustan period, however, conveys an impression of the munificence with which the Games of Apollo *(ludi Apollinares)* were celebrated in that era. As we learn from the inscription on the tomb of Aulus Clodius, not only was he duumvir for three terms, *quinquennalis,* and *tribunus militum a populo,* but he also financed the procession *(pompa)* in the forum, and bulls, bullfighters and their attendants, three pairs of *pontarii* (gladiators), a team of boxers, individual boxers, and various stage performers for the games (*CIL* X 1074).[73]

The rituals and some of the performances listed on his tomb took place in the forum, which was directly connected with the Temple of Apollo through great gateways opened on festival days. In recent years various scholars have rightly stressed the importance of visualizing the architecture in combination with such rituals if we are to assess its full effect properly.[74] The inscription containing information on how the Games of Apollo in Pompeii were celebrated provides one valuable opportunity to do so.

POMPEII

Figure 33 Model of the Temple of Apollo and the forum (Pompeii Museum). The forum was lined on three sides by religious buildings. Several structures devoted to the cult of the imperial family were added on the long eastern side in the early years of the Empire, joining the older precinct of Apollo and the Temple of Jupiter, which dominated the square.

The Cult of the Emperor

Augustus' program of *pietas* in Rome was intended to honor the full pantheon, but the gods most closely associated with him naturally received the greatest reverence. It was to their cults above all that the magnificent new marble temples were devoted. In Rome Augustus limited the cult of his own person to an indirect manner; his *genius* could be honored only in combination with the Lares. However, he clearly had no objection if the designation *augustus* was added to the names of certain divinities, especially those who personified the virtues being so vigorously promoted. Magistrates in smaller towns throughout Italy followed his lead. A large majority of the many new shrines and temples built in the early Augustan age were intended to honor the emperor in this indirect manner. And it was possible to celebrate the superhuman attributes, indeed the divine nature of the ruler's power, far more openly in the provinces than in Rome itself, in the emperor's own presence. One could even go so far as to say that the official elites of Roman towns in the western half of the Empire found a new source of identity for themselves in the many gifts they made to honor the imperial dynasty. Because of the large number of inscriptions and monuments preserved there, Pompeii offers the best example of this development.

The first sanctuary built in Pompeii to honor the emperor in this broad sense is the Temple of Fortuna Augusta (figs. 34–36).[75] It was erected by M. Tullius, one of the town's most influential citizens, who was probably at the height of his career in the earlier part of the Augustan era (25–5 B.C.?) and served as duumvir for several terms, as *quinquennalis,* and as *tribunus militum a populo;* he also held a lifetime appointment as augur.[76] The post of tribune was an honorary one, awarded by the emperor to nominees proposed by the civic leaders of Italic cities. M. Tullius, along with the M. Holconius Rufus who sponsored the renovation of the theater, numbered among the Pompeian officials who were elevated to the nobility in this fashion and were thereby able to enter into direct contact with the imperial dynasty.

M. Tullius sponsored construction of the marble-faced Temple of Fortuna Augusta on his own land and at his own expense *(solo et pecunia sua).* For its site he chose a location just north of the forum, at the intersection of two of the town's most important streets. The podium of the pseudoperipteral temple jutted out into the street. Later an attempt was made to integrate it with the forum by adding a narrow portico. Most likely its construction was prompted by Augustus' safe return from a journey, either to the East in 19 B.C. or to the West in 13 B.C. Altars and shrines to Fortuna Redux were built in Rome and many other cities at that time, and in addition the Corinthian style of the marble capitals (plate 7) argues for such an early date.[77]

We may well ask why M. Tullius did not build his temple in the forum itself. Was he unable to acquire a lot on the forum's long eastern side, the only location still available for this purpose? Or were the buildings associ-

ates 1 and 2   Two mosaics from the House of the Faun (VI 12). In the Oscan era the taste of the
ban elite in Pompeii was decisively influenced by the culture of Hellenistic cities in the eastern
editerranean. Furniture, implements, and works of art—such as the bronze statuette of the "dancing
un" after which the house is named—were imported or commissioned from itinerant Greek arti-
ns. The mosaics in grand reception rooms also bear a close resemblance to those found on Delos and
other Greek cities. Erotic scenes with satyrs and nymphs were one of the most popular subjects of
e Hellenistic art, as in this floor mosaic from a bedroom off the Tuscan atrium (fig. 5, no. 2).

Plate 2   Mosaic depicting fish and other sea creatures. Like most of the motifs in the mosaics of the House of the Faun, it is based on a famous model, in this case one thought to have been in the Museum, the center of learning at the court of Alexandria. The careful depiction of the creatures reflects an interest in natural phenomena; at the same time, however, many of the fish shown were culinary delicacies, so that the motif would have been suitable for a dining room (fig. 5, no. 3).

Plate 3.1   Dedicatory inscription of the Odeon *(theatrum tectum)*. The two chief officials of Pompeii, the duumviri C. Quinctius Valgus and M. Porcius, supervised construction of the building, which had been commissioned by the town council, and carried out the final inspection: *C. Quinctius C. Valg(us), M. Porcius M. f.. duovir(I) dec(urionum) decr(eto) theatrum tectum fac(iundum) locar(unt) eidemq(ue) prob(arunt)* (Degrassi, vol. 1, no. 646).

Plate 3.2   Aerial view of the amphitheater *(spectacula),* showing clearly how the city wall was used as a support on one side. To the left is the field enclosed with colonnades in the Augustan period, perhaps as a *gymnasium,* a sports ground for the boys and young men of Pompeii (cf. figs. 59, 60).

Plate 5   Tombs along the road outside the Nucerian Gate. The custom of self-promotion in the form of exhibitionist funeral monuments was brought to Pompeii by Roman colonists. The size and cost of the tombs were intended to reflect the prestige and rank of the deceased and their families, and it was also important to secure a good site (as close as possible to one of the heavily traveled roads near a city gate). Dimensions and artistic embellishment of the monuments were key criteria as families vied to outdo one another.

Plate 4   Odeon (*theatrum tectum:* cf. fig. 27). One of the two satyrs whose backs support the walls *(malemmata)* surrounding the auditorium *(cavea).* The same stonemasons appear to have built the theater in Pietrabbondante, where the Samnites living in the mountains used to assemble.

Plate 6 View of the reconstructed portion of the colonnade, Temple of Apollo. The temple under
went extensive renovation in the Augustan period, and many embellishments were added. Two cost
ly bronze statues, representing Apollo (see photo) and Diana as archers, were probably votive offer
ings dedicated in that period. The style and rather inferior craftsmanship suggest that they date from
the late first century B.C.

Plate 7 Two marble capitals from the Temple of Fortuna. The architectural decoration in the ne
cult buildings of the Augustan Age reflects a quality of execution never before achieved by Italic ston
cutters. Models from Rome played a key role in raising the level of skill and sophistication.

Plate 8.1   A water tower *(castellum aquae)* near the Vesuvian Gate. Water brought from the mountains by aqueduct was fed into large tanks like this and later piped to different parts of the town.

Plate 8.2   *Campus,* known as the palaestra. Consisting of three very long porticos surrounding a large grassy area, it was built in the Augustan period primarily as a sports and recreational center for the youth of the town. In the foreground are visible the hollows left by the root systems of the large trees that once stood there.

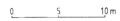

0   5   10 m

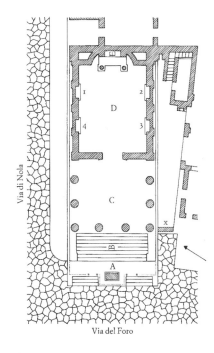

Figures 34–35 Ruins and ground plan of the Temple of Fortuna Augusta. Early in Augustus' reign M. Tullius, one of the leading citizens of Pompeii, privately sponsored the construction of this first temple dedicated to the cult of the emperor. Like many civic leaders elsewhere, he thereby followed the example of the Roman Senate, which had erected marble altars to honor the emperor's Fortuna Redux. The ground plan and lavish ornamentation are also modeled upon Augustus' new marble buildings in Rome.

Urban Space as a Reflection of Society

Figure 36 Idealized reconstruction of the Temple of Fortuna Augusta and its surroundings (after C. Weichardt, 1896).

ated with the cult of the emperor and the building of Eumachia already in the planning stage? Were the Pompeians not yet willing to sacrifice the shops south of the market for a project connected with a political cult in the early days of the principate? It is to be hoped that J. J. Dobbins's "Pompeii Forum Project" will provide some answers to these questions.

The temple's form and manner of construction show that the builder and architect were familiar with the new principles of sacred architecture in Rome, although no specific models existed as yet for them to imitate. The costly white marble reflected the lavishness fitting for the gods, and also measured up to new standards of craftsmanship and aesthetics. The emphasis of the façade with podium and integrated altar (fig. 35, A) matched the highly effective symbolism of the *aurea templa* in Rome.[78] The long sides of the *cella* were designed to contain niches for statues of the benefactor and his family, and perhaps also members of the imperial house (1–4). The statue of a toga–clad figure from the Augustan era found here might possibly depict M. Tullius, while a female figure might represent a member of the dynasty upon whom the sentence of *damnatio memoriae* was later pronounced, perhaps Julia, since the original face was destroyed and replaced by another. Construction of new temples for the cult of the emperor provided local officials with effective opportunities to draw attention to themselves and promote their own careers.[79] Just like the members of the imperial family, whose statues were now placed everywhere in temples both old and new, so too these local dignitaries acquired something of the aura of the ruler and of the divinities associated with his cult.

We find the same kind of self-promotion in the aedicula of the market (figs. 37 and 38).[80] This was a recess containing steps up to a raised platform, which was created at the eastern end of the new market building. (To the left was a meeting room for officials of the cult; to the right was the fish market.) At the time of the earthquake the recess contained a statue of the emperor, of which unfortunately only one arm has been found. (The globe held in the hand shows that the emperor was seated, like the frequently depicted "Jupiter on his throne.") The two statues found in the niches to the right, from the reign of Nero, no doubt honor officials who had performed valuable services on behalf of the market. The man (fig. 39), probably already deceased, is shown naked except for a drape around his hips, in the heightened heroic pose of rulers and princes, while the woman (fig. 40) is depicted in the robes of a priestess, wearing a wreath on her head and holding a small box of incense. She may have been one of the public priestesses (*sacerdotes publicae*) who played such a large role as civic benefactors in Pompeii in the early years of the Empire.[81]

To the south of the market, the old shops were razed to make room for two new buildings associated with the cult of the emperor. The Sanctuary of the Lares (figs. 41 and 42) presumably dates from the period between the death of Augustus and the earthquake.[82] It was not still under construction, as Maiuri thought; instead the shrine was stripped of its valuable marble facing by robbers during the long period when the forum lay in ruins. One good indication for the validity of this hypothesis is the discovery of the remnants of a marble floor during excavation. The Sanctuary of the Lares is an unusual structure, with a central apse that is flanked by square exedrae and has many niches for statues. Whether the sanctuary was roofed or open to the elements remains a matter of controversy. It also had its own portico,

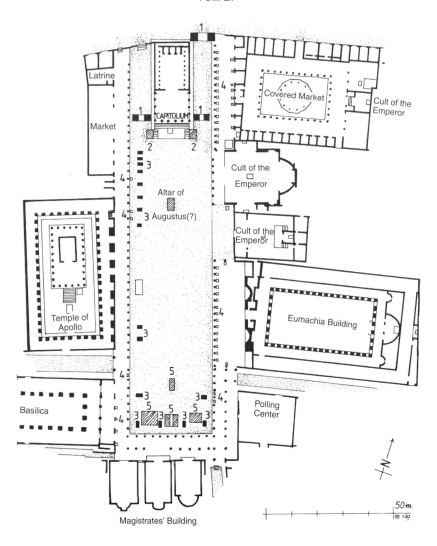

Figure 37 The forum as it appeared in the early Empire. Some elements of the plan are speculative. By this time the space had become entirely dominated by monuments to the imperial family. Presumably an altar to Divus Augustus stood in the center opposite the two small temples for the cult of the emperor.

1: Arches. 2: Equestrian statues of imperial princes (?). 3: Equestrian statues of local magistrates. 4: Honorific portrait statues. 5: Imperial monuments.

Figure 38   The market with an exedra for the cult of the emperor. In the Augustan era even the market building had a chapel added to it for the cult of the imperial family. A statue of the seated emperor, modeled on similar statues of Jupiter, stood in the center.

which was open at both ends and used as a passageway along the forum. From the beginning this building's main purpose appears to have been to display a large number of statues, most likely members of the imperial family, similar to the collections found in so many cities of Italy and the western provinces. An altar stood in the center, where citizens could pay homage to the Lares of the city, as well as to (obviously) the emperor. Recently, J. J. Dobbins has dated the building in the period after the earthquake of A.D. 62, proposed that it had an elaborate dome, and connected the construction with a workshop of Roman stonemasons.

Several features of the Temple of Vespasian (fig. 43), located to the right of the Sanctuary of the Lares, suggest that it was constructed during the Augustan period.[83] The niches on the inside of the surrounding wall exhibit motifs similar to those on the southern façade of the Eumachia Building, providing a rough indication of their date. The appearance of the altar,

Figures 39–40 Marble statues from the market. These statues of two members of a leading Pompeian family flanked the larger-than-life-size statues of the imperial family; probably the man and woman depicted belonged to the family that donated the new chapel. The woman's

wreath and box of incense mark her as a priestess, while the man is shown in a heroic pose also used for members of the ruling dynasty. On the basis of the hairstyles the statues can be assigned to the period around A.D. 60.

Urban Space as a Reflection of Society

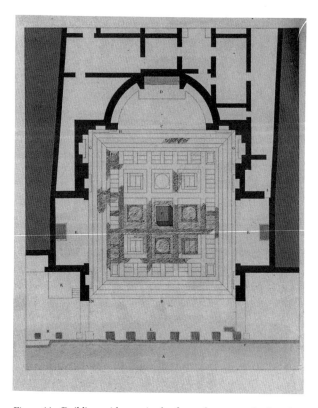

Figure 41 Building with apse in the forum known as the Lararium, with a reconstruction of the tile floor (after Mazois). The many niches of this singular structure suggest that it was designed to hold a gallery of statues of the imperial family, such as are known to have existed in many other towns. The floor tiles of various colored marbles, some of them imported from great distances, offer a good example of the costly fittings used in such ceremonial buildings.

which was renovated and partially replaced after the earthquake, also agrees with this dating (fig. 44).

The shrine consists of a forecourt, an altar, and a small peristyle temple with four columns on a tall podium, accessible by a staircase on either side. The motifs on the altar—a shield *(clipeus virtutis)*, an oak wreath *(corona civica)*, garlands of laurel, and the sacrifice of a bull—document the shrine's connection with the cult of the emperor.[84] In the nineteenth century Fiorelli connected the well-known inscription of Mammia with this build-

Figure 42 Building with apse in the forum (Lararium). Reconstruction of the elevation (after Mau, 1902).

Figure 43 Shrine for the cult of the emperor, with altar and temple known as the Temple of Vespasian. The small shrine, presumably dedicated to the genius of Augustus, is thought to have been first erected in the Augustan era; it was repaired after the earthquake. The little temple with four columns in front stands on a tall podium accessible only from the sides.

Urban Space as a Reflection of Society

Figure 44 Marble altar in the precinct for the cult of the emperor. The relief shows a bull being sacrificed, a frequent ceremony in the cult. A temple with four columns can be seen in the background below the drapery; on the pediment is the *clipeus virtutis* characteristic of worship of the emperor.

ing. This inscription on a marble epistyle, now in the Museo Nazionale in Naples, reads: *M[a]mmia P. f. sacerdos public(a) Geni[o Aug(usti) s]olo et pec[unia sua].*[85] It was soon recognized that this dedicatory inscription on the temple should probably be seen in connection with the homage paid to Augustus in the shrines to the Lares in the different districts of Rome from 7 B.C., and the date of the Pompeian temple reckoned accordingly.

Mammia belonged to an old established family in Pompeii.[86] She must have earned the city's gratitude, for the town council honored her after her death with a burial plot inside the *pomerium* directly in front of the Herculaneum Gate and next to the tomb of M. Porcius.

The largest building by far to be constructed in the forum in the Augustan age was also the work of a public priestess (figs. 45 and 46).[87] Eumachia dedicated it to Concordia Augusta and Pietas in her own name and in the name of her son, M. Numistrius Fronto, who is probably identical with the duumvir of A.D. 2/3 (*CIL* X 810). This suggests that we should understand the large gift to the town in the context of his election campaign. Architecturally the structure is a somewhat strange combination of the heterogeneous elements listed individually in the inscription: *chalcidicum, crypta, porticus.* The inscription itself was carved in giant letters on the frieze above the short Doric columns of the façade and below a presumed second order of Ionic columns.

The term *chalcidicum* refers to the portico. It is as deep as the double colonnade in front of the *comitium,* but it did not serve as an extension of the latter, since the southern end was blocked by a statue base and a metal grating. It thus appears that the donor wished to have the building stand on its own as a single, unconnected entity that could be entered only from the side facing the forum. The interior, faced with the most expensive kinds of marble, must have been impressive, but unfortunately most of it was plundered after the earthquake.

Surviving traces indicate that the decor alluded to some of the lofty themes of Augustan ideology; these include the two laudatory inscriptions *(elogia)* to Romulus and Aeneas set into the wall below the small niches on the sides of the semicircular exedrae. They represent "quotations" from the program of images and inscriptions of the *summi viri* in the Forum of

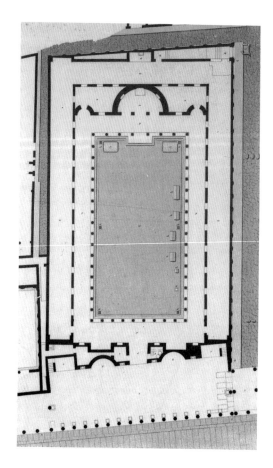

Figure 45 Ground plan of the Eumachia Building in the forum. Eumachia, together with her son, dedicated this very lavish building to Concordia Augusta and Pietas. The building consists of various parts, which presumably served different functions. There was a gallery of statues in the portico. The cryptoporticus and garden may have served as a meeting place and center for recreation, as in Rome. The cult statue stood in the exedra.

Augustus.[88] One would like to know whose statues stood in the two niches on the right. A further odd feature of the building consists in the two rectangular exedrae, each containing a flight of steps (though only the flight on the left actually gives access to the podium). Were these *podia* meant as auctioneers' platforms, as has been supposed, or is it not more likely that they represented platforms for commemorative oratory on festival days honoring the emperor (and that the one on the left was actually used for this purpose)?

The grand style of the *chalcidicum* is revealed by the long row of identical statue bases behind the columns. They must have held a gallery of honorific statues similar to those in the forecourt of the market. Were they

Figure 46 Portico of the Eumachia Building, with a view of the doorway. This door frame, made of marble slabs with the well-known acanthus scroll motif, was reconstructed after excavation.

perhaps *summi viri* modeled after those in the Forum of Augustus, or were they memorials to deserving former municipal officials? The best clue we have to the donor's extravagance is the magnificent door frame with carved acanthus scrolls (fig. 47). It resembles the reliefs of the Ara Pacis so closely and is of such high quality that it may be justifiably assumed to have

Figure 47 Detail of the marble door frame (?) in the Eumachia Building. The style and quality of the scroll frieze make it comparable to the Ara Pacis in Rome. The donor probably commissioned it from a Roman workshop. Later the door frame was joined to the building for the cult of the emperor to the left of the Eumachia Building.

come from a workshop in Rome. As it does not fit the opening in the wall exactly, K. Wallat has recently suggested that it may originally have adorned the entrance to the Temple of Vespasian.

The interior of the building consists of a four-sided colonnade *(porticus)* around a central courtyard, with a large apse devoted to Concordia

Augusta at the rear, flanked by two small semicircular *exedrae*. Behind this colonnade lay the three-sided *crypta* (covered gallery); from the short side behind the apse one could look from the *crypta* onto the two small spaces on either side of the apse that were planted as gardens. From the way in which various architectural elements are combined, it is apparent that this lavish building served a variety of leisure-time purposes. Clearly Eumachia wanted her building in the forum to bring a touch of urban flair to Pompeii. As the flat terrain in no way necessitated the construction of a cryptoporticus, it seems that the donor was motivated by the Augustan theme of *publica magnificentia,* and wished to create a particularly impressive example of it. In such a context the combination of a *porticus* with a *crypta* and gardens had far more dash than a simple colonnade.

Eumachia's gift to the town appears to have been inspired by the Porticus Liviae in Rome, a form of "community center" built by Livia and her son in the densely populated area of the Subura. The latter was dedicated in 7 B.C. and also consecrated to Concordia Augusta. Eumachia probably followed Livia's example only a few years later, whereby her chief aim seems to have been not so much to imitate the Roman building's celebrated architecture as to rival Livia's civic-mindedness and piety.[89]

Of course in this instance the piety was directed toward the imperial family itself. In the large apse of Eumachia's building stood an elaborately carved statue of Concordia with a gilded cornucopia (fig. 48). The goddess was probably depicted with Livia's features, a frequent form of homage. This is suggested by the simple relief on the fountain facing the side entrance to the building, which shows Concordia with Livia's fashionable hairstyle (fig. 50).[90]

Eumachia offers another instance of a donor's using a building for direct self-promotion. A statue of her was found in the *crypta* in a niche directly behind the chapel to Concordia. Presumably Eumachia arranged to have this statue, space for which was included in the original plan of the building, dedicated to her by the *fullones,* the cloth fullers and dyers; obviously they owed her a particular debt of gratitude. It depicts her as a priestess and holy woman, with her head covered (fig. 49), and was executed in the classical style.[91] This is noteworthy, because the sculptor was not a particularly skilled craftsman. Both face and body are depicted entirely in the

Figure 48 Statue of an Augustan divinity with the features of Livia (Ny Carlsberg Glyptotek, Copenhagen). Several indications suggest that the cult statue in the Eumachia Building must have resembled it (compare figure 50). The imperial family is here celebrated as the source of all prosperity, in the form of a goddess with a cornucopia.

Figure 49 Statue of Eumachia (Museo Nazionale, Naples). The statue of the benefactress was found in the niche behind the large exedra for the cult statue. It was donated by the *fullones,* the cloth fullers and dyers; Eumachia may have been their employer. The veil over her head alludes to her piety and to her office as civic priestess *(sacerdos publica).* The two statues of the goddess/empress and the local benefactress were thus placed in relation to each other, despite their separation by a wall.

Figure 50 Fountain at the side entrance to the Eumachia Building. The rather crude relief made by a local stone carver is presumed to be an imitation of the lost cult statue of Concordia Augusta inside.

idealized forms of the late classical epoch. The movement of the body expresses reserve and grace *(charis)* in equal measure, and the rendering of the face reflects no attempt to portray the real Eumachia, whose appearance must have been familiar to all. The statue's features are completely idealized. This classical vocabulary had ethical connotations for Augustan ideology, associations with which the Pompeians who commissioned the work must have been acquainted.[92] But visitors to the splendid building no doubt felt that this exalted language of form, familiar to them from statues of the imperial family, elevated and ennobled their neighbor Eumachia. Thus we see that even the few finds from the priestess's building offer important evidence showing how the new visual symbolism of the Roman state was absorbed and reworked on different levels.

In the course of only a few decades four imposing buildings (or perhaps only three, if Dobbins's theory is confirmed) were added to the eastern side of the forum, all faced at least in part with marble, and distinguished by their elaborate decoration and light travertine façades. These features gave them a certain substance in comparison with the older buildings made of tufa. Even more important, however, each of these new structures had direct or indirect ties to the worship of the emperor and his family; again and again, the particular rituals and festivals associated with each one drew the inhabitants' attention to the buildings and their cults.

New research has shown that the forums of many cities underwent similar profound changes in appearance in the early years of the Empire. Many such buildings were erected during Augustus' reign, others during the reigns of his immediate successors. The location, size, and decoration of these shrines varied from place to place, for they were built by local officials to demonstrate their loyalty. In this instance townscapes offer a unique reflection of the political changes that were occurring, and prove the extent to which society identified itself with the new system. In many cities builders and architects were able to create far more impos-ing ensembles than in Pompeii; indeed, in cities founded in this era the buildings associated with the cult of the emperor dominate all the rest.[93] The case of Pompeii is particularly valuable, however, because here we are able to gather some impression of how the transformation pro-ceeded.

It is significant that each such building resulted from individual initia-tive. There was no overall plan, not even for integrating the new structures into the existing ensemble. Although this seems amazing, we know it is the case, since not one of the façades is flush with any of the others. In conse-quence there was also no continuous portico on the eastern side of the forum; instead the forecourt of the market, the Sanctuary of the Lares, and the Eumachia Building all presented the square with façades of differing sizes and styles.

Honorific Monuments in the Forum

The area of the forum itself acquired new features in the early Empire.[94] After the colony was founded at Pompeii, it appears that equestrian statues of a certain size came into fashion as tributes to the town's highest officials; this is suggested by the old pedestals on the western side of the forum and in front of the municipal offices to the south (fig. 51). Some of these were removed as early as the Augustan era, however, to make room for an arch, which may have been surmounted by a statue of the emperor driving a four-horse chariot *(quadriga)* like the famous one in the Forum of Augustus in Rome. Later two enormous monuments on rectangular plinths were added flanking the arch, probably also *quadrigae,* as well as a colossal equestrian statue farther toward the center of the forum on its long axis. Presumably the equestrian statues that had previously been lined up at the southern

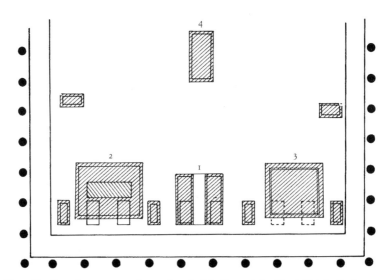

Figure 51   Bases for statues on the south end of the forum (after Mau). Originally there was a row of equestrian statues there, but most of them were taken down to make room for monuments to the imperial family on three huge bases (1–3).

end were removed and re-erected elsewhere in the square, but the over,
effect in creating the new monuments—which doubtless honored mem
bers of the imperial family—was to marginalize the town's most illustrious
citizens; their lesser significance was also reflected in the figures' relative
size.[95]

The position directly in front of the main town offices at the forum's
southern end clearly had the highest status; this probably came about because it was the busiest part of the square. It does in fact appear as if the
imperial monuments were aligned facing the path that would have been
taken by traffic between the Via dell'Abbondanza and the Marine Gate.
The long western side conveyed less prestige, as is obvious from the smaller
size of the pedestals. The few statues of standing figures along the steps of
the portico would have been completely overshadowed. The surviving
inscriptions indicate that these were honorific statues of local officials. It
thus emerges that a clear hierarchy existed in the location of imperial and
municipal monuments.

The north end of the forum was dominated by more monuments to the
imperial family no less impressive than those to the south. Two arches were
erected, one on either side of the *capitolium,* modeled on those on the east
side of the Forum Romanum and in the Forum of Augustus; they presumably honored princes of the imperial house (fig. 52). Later the arch on the
right was moved all the way back to the street running behind the *capitolium,* both to keep it from blocking the new forecourt of the market and
to create a better visual link to the Temple of Fortuna Augusta and the
portico leading to it. When still later a further arch was built next to this
temple in the line of sight from the forum arch, it created an effective
receding vista reminiscent of far larger cities (see fig. 54).

The arches' proximity to the temple façade elevated to the religious
sphere the statues of the family members thus honored; they also drew the
old *capitolium* into the ensemble, virtually making it part of the encomium
to the emperor. This effect was increased by placing equestrian statues on
both sides of the steps, as shown on the relief in the lararium of the house
of Caecilius Iucundus (fig. 54a).[96] No doubt these, too, honored members
of the imperial dynasty.

Figure 52 A reconstruction of the north end of the forum (after D. Scagliarini Corlàita). This side of the square was also dominated by monuments to the ruling dynasty. As in the fora of other Italic cities, they were displayed in two places: flanking the steps to the Temple of Jupiter, and on top of the two triumphal arches adjoining the temple.

The forum itself was repaved with travertine, probably in the early imperial period; the new surface must have created a far grander impression than the old blocks of tufa that it replaced.[97] An inscription set in the pavement near the *suggestum* (platform) and running the width of the forum named the donor. It is reminiscent of the inscription in the Forum Romanum naming the Praetor Surdinus and similar pavement inscriptions in other Italic cities. Unfortunately, only a few letters of this bronze inscription can be reconstructed, but even this much suffices to show that the donor was as little inclined to modesty as Eumachia. The lettering is larger than in Surdinus' inscription in Rome! The occasion of the repaving may have been used to arrange the commemorative statues in a more systematic way. Perhaps the town magistrates decided then to remove all the pedestrian statues from the forum and reassemble them in the *chalcidicum* of the Eumachia Building and the forecourt of the market (see fig. 53). The identical bases in both places suggest a kind of portrait gallery, similar to the *summi viri* in the Forum of Augustus in Rome.

If we now turn our attention to the effect created by the forum as a whole, we see that the space in the center was kept free of honorific monuments. But at about the height of the two buildings devoted to the cult of the emperor are the remains of a tall rectangular base on the long axis of the square (see fig. 37). Its dimensions have led to speculation that it was an altar, and I believe this is correct. It could not have belonged to the *capitolium,* however, for its altar, once located in the forum but closer to the temple, was moved to the temple podium in the Augustan era, as it is shown in the lararium relief of the House of Caecilius Iucundus (see fig. 54a). There is good reason to suppose that the base in the center of the forum represents the remains of an altar dedicated to the emperor, which would then have been surrounded on three sides by buildings for his cult or monuments in his honor. The altar's orientation with regard to the cult buildings would then seem to indicate a shift of focus in the forum, in a

Figure 53 A reconstruction of the portico in front of the market (*macellum;* after Weichardt, 1896). A series of similar statue bases stood in front of the market and in the portico of the Eumachia Building. Perhaps the earlier statues of civic leaders of Pompeii were re-erected here after the places of honor in the forum were appropriated for monuments to the emperor and his family. In reality, however, the effect created by these porticos was not quite as grand as was imagined by this illustrator in the late nineteenth century!

Figure 54 A view from the forum to the arch adjoining the Temple of Fortuna Augusta (A. Gaeta). Later on a small triumphal arch that served to distribute water as well was erected next to this temple. The vista gives an impression of the impact made by the new ceremonial buildings and honorific monuments.

Figure 54a Relief from the lararium in the House of Caecilius Iucundus (V 1.26) showing the Temple of Jupiter during the earthquake, with the presumed altar for the cult of the emperor to the right and an honorific arch to the left.

POMPEII

manner of speaking, toward the grand new structures associated with the emperor. We may then consider whether the large altar shown in the center of the lararium relief may not in fact represent this very monument.

Seating by Rank in the New Marble Theater

M(arcus et) M(arcus) Holconii Rufus et Celer
cryptam tribunalia theatrum s(ua) p(ecunia)

The above inscription (*CIL* X 833–34), several copies of which survive, refers to the large-scale renovation of the Hellenistic theater in the Augustan era (figs. 55, 56).[98] It was placed above both side entrances *(parodoi)* and probably on the façade of the stage-building as well, where audiences would have in view a constant reminder of the generosity of the Holconii. The word *crypta* refers to a considerable enlargement of the curving cov-

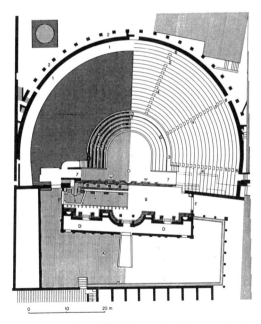

Figure 55 A plan of the theater after its renovation in the Augustan era.

Figure 56 Reconstruction of the large theater after its enlargement and embellishment in the Augustan era (after de Franciscis). In the later part of Augustus' reign the original theater from the second century B.C. was enlarged and refurbished by the Holconii brothers. The renovation reflected not only the general desire for impressive public buildings, but also the increased emphasis on social distinctions in the Empire. Spectators now sat in clearly demarcated sections according to their social rank, and the official sponsors sat in prominent view on newly installed tribunals. Presumably the façade of the stage-building was decorated with statues of the imperial family, as in many other cities.

ered gallery around the auditorium; after the renovation it became a passageway dividing the old seats in the lower rows from the new, more closely spaced rows on top (*summa cavea;* see fig. 55, no. 1). The word *theatrum* must refer among other things to the renovation of the auditorium—so substantial it must have almost amounted to complete reconstruction—that was necessary before the steps and seats could be faced with marble (see fig. 55, nos. 3 and 4).

The side entrances had been covered with vaulting in the Sullan period; now, with the addition of two seating platforms (*tribunalia,* no. 7) above them—also faced with marble, of course—the old theater from the second century B.C. had become thoroughly Roman in appearance. It enabled the magistrates sponsoring the performances to be seated in elevated boxes, as befitted their rank and dignity, where they could be seen by everyone in the theater. The general renovation must have included facing the stage-building or *saenae frons* with marble as well. The many theaters of the early Empire and their stage walls with two- and three-story orders of columns are well known. Unfortunately, very little of the marble facings survived in the theater at Pompeii, and it has not been possible to reconstruct the exact appearance of the stage reliably.[99] Perhaps we may imagine it as similar to the one in the theater at Herculaneum. In any event we may safely assume that some of the statue bases found in the theater once stood between the columns of the stage front, which in Pompeii may also have contained statues of the emperor and his family in the center. The customary hierarchy of rank would dictate that these were flanked by portraits of the Holconii, at least three of which have been positively identified.

M. Holconius Rufus was the leading citizen of Pompeii in the middle and late Augustan era (compare fig. 58).[100] He was descended from an old family that produced excellent wine and even had a type of grape named after them. M. Holconius Rufus' political career must have begun about 20 B.C., for at the time the theater was built in 3/2 B.C. he had already served as duumvir four times, as *quinquennalis* once, and been awarded the honorary title of *tribunus militum a populo* by the emperor. In addition he held the office of priest in the cult of the emperor *(sacerdos Augusti).* He later received the title of "patron of the colony" *(patronus coloniae),* the highest honor that the town of Pompeii could bestow.

The relative by the name of Celer mentioned together with M. Holconius Rufus in the inscriptions must have been considerably younger: he was not chosen duumvir until A.D. 13/14, although by that time he was *quinquennalis* designate and *sacerdos Augusti.* Still later he became *sacerdos divi Augusti.* Probably he was Rufus' son. As in the case of Eumachia's splendid donation, this gift was intended, among other things, to advance the career of a younger member of the family and thus help to maintain a leading family's status.

Like construction of the buildings for the cult of the emperor, the extensive renovations in the theater offered the sponsors ample opportunity for self-promotion. The honorific monuments placed there by the citizens should once again be seen in the living context of festivals and performances. Members of the *gens Holconia* occupied places of honor not only at the dedication of the refurbished theater, but later on as well; as magistrates or priests of the emperor's cult they would have had places in the seats reserved for officials, or on the new seating platforms as sponsors of performances. The particular prestige M. Holconius Rufus enjoyed in Pompeii is revealed above all by a monument that stood on the lowest step of the middle tier along the central axis of the auditorium, accompanied by an inscription listing his complete *cursus honorum* (fig. 57). The pattern of the holes drilled in the step to attach the monument suggests it may have been a bronze curule chair *(sella curulis),* a form of honorific monument later documented for members of the imperial family.[101] In this way audi-

Figure 57 Inscription honoring the benefactors, the Holconii brothers, in the center of the seating area in the *cavea.*

POMPEII

Figure 58 Honorific statue of M. Holconius Rufus. Citizens honored Pompeii's most important political figure in the late Augustan era with this monument showing him in armor. It stood outside the Stabian baths on one of the busiest streets in town. The military nature of the statue refers to Holconius' status as *tribunus militum a populo*, an honorary title bestowed by the emperor on leading citizens of Italic cities who had performed some outstanding service (*CIL* X 830).

ences would have had before their eyes a conspicuous reminder of the honorand's outstanding career in office.

The case of the Holconii offers us unusually good insights into the process by which the prominent families in Roman cities functioned as intermediaries. It was these leading families who led the campaign for Augustus' program of cultural renewal and created corresponding symbols with their donations. Like M. Holconius Rufus, most of them had direct political connections with Rome, and even with Augustus himself. They were certainly very well informed about the new political guidelines and prepared to identify with them. Political leadership, observance of the cult of the emperor, and interest in improving the appearance of their home towns went hand in hand. M. Holconius Rufus is the first securely documented instance of a priest of Augustus (without the slightest euphemism in his title, incidentally: *Augusti sacerdos*). The emperor had honored him personally, awarding this man with no military connections the high-sounding title of *tribunus militum a populo*. Among other privileges, this entitled Holconius to a particularly prominent seat among the *equites* on his visits to the theater at Rome. When the citizens of Pompeii erected a statue to him at a busy intersection in front of the Stabian baths, they commissioned it from a workshop in Rome. It is likely that Holconius, who knew Rome well, also had a hand in this selection. The type of monument chosen—a copy of the cult statue of Mars Ultor from the Forum Augustum—provided Pompeii with a further important portrait. It gave the highly honorific title a concrete pictorial form, while at the same time proclaiming the importance of manliness and the military.[102]

By refurbishing the theater in marble, M. Holconius Rufus contributed substantially to Pompeii's appearance—another case in which public magnificence was the main theme. New theaters on an ambitious scale were going up everywhere in Roman cities at that time, in central locations inside the walls. In Rome Augustus himself had acted as the sponsor. One function of such institutions was to embody and express the cultural aspirations of the new era. At the same time the members of the upper class in the cities wished to create appropriately elegant settings where they could gather and enjoy themselves. This aim was furthered by the theaters' elaborate and costly decoration with marble, columns, and ornamental statuary, and also by the fact that citizens were expected to wear their best clothes when attending.[103]

One might ask why the Pompeians, who had had two attractive theaters at their disposal for some time, did not consider them sufficient to fulfill this aspect of Augustus' program. Presumably the problem was the lack of marble, which rendered the old theater ugly in their eyes in comparison with the new buildings going up elsewhere. The renovations resolved this difficulty, but the inscription on the refurbished theater reveals that the Holconii had specific sociopolitical aims in view as well. The new *crypta* created additional seating for the lowest-ranking members of the audience (visitors, slaves, the poor, and possibly also women), but was constructed so as to keep them apart from the rest. These seats in the highest tier were accessible only by staircases—quite crude ones, incidentally—leading up directly from outside the building, and there was no connection with the middle tier, where the middle classes sat, preventing this section of the audience from mingling with the others. Such an arrangement reflects perfectly the political concept behind Augustan regulations regarding the theater: the number of those privileged to attend was meant to be increased—to include deserving slaves, for instance—but at the same time distinctions of rank were to be made clearer than ever.

In this connection reconstruction of the *crypta* served a second important purpose, namely, altering access routes to the middle tiers of seats. Thanks to the new *crypta,* there was now separate access to the middle and the bottom tiers *(ima cavea).* The free citizens of the town could reach the twenty rows of seats allotted to them in the middle tier by six staircases leading down from doors in the *crypta;* this allowed the orchestra entrance to be reserved for the aristocrats, who sat in the bottom tier closest to the stage. Probably further divisions existed within the middle tiers for special groups such as members of youth brigades or the army, and in all likelihood the provisions of the *lex Iulia theatralis* created additional categories of privilege and exclusion, as they did in Rome and elsewhere.[104] The only seating divisions preserved in Pompeii are the lines (with matching numbers) on the marble seating indicating that the width allotted per seat was a little over fifteen inches. In sum, it is evident that thanks to the efforts of the Holconii the theater in Pompeii, too, became a setting in which the members of society could experience their own hierarchical order repeatedly and in an enduring fashion, just as their emperor desired.

An "Athletic Field" for Young Men

One further public building in Pompeii from the Augustan era demonstrates the citizens' eagerness to follow the example of the emperor in Rome: the large palaestra next to the amphitheater (figs. 59 and 60).[105] Improving the physical and moral condition of young men in the upper classes was one of Augustus' main concerns; as a means of reaching this goal he promoted equestrian sports, parades, and an annual inspection *(probatio equitum)*. The Troy Games had been revived, and the young men of Rome practiced for them in public view on the Campus Martius. When Augustus' adopted sons Gaius and Lucius were awarded the honorary titles *principes iuventutis* and took on leading roles in the games, these activities acquired even greater significance. The Roman example had an invigorating influence on other towns, where organizations for young men were revitalized and began to sponsor similar competitions. The provision of new training grounds showed how seriously the matter was taken.[106]

The large palaestra is without doubt Pompeii's version of the athletic field. It consists of a very large park-like area (458 by 347 ft.) surrounded on three sides by a colonnade. The front side, which faced the amphitheater, had three entrances surmounted by pediments, with merlons along the walls (fig. 60). The last feature alluded to the structure's function, in theory

Figures 59–60 Ground plan and front view of the *campus* known as the "palaestra." This sprawling sports ground for boys and young men reflects another aspect of Augustus' program of cultural renewal. The park-like area was surrounded by a front wall with three gates and a three-sided colonnade, and had a large swimming pool in the center. The decorative merlons on the wall are an architectural allusion to the underlying ideology of preparedness for battle. In fact, however, under Augustus young men were no longer required to give proof of their fitness for military service, since battles were fought by the professional troops of the Empire.

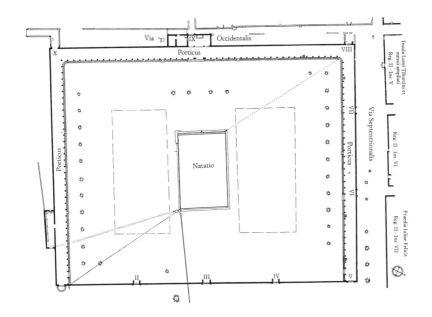

at least: the sponsors—whose identity is unfortunately not known—intended it as a site where the young men of the town could be trained in the basic military arts and keep physically fit. In practice, however, young men in Italy were hardly ever called upon to serve; increasingly, the emperor relied on professional soldiers and barbarian auxiliaries to defend the borders of the Empire. If the donor of the training ground *(campus)* nonetheless insisted on giving it a touch of the fortress, architecturally speaking, it was to serve as a reminder of the cult of *virtus* ("manliness"). A militarization of imagery can be observed in various areas in the early Empire. It both expressed and served to stabilize an outlook that had spread throughout Italy as a result of Augustus' cultural policies, the awareness of being a ruling power.

In actual fact the *campus* was used for a variety of leisure-time activities. There was a large swimming pool *(natatio)* that must certainly have been welcome in the summer, and two rows of plane trees that offered cool places in the shade to rest in between dips. The thick roots of these trees provide an important clue to the age of the structure.[107] At the time of Pompeii's destruction the trees were almost 100 years old (plate 8.1), so that the *campus* dates from the early years of Augustus' principate.

The colonnade, measuring 1,160 feet in total length, has no annexes except for a latrine on the south side and a small shrine, perhaps for the cult of the emperor, in the middle of the long western side. From this we know that no institution such as a *collegium* was permanently established there. However, evidence that the palaestra was actually used as a site for games and athletic contests does exist in the form of several graffiti. Most of these scrawled comments reflect other activities, such as the verses written by a schoolmaster complaining that he has not been paid. Others wrote lines of poetry they had memorized, and of course many graffiti refer to the gladiators' contests that took place next door in the amphitheater. The palaestra was probably heavily frequented by spectators during breaks in the games. And there is no lack of other messages—such as price lists, recommendations for barbers, and naturally the ubiquitous obscenities—indicating that, fortunately, everyday life often diverged greatly from the austere ideals of the reigning ideology.

Small Amenities around Town

After Augustus transformed Rome into a "city of marble," even smaller towns in the western part of the Empire put up expensive public buildings with marble facing. For his contemporaries marble was more than just a means to improve the appearance of their cities; it became a symbol of the new era and acquired a variety of connotations. Buildings made of marble proved that Romans need no longer fear comparison with the beautiful Greek cities of the East. It also stood for a new political culture and morality. In the past only the palaces and villas of the wealthy had been adorned with marble, but now civic buildings were gleaming white, too. The emblem of private luxury was transformed into a symbol of public magnificence, reflecting the priority of communal interests over individual self-indulgence. The new buildings proclaimed the solidity of the new order, from which each citizen's personal security was derived.

Of course not every community could afford marble. Sometimes people had to make do with the lighter shades of limestone or artful stucco work. The Pompeians often fell back on such substitutes, as in the case of the columns for the large palaestra, which were made of stucco-covered bricks. But the values behind the symbol remained potent, and for this reason even small marble embellishments or decor imitating marble had great significance. They accented the appearance of streets and buildings, functioning as encapsulated references to the larger phenomenon of "cities of marble." Pompeii was full of such minor allusive embellishments.

Some were purely small amenities, such as the two marble sundials in the courtyard of the Temple of Apollo and the sacred precinct near the theater. The temple sundial stood on a short column, while the one at the archaic temple was combined with a semicircular bench *(schola)*.[108] In the covered theater the duumvir M. Oculatius donated a new floor in the orchestra made of variegated marble paving.[109] Probably the *tribunalia* and the marble veneer of the *scaenae frons* also date from this time. Over a period of years a number of magistrates donated new rows of seats in the amphitheater.[110] In contrast to those in the theater, however, these were made only of tufa. In the Augustan age the amphitheater ranked far below the other entertainment sites in cultural importance. The two public baths also underwent renovation and had improvements added. In the forum baths, for instance, the duumviri of the year A.D. 3/4 donated a large marble basin (*labrum*, fig. 61).[111]

These examples show that men and women chosen for public office were virtually required to become donors as well. Especially wealthy officials could afford to attach their names to entire structures, like Eumachia and the Holconii, but also M. Tullius and Mammia. But the less affluent could still commemorate themselves in marble in some smaller way. As a result the townscape presented itself to the eye as a communal achievement, but one in which distinctions of social and political rank were preserved all the same. The overall impression must have been one of manifold and ceaseless activity; the citizens felt the town was "on its way up," and everyone contributed to the general effort.

Supplying Water to the Town

Improvements to the infrastructure greatly affected people's outlook. In Pompeii, as in many other places in Italy at this time, streets were repaired and the sewage system was improved.[112] Above all a constant supply of fresh running water was made available to the town's inhabitants. This is thought to have occurred early in Augustus' reign.[113] Unfortunately, we do not know much about how this ambitious project was carried out. The main aqueduct carrying water to the naval port of Misenum had a branch that supplied Pompeii; the water was fed into the main tank standing at the highest point in town, next to the Vesuvian Gate (plate 8.2). From there three large pipes carried it to different neighborhoods. The sloping terrain created considerable water pressure, which was regulated in columnar water towers up to nineteen feet tall.[114] To date fourteen such secondary tanks (*castella secundaria*) have been found; they can be spotted all over town, sometimes standing on sidewalks, and supplied the immediate vicinity with fresh water. It is astonishing to see how many houses were connected to the system and had running water; a large portion of the population profited directly from the new convenience. The supply was also

Figure 61 Marble basin in the caldarium of the forum baths, donated by the two duumviri who served in A.D. 3/4. The basin is one of the small amenities typical of urban improvements in the Augustan period.

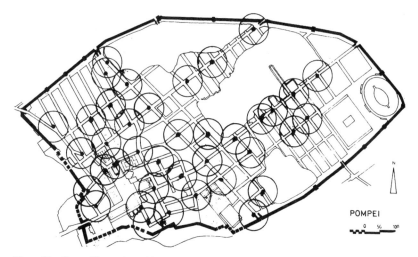

Figure 62 Sites of fountains with running water in Pompeii (after Eschebach). Piped water and a sewage system were standard facilities in the modernized infrastructure of Roman towns. The equal distribution of water pipes throughout the town improved the quality of life of all the citizens. Filled dots indicate street fountains; circles around them show supposed range of supply.

abundant; in the houses of the more affluent we find decorative basins *(nymphaea)* and fountains everywhere, and even some private baths *(thermae).*

But even those too poor to have their houses connected to the city system could enjoy fresh water piped from the mountains, for no fewer than forty public fountains have been discovered in all parts of the town (fig. 62).[115] They tend to be of a standard shape and dimensions, but the details can vary considerably, especially the pretty decorative reliefs carved by unassuming local craftsmen (compare fig. 50). Most of these fountains are made of lava slabs, with a few exceptions fashioned of carved travertine or marble. The more elaborate ones may have been financed by private donations (fig. 63).

When we recall that before introduction of this system the Pompeians were dependent on deep wells and rain-collecting cisterns for their water, it is easy to imagine their joy over the new amenity, which truly represented a substantial improvement in their quality of life.

120

Figure 63 Fountain with running water at a street corner (after Mazois, around 1830). The spouts of such fountains were usually decorated with simple reliefs: compare figure 50.

While the general assumption is correct that the aqueduct going to Pompeii was a subsidiary branch of the imperial aqueduct that carried water to the new harbor facilities and the fleet in Misenum, the townspeople had the emperor to thank personally for authorizing the diversion of part of the supply. Augustus also had aqueducts built to supply many other towns, or contributed toward their construction.[116] Agrippa had set an example with his renovation and expansion of the water supply system in Rome beginning in the late 30s. The Pompeian installations must also be seen in this context; the Roman example was followed everywhere, down to the decorations on the public fountains. And, as in Rome, the new water supply led to increased luxury in the public baths. Here and in other instances of improvements paid for by the Pompeians themselves, the new aqueduct led them to associate such benefits with the emperor. In the last analysis, or so it must have seemed to them at the time, it was he who was responsible for the fact that life was getting better.

Honorific Tombs as Expressions of Civic Pride

In concluding this survey of Pompeii in the age of Augustus, we must look at an area outside the walls, where Augustan ideology led to another alteration in the townscape: the tombs in the form of benches *(scholae)* studied by V. Kockel (fig. 64).[117] Thus far eight of these unusual tombs, consisting of a semicircular bench made of tufa, have been found outside the Herculaneum, Vesuvian, Nolan, and Stabian Gates.

They were honorific tombs for former duumviri or their relatives, to whom the town council had given special permission to build within the

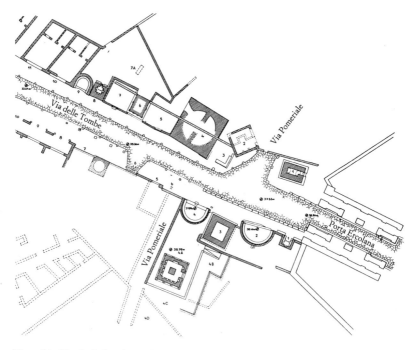

Figure 64 Tombs lining the road outside the Herculaneum Gate (after Kockel/Weber). The most meritorious citizens were honored with grave monuments in the form of exedra near the town gates.

Figure 65 Tomb of the priestess Mammia outside the Herculaneum Gate (painting by Jacob Philipp Hackert, 1793; Goethe Museum, Weimar). During the Augustan era a new form of roadside tomb for distinguished families came into fashion, in the form of a large, exedra-shaped bench on which passers-by could rest. The tomb honoring an individual thus served simultaneously as a decorative amenity for the town. Its worn steps reveal how much it was used by both residents and travelers.

ninety-foot-wide sacred perimeter *(pomerium)*. Honorific monuments of a related type have been found in Greek sanctuaries, but Pompeii is the only place known where they serve as tombs. Some of the *schola* tombs, like the Greek monuments, enclose a base in the middle to support a column or altar. Since no burials have been found at the site, it seems likely that the column or altar held an urn with the ashes of the deceased.

All the people for whom these tombs were built belonged to the leading families of Pompeii. Mammia's name was chiseled into the backrest of her *schola* tomb in huge letters (fig. 65). The group that allowed itself to be honored in this manner for its achievements was a closed social circle. Whoever had the opportunity to compare these commemorative monuments with the flashy tombs of the "colonial era," particularly the altar graves and aedicula graves, some of them in marble, could not help being struck by their simple dignity. In addition, a special effect was created by the fact that these civic leaders designed their graves as places for fellow citizens to sit and rest, an unusual idea fully in keeping with the spirit of Augustan reform. The worn steps of Mammia's grave reveal how often people sought out the semicircular benches. The slightly raised seats of the *scholae* offer a good view of passing traffic; in addition to providing travelers with a convenient resting spot, they must have been the site of countless conversations, where Pompeians could keep an eye on all that was going on and pass along the latest news.

Most of the building activity observable in Pompeii in the early decades of the Empire has parallels elsewhere. Many cities in Italy and the western provinces did not acquire their major monuments until the reigns of Augustus or his immediate successors. The smaller towns especially tended to retain this appearance with few or no major changes down to late antiquity.[118] The high concentration of lavish public building in this epoch would have been incomprehensible without the impetus provided by Augustan cultural policies.

In many places the new buildings were more elaborate and architecturally more interesting than in Pompeii. But nowhere else can we distinguish so many separate initiatives or learn the identities of so many important benefactors. Pompeii also offers us a unique opportunity to observe in detail the social interaction that made it possible to carry out Augustus' policies with the limited means available to smaller cities.

The City's Final Years

We must now turn briefly to the state of the town after the devastating earthquake of A.D. 62 (fig. 66). In A.D. 79 many parts of Pompeii still lay in ruins, despite all the efforts of the intervening years.[119] The inhabitants seem to have been left on their own, without any significant assistance from Rome. They concentrated on making those repairs that were absolutely necessary, and beyond that clearly chose to rebuild the places with the greatest significance for them. To obtain a picture of this period we should start with the shops, workshops, and dwellings, for this was the area in which reconstruction was furthest along. We have a far more compre-

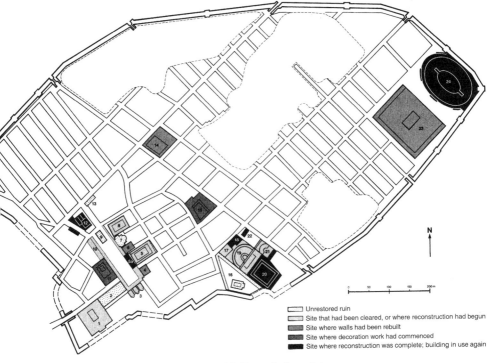

Legend:
- Unrestored ruin
- Site that had been cleared, or where reconstruction had begun
- Site where walls had been rebuilt
- Site where decoration work had commenced
- Site where reconstruction was complete; building in use again

1. Temple of Venus
2. Basilica
3. Administration building
4. Comitium
5. Eumachia building
5a. Chalcidicum
6. Building for the imperial cult
   (Temple of Vespasian)
7. Forum exedra (Lararium)
8. Market
9. Capitolium
10. Produce market *(Forum holitorium)*
11. Temple of Apollo

12. Forum baths and cistern
13. Temple of Fortuna Augusta
14. New central baths
15. Stabian baths
16. Triangular forum and archaic temple
17. "Samnite" palaestra
18. Temple of Isis
19. Large theater
20. Presumed gymnasium
21. Covered theater
22. Temple of Zeus Meilichios
23. Campus
24. Amphitheater

Figure 66   Public building activity in Pompeii after the earthquake of A.D. 62. New priorities are reflected in the order of projects chosen for rebuilding. Compared with earlier times, the main political centers, including temples connected with the cult of the emperor and the old civic temples, have declined in importance, while centers of leisure activity such as baths and the amphitheater are given top priority, along with the temples of private cults.

Urban Space as a Reflection of Society

hensive picture of Pompeii in its last phase—when its political and cultural life was dominated by a large and very homogeneous "middle class"—than for any other ancient city. Many of the restored houses had been decorated in a distinct style. Everywhere, even in the smallest dwellings, we encounter elements of the luxury associated with villas, usually on a reduced scale and often only as pictorial allusions.[120] Unfortunately, we are not able to compare the late Pompeian houses with contemporary dwellings in other towns. But it appears that being surrounded by piles of rubble after the earthquake inspired the inhabitants to make their houses as beautiful and their lives as pleasant as possible.

The center of daily activity had shifted from the badly damaged forum to certain streets, mainly the Via Stabiana, Via dell'Abbondanza, and the Via degli Augustali. The stretch of the Via dell'Abbondanza that widens almost into a square in front of the Stabian baths seems to have become an important focal point of city life.

In contrast to private dwellings, on which reconstruction work was well advanced, a number of important public structures still lay in ruins seventeen years after the earthquake. Repair work had begun on some, and others were nearly finished, but only a few were back in full use again. Their state of repair clearly reflects the priorities that had been established by the inhabitants of the town (see fig. 1).

Although the numerous shrines to the Lares and altars in and adjoining private homes show that the inhabitants remained basically religious, not one of the old municipal sanctuaries had been fully restored. Little or no work had been done on the *capitolium,* the Sanctuary of the Lares, the chapel in the Eumachia Building, or the Temple of Venus. The smaller of the two structures in the forum dedicated to the cult of the emperor had been rebuilt, but it was not yet redecorated. The only structure where repairs were already far advanced was the Temple of Apollo, indicating that Pompeians attached greatest importance to their oldest religious tradition, veneration of the town's tutelary god, Apollo. The fact that the Temple of Isis was fully restored is not surprising, given that the initiates of her cult constituted a closely knit and intensely devoted group (figs. 67 and 68). The wealthy freedman N. Popidius Ampliatus assumed the cost of the

Figures 67–68 View of the Temple of Isis and dedicatory inscription. The shrine to Isis, first erected in the second century B.C., was rebuilt immediately following the earthquake, in contrast to the capitolium in the forum. It is significant that the cost was assumed by a wealthy freedman, N. Popidius Ampliatus, who achieved in return the election of his six-year-old son to the city council.

work in the name of his six-year-old son Celsinus.[121] In gratitude for this generous donation the town council elected the boy a member. In this manner the father achieved for his son, at least, the social advancement denied to himself as a former slave. However, the honor also shows the political influence wielded by devotees of Isis in the town at this date.

The small temple of Zeus Meilichios or Asclepius was in serviceable condition again, although this did not require very much effort. It is likely, incidentally, that the somewhat oversized statue of Juno and a bust of Minerva found there—both late Hellenistic works in terracotta—were

Figure 69 Election slogans on the façade of a house. The colorful painted graffiti reflect the active political life of the town, which remained restricted to local affairs. The emperor and Empire had ceased to play a significant role. The religious drawings honor the old household divinities, the Lares, who were generally worshiped in the form of snakes. Apart from elections, gladiatorial contests are the only public events mentioned in wall graffiti.

POMPEII

placed alongside the clay statue of the foreign god in the early days after the colony's founding, in order to increase his resemblance to Capitoline Jupiter.[122]

The state of repair of other public buildings offers a highly revealing picture as well. Of the three structures devoted to shows and entertainment, only the amphitheater was in viable condition. Extensive damage there, especially to the vaulted passages, seems to have been repaired with donations from the two C. Cuspii Pansae, father and son, who were rewarded with honorary statues in new niches added on either side of the main gate.[123] The large outdoor theater and small covered theater remained unsuitable for use, although work was proceeding on a new marble stage front at the former. Obviously, however, the gladiators' contests in the amphitheater had absolute priority. It was for their sake, too, that the large palaestra next door, presumably part of the former gymnasium, was also remodeled into barracks housing. The many small rooms behind the colonnade were all added after the earthquake.

The citizens were prepared to spend even more money on rebuilding the baths. Both the forum baths and the Stabian baths were completely restored and refurbished with elaborate plaster decoration and wall paintings. At the Stabian baths the central water system was still not repaired, but the forum baths were open for business again—at least for male clients, who used water from the large cistern nearby. It is noteworthy, however, that repairs to the women's facilities were still not finished.

Even more revealing than these renovation projects is the construction of a third large public bath in region IX (fig. 70).[124] Here an *insula* previously occupied by private houses was turned into a bath complex modeled on one in Rome, with the same high windows designed to flood it with sunlight. The shell of the building was already complete, and the workmen had just begun putting up expensive marble columns at the time of the eruption.

This example shows that the town itself or its private benefactors were able to finance expensive projects. That makes it all the more surprising to find little evidence of interest in repairing the forum and the symbolic public buildings fringing it. The square itself had been more or less cleared

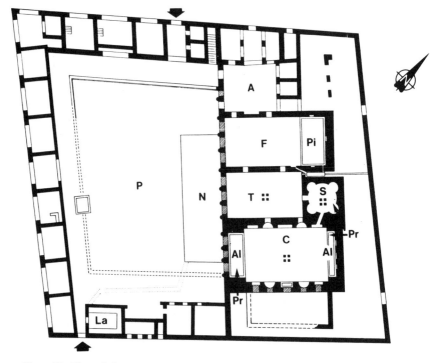

Figure 70 Plan of the central baths, as they were built following the earthquake. The architect based his plan on models from Rome, using windows high up the walls and marble columns. The result suggests that the town had no interest in cost-cutting here.

of debris, but that was all. Most of the statues had toppled off their plinths, which had themselves been stripped of their marble facing. The ruins of the *capitolium,* the Sanctuary of the Lares, and the colonnades around the forum must have been a depressing sight, surrounded by other buildings encased in scaffolding, on which work was proceeding only sporadically. Essential festivals in honor of the emperor must have taken place in the Temple of Vespasian, which had been hastily patched together. The municipal building with an apse (the office of the duumviri) was in use again, while work was going forward on the *comitium* and the two other municipal offices.

Even this rough sketch shows how much the emphasis had shifted. The low levels of interest in the town's political center and state cults combined with the great efforts made to repair structures used for entertainment and pleasure stand in stark contrast to the building boom of the early Empire. The lively campaign slogans painted on house walls show that Pompeian political life remained vigorous in the city's final years, but it was entirely restricted to local affairs.[125] The Pompeians, who had been left to pick up the pieces after catastrophe struck, must have felt abandoned by the emperor, who—understandably—was seen as a more remote figure than in earlier years. It is possible that a number of the great families—those with estates in other areas and ambitions for careers in the imperial administration—had left the city long before the eruption, leaving freed slaves to manage their property in the struggling and still endangered city. And although extraordinary efforts had been made, Pompeii's limited ability to function is evident from the breakdown of the water supply system, which had still not been restored. In all probability the earthquake had destroyed the aqueduct originally financed by the emperor, and there was no money to repair such a large-scale project. A few wealthy individuals, unwilling to give up the fountains in their courtyards, had private water supplies connected to their houses, but the source from which they drew the water has not been established.

Despite the pressures created by the exceptional circumstances, however, the priorities of the "reconstruction program" in Pompeii reveal a clear general trend. After the heady atmosphere of Augustus' campaign for cultural renewal had faded, even in the later years of his own reign, his cult and its accompanying ideology of the state had quickly become a matter of routine. Wealthy towns continued to erect temples to the emperor on an ever grander scale, but they tended to put them at ceremonial sites away from the centers of people's daily rounds. What really counted in the Flavian-Antonine era, and what determined the appearance of its cities, was a desire to enjoy the pleasures of life, be it in sumptuous houses with marble colonnades, at shows in the arena and the theater, or in lavishly decorated baths that developed into centers of leisure-time activity.

Since I originally developed this view of Pompeii, which is reflected in figure 66, new interpretations of the evidence have been proposed; investigations of the relevant structures at the site are also in progress (although not by any means complete). As a result, the picture of the town developed above may require some adjustment or refinement. The new observations are related to two areas in particular, the first being the forum. Here a number of indications suggest that immediately after the town was buried by the eruption a more or less systematic search was made to retrieve building materials for re-use. That these actions were carried out in a planned manner under the direction of a commission sent from Rome comprising *curatores Campaniae restituendae* (ministers for the restoration of Campania), as has recently been suggested, seems rather unlikely.[126]

The second area concerns the state of buildings after the earthquake of A.D. 62, and/or at the time of the eruption. Our understanding of their condition used to be derived mainly from Maiuri's investigations; now the research efforts of John Dobbins and Kurt Wallat are providing new data, which do not, however, always point to the same conclusions. Dobbins is the initiator of the large-scale "Pompeii Forum Project," which has as its goal a close examination of the buildings on the east side of the forum. At the present time, only preliminary results are available, and in my view the theories to which they have given rise require confirmation from further excavations. According to the new view, construction was undertaken along the whole east side after the earthquake, and the result was a more imposing façade than before. And whereas the *macellum,* the Temple of Vespasian, and the Eumachia Building, which pre-dated the earthquake, were only to be restored or embellished, the structure identified as the Sanctuary of the Lares was not designed and built until after A.D. 62. If these theories should prove true, then we would have to recognize that the inhabitants of Pompeii made a far more determined attempt to restore their forum than I previously assumed. In the context of my own proposals, it would be important to know how far construction on these buildings had progressed after seventeen years. Modern excavators have discovered hardly any traces of interrupted construction work. Was such work indeed interrupted by a second quake, as several scholars have assumed? Furthermore, it remains accepted that the two largest structures in the forum, the *capitolium* and the basilica, had undergone no renovation at all. Such findings would make no essential difference as regards the appearance of the forum in the Augustan or early imperial period. However, the elaborately decorated Sanctuary of the Lares, should it prove in fact not to have been built until after A.D. 62, would be evidence of considerable commitment to the cult of the emperor. Nevertheless, in the light of all we know about the forms of official involvement by the Senate or the emperor, I do not consider it possible that the sanctuary was financed by the imperial family itself.[127]

The Domestic Arts
in Pompeii

The Roman villa has long epitomized an elegant and luxurious refuge, a haven removed from the commotion of everyday life. Even in ancient times the word conveyed felicity; since the fifteenth century these associations have brought villas back into fashion again and again. In our own day the word "villa" is still used in England, for example, to suggest a touch of elegance, to imply that a house is a "residence of a superior type," when in fact the opposite is often the case.

For Romans in the late Republic and the Empire, villas and time spent at villas were synonymous with pleasure, wealth, and leisure. This was as true for broad segments of the population as it was for the fortunate few who actually owned villas; the claim applies to the Pompeians, at any rate, if the evidence of the architecture and decor of their homes is anything to go by.

In the very extensive archeological literature on Pompeian houses,[1] however, this phenomenon has received scarcely any attention.[2] Scholars, of course, frequently make mention of the villa as a model for individual elements of architecture or decor, but to my knowledge the comprehensive taste that prevailed, particularly in the final decades of the city's existence, has never been analyzed in detail. Pompeian houses represent a unique historical source for answers to such questions of taste, allowing us to draw important conclusions about the values and aspirations of a large segment of the population in the early years of the Empire that emerge only sketchily from literary and epigraphic sources.

In a study such as this, the wealth of material is best illustrated through the use of significant individual examples, entailing references to many familiar paintings and objects. In each case, the choice was dictated by the relationship each example has in common with the overall context under investigation.

The Origins of the Roman Villa

The complex origins of the Roman villa have been little studied to date.[3] The villa represents far more than an architectural category, fascinating though its variety may be. In fact it is a key phenomenon in the adoption of Hellenistic culture by upper-class Romans. At the outset I would like to sketch in the background of this process.

When Rome expanded its rule into the western and eastern Mediterranean, Roman aristocrats, who in some respects had retained their traditional simple customs, were brought into direct contact with the opulent style of life in the Hellenistic world, particularly in the dwellings and habits of Eastern potentates. They began to desire lavish surroundings to match their sense of power and dominance. In Rome itself, however, old Republican traditions blocked or hindered open espousal and display of Hellenistic luxury. Isolated country estates offered an escape, so to speak, where aristocrats could spend their leisure time in a completely private sphere. And even Cato the censor recommended adding urban amenities to simple villas on agricultural estates, in order to make the necessary inspection visits more attractive for the proprietor (*De Agri Cultura* 4). Soon afterward Romans began building country retreats in the most beautiful parts of Campania and Latium, for purely recreational purposes.[4]

This new way of life called for opening the house to the landscape and including gardens and parks in the inhabited space. Early villas tended to be built on slopes with expansive and beautiful views.[5] After Pompey's campaign rid the area of pirates, sites directly on the coast came to be preferred (Plutarch, *Lucullus* 39). Even though the ruins of many such dwellings have been excavated and become well known, they can convey only a very inadequate notion of the great villas' size and rich decoration. The best impression of the sequence of rooms and their dimensions can be gained today from the Getty Museum in Malibu, California, a reconstruction of the relatively modest Villa of the Papyri in Herculaneum,[6] and from the great villa of Oplontis (Torre Annunziata).[7] The numerous depictions of villas in Pompeian wall frescos—often in imitation of a panel painting *(pinax)*—are a valuable source for seeing how the estates were embedded in the landscape.[8]

The intent to include gardens and the landscape in the inhabited space is a consequence of the Hellenistic experience of nature. Not infrequently public buildings in the agora or in sanctuaries had colonnades and terraces that served to frame vistas (as at Pergamum, Samothrace, Lindos, and Rhodes).[9] The latest example comes from a residence, albeit a royal one, namely, the Macedonian palace of Palatitsa, which a growing amount of evidence places in the late fourth century. There a veranda with a view across the plains has been documented.[10] Hellenistic building complexes may also have inspired the ground plans of large villas; for the *villa maritima* one might think of the royal palace quarter in Alexandria, for example, whereas the fortress-like villas of Marius, Pompey, and Caesar in Baiae (Tacitus, *Annals* 14.9.3; Seneca, *Epistles* 51.11), which dominate their surroundings, are reminiscent of the palace at Demetrias.[11] Although at the present time we can only speculate about influences in specific cases, the dominant role of large peristyles and the new use of atria (occasionally redecorated in the Greek manner) speak for themselves. Yet however great or small a role one ascribes to the influence of Hellenistic models on the development of the ground plans of early Roman villas, one thing is clear: the clever orientation of porticos, dining rooms, and bedrooms to take advantage of particular vistas shows that Roman aristocrats and their architects consciously included nature and the landscape in their designs to enhance them and add a new dimension to the inhabitants' enjoyment. This takes the Hellenistic approach to an extreme.

Nature was included in another sense as well. The largest villas were often located on landed estates; in such cases, the owner had plenty of space to create sweeping parks and game enclosures, and thus live like a king.

For the imposing architectural forms of their interiors, the early villas once more probably owed most to Hellenistic courts, for there the owners' emphasis lay on creating magnificent displays. The real structural architecture of lavish Corinthian, tetrastyle, Egyptian, and Cyzicene reception rooms (*oeci*: Vitruvius VI 3.143)[12] was complemented by the architectural wall paintings of the second style.[13] These increased the effect with painted vistas showing imposing façades, palace courtyards, shrines, and luxurious parks of a royal character. Such paintings served not only to enlarge the actual space, but also to conjure up associations of magnificent surroundings. Characteristically, the owners showed little or no concern with making these vistas spatially logical or consistent in content. What mattered was to have a great variety of scenes, each one full of interesting detail. Small villas in particular often displayed the most disparate views next to one another in confined spaces. One of the best examples of this is to be found in a *cubiculum* (bedroom) of the villa at Boscoreale. Sanctuaries and sacred precincts occur with great frequency in these paintings, reflecting the religious character of gardens around the palaces of Hellenistic rulers.[14]

Hellenistic courts provided models for the furnishings of Roman villas as well. It is hardly accidental that Cicero accused Verres of trying to match the aspirant to the throne of Syria in this respect (*In Verrem* II 4.61ff.). Verres was hardly the exceptional figure Cicero made him out to be; he surpassed some of his rich friends only in the degree of his obsession and the extremes to which he was prepared to go to acquire objects he fancied.[15]

Congenial company was a requisite of villa life.[16] Cicero's letters offer us a picture of the great figures of Roman society visiting one another when the law courts were not in session, at their large estates in the hills near Tivoli or, above all, on the Bay of Naples, that "charming bowl" (*crater delicatus: Letters to Atticus* II 8.2) where they vied to outdo one another in the luxury of the accommodations and the banquets (Plutarch, *Cicero* 7). Of course, in order to enjoy the various landscapes and climates (Plutarch, *Lucullus* 39)—and also not to miss out on what others were doing—one needed to own several villas.[17] Cicero himself, who was not a particularly wealthy man but liked to keep abreast of developments, had no fewer than seven.[18]

POMPEII

For those wishing to occupy themselves with philosophical, historical, literary, or artistic matters, villas were more suitable than townhouses,[19] for at one's leisure, far from the press of business, it was possible to feel liberated from the official schizophrenic attitude toward Greek culture.[20] When Roman aristocrats conversed informally with philosophers and poets at their villas, and indulged in their own dilettante pursuits of art and literature, they were following the tradition of Hellenistic rulers, whose portraits they occasionally displayed in their colonnades next to the great Greek intellectuals. Cultural interests were deemed such an integral part of villa life that libraries and *pinacothecae* were standard amenities (Vitruvius VI 5.2), regardless of the owner's actual interests or preferences.[21] Petronius later had his satirical character Trimalchio, the self-made man, boast of the Greek and Latin works in his library (Petronius, *Satyrica* 48). It was fashionable to refer to colonnades or parts of the garden as the "gymnasium" or the "palaestra," or to name them specifically after famous sites of classical learning. Greek names were sometimes given even to lesser rooms (Varro, *Res rusticae* II 2). Collections of statuary and other decor increased the associations with classical culture, making the appellations of these rooms clear to all. The average villa owner, however, certainly did not go to the lengths Cicero did to make his surroundings match his own broad intellectual horizons; many owners were no doubt content to purchase the standard furnishings available on the market.[22] The memory of famous cities and tourist spots in the Greek world was cultivated by the names given to individual parts of the villa, along with the corresponding decoration. Hadrian's villa is the latest and richest example of this form of cultural reminiscence, a *Bildungslandschaft* ("educative landscape").[23] External similarities were not always required; any pond, watercourse, or stream could be transformed at will into one of the popular imitations of the Euripus, the strait between Euboea and Boeotia, or the Nile (Cicero, *On Laws* II 2), or a natural grotto such as the one in Sperlonga could be turned into the cave of Polyphemus.

In sum, the adoption of Greek culture by the Roman upper class manifests itself in the late Republican villa. The leisure *(otium)* associated with villas embraces a whole sphere of life in which architecture and decor were inseparably connected with certain styles, habits, and intellectual pursuits. The painted vistas must be seen in relation to furniture, other furnishings, the silver on the table, and last but not least the exquisite food served there. A herm of Aristotle in the peristyle, for instance, points beyond the specific locale and style of furnishings that may have been used; for one owner it might have served to stimulate or recall to mind a variety of educational experiences, while for another it merely demonstrated that he kept up with current fashions.

The experience of architecture and villa surroundings in connection with an extensive and multifaceted network of associations reflects the villa owners' new and ambivalent sense of identity. Their awareness of their own power and status demanded appropriately princely settings, yet at the same time the dominant Greek cultural tradition was present in every room, inspiring occupants not just to congratulate themselves on how educated they were, but also to continue learning, and to meditate on the past.

Naturally, the unbridled competition for offices, wealth, and prestige so characteristic of the late Republic had a noticeable effect in the area of domestic luxury. After the Social War, participation in an elite culture was open to a large class on the top rungs of the social ladder, including the prominent office-holding families of Italic cities and rich merchants as well as Roman aristocrats.[24] Their levels of affluence and education varied, but all felt the same need for self-promotion and display. Thus we find villas of the Republican era across a correspondingly broad spectrum, ranging from enormous complexes resembling little self-contained cities (Sallust, *Catiline* 12–13) to the compact villas just inside Pompeii's southern wall (compare fig. 71). In the first century B.C. such luxurious country estates—referred to euphemistically as "gardens" *(horti)*—had crept up to the old walls of Rome, and the lifestyle cultivated at country villas had become the norm among the upper classes in the city, too. Exploiting Rome's geography, the elite built themselves little urban villas with their own views on the Palatine and Aventine hills.[25]

The degree to which villas had come to epitomize wealth and luxury is revealed by an episode in the campaign of the tribune A. Gabinius against

Figure 71 Terrace houses in the theater quarter, region VIII 2 (after Noack and Lehmann-Hartleben). The original atrium houses with an orientation toward the street were expanded in the course of the first century B.C. to provide a view across the plain to the sea.

Lucullus. To turn popular opinion against his opponent, Gabinius had a picture of Lucullus' famous villa at Tusculum shown from the rostra (Cicero, *Pro Sestio* 93). During proscriptions, possession of a beautiful villa could seal a man's doom (Plutarch, *Sulla* 31.4).

The example set by the wealthiest and most prestigious aristocratic families in the second century B.C., when they began to adopt Greek culture, had enormous influence in the later climate of competition, when everything the upper classes did was imitated. The phase of discriminating individual selection was thus followed swiftly by one in which the market offered standardized "Greek" house and decor plans suited to every pocketbook.

This cultural and historical setting explains some key features of Roman villas, such as the haphazard assembly of decorative elements, the frequent disregard of organic harmony and proportions, exaggeration in scale and motifs, and excessive use of expensive materials (or imitations of them). This is true not only for lesser villas; even the huge collection of bronze sculptures at the Villa of the Papyri in Herculaneum and the wall frescos at the recently excavated Villa of Oplontis (Torre Annunziata) display such features.[26] The lifestyle associated with the villa proves to have been a grand and vital mixture of Greek cultural elements that formed different amalgams in each house, depending on the temperament and education of its owner.

Two Forms of Living Space

The Samnite growers and merchants[27] in the area around Pompeii had learned about Greek homes and interior decor along with the Romans, either directly, through travel in the East along Roman trade routes, or indirectly, through gradual adoption of trends from Rome, the center of Hellenism in Italy from the second century.[28] In contrast to aristocrats in Rome itself, the Samnites had no traditions hostile to indulgence in luxury. There was nothing to prevent them from investing their new wealth in large townhouses. It is characteristic of the richest families in Pompeii that they clearly identified themselves not with middle-class Greeks, such as the merchants and traders who built houses on Delos, for example, but rather with aristocrats and their opulent residences. H. Lauter has offered convincing evidence of a resemblance between the largest of the early houses, the House of the Faun (VI 12), which occupies an entire *insula* measuring roughly 31,000 square feet, and the urban palaces of the Macedonian aristocracy excavated in Pella.[29] The Italic atrium is retained in reduced form, as in the early villas, but its original function as the central living space has usually been lost in Pompeian houses. In some instances the whole ground plan is dominated by peristyle gardens. The free combination of atria and peristyles in different sizes is also characteristic of large Pompeian houses. However, in contrast to the palaces of the nobility at Pella, which are even larger than the House of the Faun, the latter contained peristyles that were surrounded by only a few large rooms: the owner of the House of the Faun in fact required far less living space than a Macedonian prince. The second peristyle in his house, for example, had no function beyond creating an impression of grandeur.[30]

Thus the House of the Faun, although not derived from the villa, contains essential elements of villa architecture, such as peristyle gardens with fountains, extensive rooms with costly mosaics (for example, the exedra containing the Alexander mosaic), and even a small bath complex.[31] This elegant, completely inward-looking house provided its occupants with the Hellenistic sense of extensive space and shifting vistas through zones of shade and light in the successive peristyles, much like a villa.

The rooms in other great Pompeian houses built around 100 B.C. display even richer forms of Hellenistic interior design. The opulent living or dining rooms *(oeci)* were probably inspired by villas, that is to say, they were one step removed from Greece; the elaborate painted architectural vistas support this view.[32] In the Corinthian room *(oecus corinthicus)* of the House of the Labyrinth (VI 11.10; fig. 111b), for example, a wall painting showed a view of a palace courtyard with a small, round Hellenistic temple in the center.[33] Ptolemy IV once enjoyed a similar view—in actuality, not painted—from the Corinthian salon of his Nile ship, which was itself constructed as a floating palace.[34] The two-story arrangement of columns explodes the spatial dimensions of the Pompeian dining room: interior architecture originally intended for a large hall or banquet room was reproduced in such drastically reduced form that the real function of the room as a dining area was considerably restricted.[35]

In the second century B.C. the wealthy Samnite elite constructed their houses clustered together in the center of town, completely closed off from the landscape. After the Roman colony was founded and the city walls ceased to have any defensive function, however, affluent Pompeians in the first half of the first century began to build on the southern slopes of town, which offered a beautiful vista across the bay to the Sorrento Peninsula. The plan of the town shows that the sites on the southwestern slopes were especially sought after. It is here that the largest houses were built, not much smaller in total area than the House of the Faun (Insula Occidentalis 19–26; see figs. 30 and 31).[36] These complexes display the same orientation toward panoramic views as the villas outside the Herculaneum Gate. While the entry area remains connected with the street, the living area extends out to elaborate terraces on different levels, opening the house to the landscape. A present-day visitor can gain a sense of the size of different areas in these new "urban villas" from the portico of the Villa Imperiale next to the Marine Gate below the old museum (VIII 1).

More modest houses were added to and remodeled, spreading down the southwestern slopes toward the theater quarter (VIII 2; see fig. 71). K. Lehmann-Hartleben's study of these houses, based on Noack's notes and published in the 1930s, is a model analysis still of considerable interest for social historians today.[37] His research shows that the early first century B.C., the peak period of villa construction in Campania, was also the time when most of these houses were rebuilt as villas to take advantage of the view. Lehmann-Hartleben's drawings of them as they must have looked convey an impression of the sides facing the sea, with staggered porticos and balconies on different stories (fig. 72).[38] The extensive excavation and foundation work required for the additions suggests once again that the owners of these houses were well-to-do, but nonetheless they are clearly smaller in scale and less ambitious than the large villas on the western slopes. Although they could not compete with the type of villa that spread out into

Figure 72 Reconstruction of a terrace house in the theater quarter (after Noack and Lehmann-Hartleben). The architecture of the additions at the rear imitates the terraces and withdrawing rooms of Roman villas.

POMPEII

the landscape, these mini-villas nevertheless provided their occupants with an essential element of the new style, namely, a beautiful view.[39]

In a few houses in the town center we find renovations and additions dating from the late second and first centuries B.C., showing that here, too, the villa served as a model for cultivated living. They include such features as the bath complex and cryptoporticus in the House of the Cryptoporticus (I 6.2–4),[40] and the small bath complex and exedra with two apses in the peristyle of the House of Menander (I 10.4; fig. 111c).[41]

A Miniature Villa in the Town

As we have seen, the imitation of villa architecture in Pompeii in the first century B.C. was mainly limited to exploitation of sites with the best views on the surrounding slopes and isolated cases of luxurious interior renovation in the grandest houses in town. In the last decades of Pompeii's existence, however, the effect of villas and the decor and lifestyle associated with them spread to a very broad segment of the town's inhabitants. We find many different elements of villa architecture and decor in houses restored or remodeled[42] after the earthquake of A.D. 62,[43] although some of these features might not be recognizable at first glance as having been derived from this source.

As a rule the renovation or remodeling work was limited to the houses' gardens and peristyles. Let us begin by looking at a well-known house in the Via dell'Abbondanza (II 2.2; figs. 73 and 74) named after Loreius Tiburtinus, a fictional character.[44] The sloping lot covers almost an entire *insula,* more than two-thirds of which is taken up by the garden. When viewed from the bottom of the garden, the living quarters appear mounted on a platform reminiscent of a *basis villae* (foundation wall; Cicero, *Letters to Quintus* 3.1.5). The structure is an instance of renovation in an older, medium-sized atrium house, which in the final period of the town's existence had a tavern occupying the front section. After the earthquake the house underwent extensive remodeling, most of it concentrated on the garden and the rooms adjacent to it. This work was not yet completed at the time of the eruption.[45]

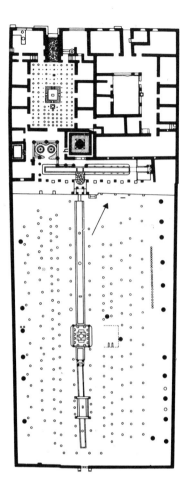

The main room or *tablinum* behind the atrium was replaced by a kind of truncated peristyle, leading to a large, almost square dining room (*triclinium*, with three couches) on the left, and to two smaller rooms, one containing a shrine *(sacellum),* to the right. The plaster-covered columns of varying diameters stand at irregular intervals determined by the adjoining rooms. This truncated peristyle connects—but also collides and competes—with two further rows of roof supports, bringing utter confusion into the ground plan. A regular porch *(pronaos)* in front of the shrine has two columns between piers with engaged columns. The pier on the garden side is flush with a row of sturdy brick supports for the more than sixty-five-

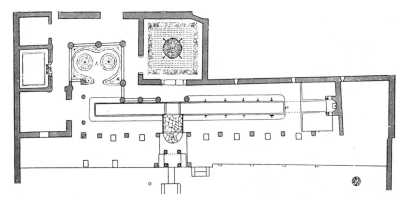

Figure 74 Plan of the terrace at the "miniature villa." Several elements of villa architecture are combined here in such a small space that they partly overlap.

foot-long pergola extending across the rear of the house (fig. 75). The pergola shades a small ornamental canal, only about three feet wide, which runs along the axis of the shrine; it is spanned by two bridge-like structures and ends in a *biclinium* (dining area with two couches) with a fountain at the other end of the terrace.[46] We know from the collection of statues found here that the ensemble re-created in miniature the type of water-course *(euripus* or *nilus)* already popular in the villas of Cicero's era.[47] A surviving example on a monumental scale is the Canopus at Hadrian's Villa.[48]

A total of five elements derived from villa architecture and reduced to miniature size are thus combined and compressed, sometimes one inside the other, onto a terrace that is only twenty-two feet wide: (1) the trun-cated peristyle with the *triclinium* and day rooms *(diaetae);* (2) the shrine; (3) an aedicula to Artemis behind the fountain and above a *nymphaeum* (dis-cussed below); (4) the watercourse associated with the pergola; and (5) the *biclinium* with the fountain-aedicula (fig. 76). All five are components of the expansive type of villa that opened up the house to the surrounding views and landscape and had become popular by the mid–first century B.C. at the latest.[49] The villas of Pliny the Younger are good examples of this type, as are some of the excavated houses in Campania and those depicted in wall paintings at Pompeii.[50] On the terrace of this particular house,

Figure 75 An old photograph of the terrace at the "miniature villa," showing the collection of garden statuettes (now missing) lined up along the watercourse *(euripus)* spanned by a little bridge. The whole terrace is surmounted by a pergola stretching from a small shrine to Isis at one end to two masonry couches at the other. The paths are too narrow to permit two people to stroll side by side or in groups, an integral feature of the Roman villa.

however, the various components are squeezed into such a small space that two people cannot walk next to each other under the pergola without running up against a fountain, little bridge, pillar, or post at every turn, or tripping over the statuettes in the grass. A portion of the architecture has lost its original function.

The sense of constriction is increased by the excess of decorative painting and statuary. In the large *triclinium* there are two friezes above a wide panel painted to look like expensive multicolored marble incrustations.[51] A raised curtain painted in at the top of the picture is intended to heighten the illusion that the friezes are valuable Greek originals, and it gives the room the aura of a *pinacotheca* (fig. 77). The upper frieze (approximately two and a half feet tall) shows the labors of Hercules—probably following a Hellenistic model; the smaller frieze below contains scenes from the *Iliad*.

148

This room, distinguished from others in the house by its very elaborate decoration, offered occupants a view through the Artemis aedicula and the lower part of the garden to the city and mountains beyond (plate 9). The *sacellum,* set off by two columns between piers with engaged columns, is also painted elaborately in the fourth style, this time depicting a wall. The figure of a priest of Isis on one of the inner walls and the diptych of Diana and Actaeon on the façade (along with the Egyptian terracottas found in the little garden in front of it) all suggest that the shrine was devoted to Isis/Diana. Her image probably stood in the niche on the back wall.[52] The architect had to dispense with a gable for the shrine, however, since it would have interfered with the pergola.

Small shrines, sometimes located in a garden, were quite common at

Figure 76 Masonry couches at the "miniature villa," with a "view" over the *euripus.* In the foreground one can see the slanted surfaces on which mattresses were placed. Behind them are an aedicula and two frescos with mythological motifs designed to look like framed paintings.

Figure 77 Wall painting in the reception room opening onto the terrace at the "miniature villa" (after Spinazzola; compare fig. 74). This *triclinium* was the most opulently decorated room in the house, and the owner could display his taste and learning in the frescos. The lower part of the wall imitates costly multicolored marble; it is surmounted by a frieze with scenes from Homer's *Iliad*. The main zone depicts the labors of Hercules. A painted raised "curtain" above these scenes is intended to suggest that they are valuable "paintings" that need to be protected from light, just as in some modern museum displays.

larger villas; one need only think of the "Amaltheion" that Cicero so admired on the country estate of his friend Atticus in Epirus.[53] In the house we are concerned with here, the shrine was used as a kind of gazebo, from which one could look out the door toward the terrace and the watercourse, or through the window on the other side toward the lower part of the garden.

The statuary along the "banks" of the watercourse was adapted to the small format of the architecture.[54] The muses mounted on bases (fig. 78) are of normal statuette size—although there was apparently never a complete set—but the various figures in a seated or recumbent position and scattered about the grass are definitely miniatures (see fig. 75). They are

POMPEII

also associated with a variety of different themes. The recumbent river god and the Sphinx are part of the usual watercourse decor; the herms were usually placed along garden paths. The little seated satyr belongs in a Dionysiac park, while the two sets of figures depicting hounds and quarry belong in a *paradeisos* (preserve for wild animals). The statuettes of the muses themselves belong in a *museion* (museum) of the type so frequently found at villas.[55] To this collection we should also add the little satyr in the

Figure 78 Statuettes of two muses that stood along the *euripus* at the "miniature villa." They are copies of two statuettes from a famous Hellenistic group of all nine muses. As in the case of copies of paintings, such decorative statuary was intended to awaken associations of "Greek sculpture" and "art collections" in visitors.

pose of Atlas supporting the fountain, and there must have been a statue of Artemis/Diana intended as a cult image for the aedicula, since its gable bears a portrait of her (fig. 79).

In addition to these numerous sculptures there was no lack of wall paintings. The fountain aedicula, lined with pumice stone, is flanked by two large mythological scenes, one depicting Pyramus and Thisbe and the other a seated Narcissus (plates 10.1 and 10.2).[56] An artist named Lucius proudly signed his name to them, although their quality is undistinguished. These frescos in the manner of panel paintings call to mind the passionate art enthusiast and collector Hortensius, who at his villa Tusculum made a shrine *(aedem fecit in Tusculano suo)* for Kydias' painting of the Argonauts (Pliny, *Natural History* 35.130). And there was still more: the entire length of the wall (over twenty-three feet long) to which the pergola was attached was covered with frescos depicting a variety of scenes—Orpheus charming the beasts, a hunting scene in a *paradeisos,* and Venus hovering above a shell on the sea.[57] These paintings and the statues of the muses on elaborate plinths were intended to give the airy pergola the flair of a lavish portico.

All this decoration and elaboration, however, represents only the upper level of the plan. From the terrace a flight of steps led down to the garden some three feet below, which measured approximately 180 by 95 feet. It was enclosed by a high wall and, like the terrace, bisected by a type of *euripus.* Pergolas and rows of shrubs and trees were arranged parallel to it. Similar paths ran along the brook on Varro's estate near Casinum (*Rustica* 3.9). The remains of a marble table indicate that there was a round seating area, and a recumbent hermaphrodite must be the sole remnant of a group of sculptures placed in the borders.[58] As mentioned above, the *euripus* ran not down the middle of the garden but rather along the axis of the large dining room decorated to look like a *pinacotheca.* This canal was interrupted or spanned by several structures, and was also linked to the terrace pergola by a hybrid two-story construction, the upper portion of which we have already encountered as the Artemis aedicula. The lower story contained a miniature *nymphaeum*[59] with a fountain connected to two water spouts: a mask of Oceanus and an Eros with masks sitting above the steps down which the water flowed.[60] There were also fish painted on the upper basin.

Figure 79 Aedicula with a *nymphaeum* in the garden of the "miniature villa." The aedicula, which was accessible from the garden terrace, originally contained a statue of Artemis, the goddess of hunting. The goddess was placed there in part as an allusion to the hunting preserves connected with great landed estates. The lower story of the structure, accessible only from the garden, is fitted out as a miniature *nymphaeum*. Such a composite, multipurpose structure is characteristic of the overall architectural and decorative style of the house.

To one side of the fountain Actaeon is shown watching Diana bathing, and as if all these were not enough mythological trimmings for one small fountain, on the narrow sides the artist added some small framed landscape scenes with shrines to Apollo and Diana. The room itself measures only about 9.7 by 3.2 feet, and with the fountain in it does not have space for even one couch.

At about the same time that this house was being remodeled, an owner of one of the terrace houses in the theater quarter (VIII 2.28) was building a *nymphaeum* on his property, in the form of a grotto just large enough to use and carefully placed to take advantage of the mountain view across the bay.[61] Thus, the borrowing of elements from villa architecture proceeded in steps, and models for some features could already be found within the town.

To return to the miniature villa: the more than 160-foot-long water-course below the *nymphaeum* is divided into several sections. The water flowed first into a channel approximately 80 feet long with three jets of water spaced along it. Below this was a large pool lined with marble containing a square fountain in the middle, with steps on each side for the water to flow over and bases for twelve statuettes or vases around the edges (fig. 80).[62] Only 12 feet further on the channel is spanned by a decorative baldachin bridge, much too small for actual use. Below the bridge the watercourse then shifts direction slightly to point toward the gate in the wall at the bottom of the garden. Clearly there was already a path up to the house from this gate, and the watercourse was designed to run alongside it. By continuing his watercourse down this far, the owner also enabled passers-by to catch a glimpse of it through the gate. The lower channel below the canopied bridge is interrupted once, too, by a wider basin. Both it and the square pool higher up were probably shaded by arbors.

Thus the watercourse actually consisted of a series of separate pools of varying sizes connected by overflow troughs.[63] Once this has been recognized, the function of the pools becomes clear: they were fish ponds of the type popular at large seaside villas. Most likely they were painted in distinctive colors.[64] Varro and Cicero mention both the profits that could be made by raising fish and also the grotesque excesses to which some of these

Figure 80 Marble fountain in the lower part of the watercourse at the "miniature villa" (compare fig. 74). This fountain interrupts the flow of the *euripus* and is too large in proportion to the other elements of the garden architecture. In the background a further aedicula is visible.

piscinarii were led by their passion for their favorite breeds.[65] Fish ponds represent another feature of villa life imported from the courts of Eastern potentates.[66]

In the case of the miniature villa in Pompeii, the clever arrangement of the fish ponds gave the owner a second watercourse! As we have seen, this excess was characteristic of the villa owner. We find the same principle of overkill with some miniaturized elements of villa architecture in the garden as on the terrace; in both places too many separate structures have been crammed into too small a space. Instead of distributing the decorative features around his garden—as the villa model would have suggested and his good-sized lot allowed—he first turned his fish ponds into a *euripus* and then added the *nymphaeum,* marble fountain, baldachin bridge, and pergola. His method did have one advantage, of course: it enabled him to survey the full complement of architectural splendors in his garden from the door of his dining room. Furthermore, the perspective made the entire layout seem larger than it was (although perhaps too much emphasis has been placed on such effects in recent studies).[67]

In this manner a country villa was re-created in miniature in Pompeii during the last decade of the town's existence. Perspectives actually intended for wider views are cunningly inverted—architectural elements borrowed from villas in the country or by the seaside are crammed together into a Walt Disney world. The elaborate garden is wholly out of proportion to the quite modest size of the actual living quarters; the remodeled section of the house is also characterized by a poor sense of proportion and a low level of artistic skill, in contrast to the "Neronian" wall paintings in the fourth style in the older section. The owner, eager to imitate the lavish world of villas he so clearly admired, preferred quantity over quality.

A Courtyard with a Large Marble Fountain

The miniature villa with the features discussed above is by no means unique to Pompeii; it is only the richest and best preserved example of a widespread taste in domestic environments. Proof that it is no exception is offered by another instance of remodeling in the last decades before the eruption, in a smaller house with a far less advantageous site that appears to have been acquired in bits and pieces. The House of Apolline, located directly in front of the town wall (VI 7.23; fig. 81), was excavated between 1810 and 1840 and, like most of the houses discussed here, is in deplorable condition today.[68] The marble fittings discovered by the excavators have now virtually all disappeared, and if the team had not jotted down at least a few notes we would not be able to interpret the site today. A small atrium without *alae* (wings) leads to the main room, which in turn gives onto a narrow courtyard almost filled by an elaborate marble fountain similar to the one above the lower watercourse at the miniature villa (fig. 82).[69] Around the fountain the excavators found double herms and marble vases decorated with reliefs; we should picture these arranged on the surrounding ledge. The scale of the whole ensemble was completely out of propor-

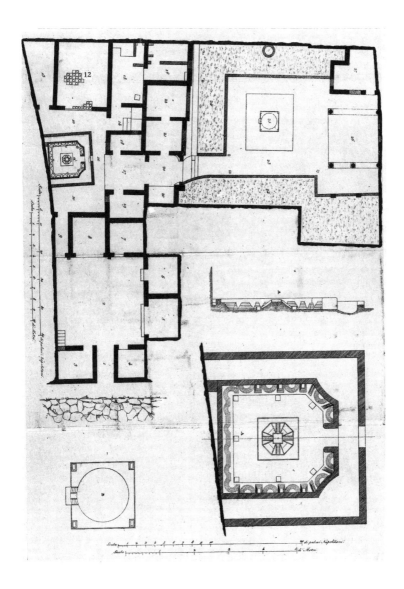

Figure 81   Ground plans of the House of Apolline (VI 7.23) and its two fountains. This is another case of a modest atrium house combined with a large garden, some of which was bought up and added to the property at a later date. The very large reception room at the western end (12) opens onto a court with a large fountain. The actual villa garden was enclosed by porticos and contained a *nymphaeum* and enclosures with couches.

The Domestic Arts in Pompeii   157

Figure 82 Marble fountain in the courtyard of the House of Apolline. The fountain was originally decorated with double herms and marble vases carved in relief. The wall at the left was decorated with a large painting depicting a villa garden.

tion to the small courtyard (off which lay a rather large dining room, the kitchen area, and two further rooms in addition to the main room). On the wall behind the fountain the owner commissioned a large painting of a garden scene, no doubt to give the illusion of greater space. Its depictions of a park with many different kinds of birds, a fish pond, and a statue of Diana were no doubt intended to call up associations with villas.[70]

The real garden, as opposed to a painted one, is located on a plot of ground to the north that was probably acquired after the house was built and measures only a little over 3,000 square feet. Passing through what used to be two rooms in between, one comes down a few steps into the garden, which was enclosed by a kind of terrace on three sides. The terrace, which varies in width, lies about three and a half feet above the ground and hides a cistern beneath it on the western side. The paintings and mosaic on the walls behind make it seem likely that an arbor ran the entire length of the terrace.[71] The "sunken" garden had a second marble fountain in the middle, this time round in shape, but like the courtyard fountain it was surrounded by marble herms. The figure in the center and

POMPEII

a flight of marble steps face to the north, where on the far wall three intersecting structures were squeezed together (fig. 83).[72] The middle structure was open on each side, where two columns and one engaged column supported an architrave. The line of its roof is still visible in the garden wall. The wall contained three niches for statuettes; both it and the outside wall of the *cubiculum* to the left had a pumice-stone facing above and marble veneer below, while the columns were decorated with mosaic and shells in elaborate patterns. All these features indicate that the structure was conceived as a kind of open *nymphaeum*.[73] The few fragments found at the site suggest that it was lavishly fitted with marble, herms, and the like.

To the right of the *nymphaeum* two posts show that there was probably a deck under a pergola. To the left a door led to a "summer room" lit by two windows and containing two alcoves for beds. This charming room is a modest imitation of the tiny garden houses described by Pliny the

Figure 83 View of the *nymphaeum* and garden rooms at the House of Apolline (from an old photograph). The roof line of the *nymphaeum* can still be discerned in the bricks of the rear wall, whose three niches were designed to hold statues.

The Domestic Arts in Pompeii

Younger, located in the grounds of large villas away from the bustle of the main house (*Epistles* II 17.20).[74] It seems odd today that a space designed for withdrawal and contemplation should have walls covered with large perspective paintings of stage sets. These are so out of proportion to the room's actual dimensions that the overall effect is disorienting.[75] Just as in the case of the miniature villa, allusions to Greek culture formed part of the standard decorative repertoire. The same applies to two statues of philosophers, now lost, which stood somewhere in the garden.

A Garden as Sanctuary

The discrepancy between a householder's ambitions and the actual possibilities for realizing them is particularly striking in cases where the goal was to re-create the atmosphere of a grand and sprawling villa in a very confined space. Another owner of a medium-sized house achieved a far better effect by limiting his borrowing to a single villa element, but then incorporating it into his property on a lavish scale. The foundations of the House of the Black Anchor (VI 10.7; figs. 84, 85, and 112c)[76] date back to the first century B.C. At the time of the eruption the owner was in the process of constructing a very grand two-story peristyle to replace the former garden or courtyard at the bottom of the property; work on it was not quite complete (fig. 85 and plate 11.1). The builder had found a clever way to compensate for the difficult sloping terrain. The garden, only about 1,000 square feet in size, lay off a small atrium and down a staircase; originally it was enclosed by a vaulted arcade. Later the arched openings of this arcade were bricked up, creating a cryptoporticus. This was then lined with a series of stout square pillars, two stories high. In the upper story these pillars alternate with brick columns on the two long sides, whereas on the southern side, at the far end from the house, there are only round columns. The two phases of construction appear to have followed one another in quick succession.[77]

It is evident that the owner did not have the services of a first-rate builder or architect, but he clearly wished the final impression to be very imposing: pedestals reveal that the blind arches were to contain statues or

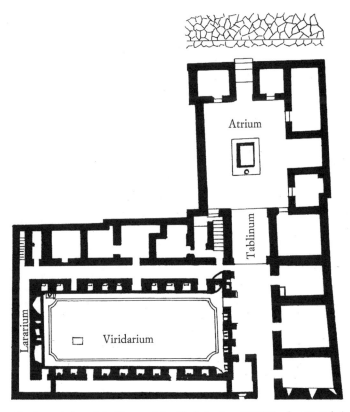

Figure 84 Ground plan of the House of the Black Anchor (VI 10.7; after W. Zahn). Here the small atrium house has a garden in the form of a sanctuary. The reception rooms lay to the north with the best view of the garden architecture.

ornamental vases. The southern end is designed as an ornate façade, with two oversized fountain aediculae[78] flanking an aedicula to Fortuna or Venus Pompeiana framed by stucco rudders.[79] This central aedicula, which is proportionately too small, gives the garden the character of a sacred precinct. When the occupants and their guests gathered in the only large room of the house, this is the façade that lay in view on the far side of the peristyle. Owing to the modest size of the house, however, this *triclinium* was situated above the stable and the rear gate, where carts pulled up to load and unload. Comparably grand peristyles would have been found only in opulent villas like Hadrian's. The evidence of landscape paintings in the

Figure 85 View of the garden at the House of the Black Anchor. The garden peristyle was two stories high, with a cryptoporticus behind the pillars on the ground floor. Only a few remnants of the masonry and plaster columns on the second story remain.

second style shows that the combination of a two-story peristyle with a shrine was once again originally derived from Hellenistic palace courtyards.[80] By contrast, the "sunken" peristyle and the orientation of the garden to make it visible from one main room in the house can be considered typical elements of villa architecture.[81] The Villa of Diomedes, only a few minutes away outside the Herculaneum Gate, may serve as an example; its garden area as a whole is comparable, although the design is far simpler.[82]

The enormous size of the garden peristyle in relation to the rest of the House of the Black Anchor, with its few modestly proportioned rooms, shows how much significance the owner attached to the impression made on guests, and the expense he was prepared to incur to this end.

As in the case of the tiny villa on the Via dell'Abbondanza, the miniaturization of some of the borrowed architectural elements robs them of

View from the door of the main reception room of the "miniature villa" in the Via ll'Abbondanza (compare fig. 73). The various elements of the garden architecture are strung like eads" along the observer's line of vision, producing a more impressive view than if they had been ttered throughout the garden.

Plates 10.1 and 10.2

Two "framed" paintings from the wall behind the *biclinium* on the terrace of the "miniature villa." They show Narcissus admiring his own reflection and the unhappy lovers Pyramis and Thisbe. The paintings are reminiscent of the Greek panel paintings that hung in the villas of the wealthy and, despite their modest quality, are intended to evoke the flair of literacy and aesthetic culture.

Plate 11.1 View of the garden at the House of the Black Anchor (VI 10.7). The garden of this small house was designed as a miniature sanctuary with elaborate architecture (compare fig. 84).

Plate 11.2 Painting of frescos at the House of Sallust (VI 2.4; watercolor by F. Morelli, 1809). These frescos discovered by excavators on the back wall of the garden have now been completely destroyed through exposure. They extended the relatively small garden by opening a vista into a park inhabited by rare birds. The painted architecture suggests an open hall decorated with festive garlands.

Plate 12   Garden at the House of the Small Fountain (VI 8.23–24). Note the current state of the large landscape painting next to the fountain (compare fig. 104 for the original effect).

Plate 13   Fountain at the House of the Large Fountain (VI 8.22), completely covered with mosaic decoration. The water splashed down the marble steps into the pool. Originally there was a theatrical mask on each side of the fountain. The missing mask depicted a tragic hero; the mask on the right shows Hercules wearing a lion's skin over his head. Both were intended as allusions to "classical education."

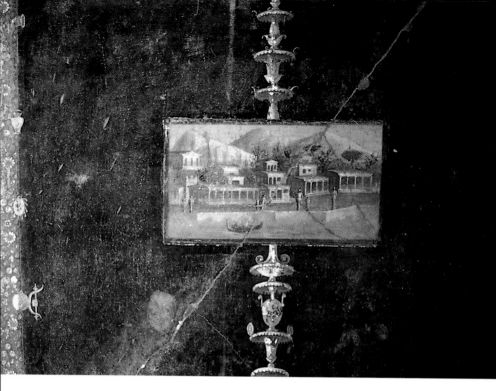

Plate 16   Fresco imitation of a small panel painting in the *tablinum* of the House of M. Lucretiu Fronto (V 4.11), showing a seaside villa. Depictions of luxurious villas are ubiquitous in Pompeian houses as symbols of a moneyed and cultivated lifestyle. Constant allusion to the world of the very rich remained characteristic of domestic decoration in Pompeii throughout the imperial era.

Plate 14.1   Painting of a fresco at the House of the Amazons, now destroyed (VI 2.14; watercolo by F. Morelli, 1812). The illusionist character of the fresco is strengthened by the vista of island villa in the background. In the foreground between palm trees is an aedicula with statues of the Egyptian deities Isis and Osiris.

Plate 14.2   Fresco from the House of Orpheus (VI 14.20), from a lithograph of 1875 that distort the colors. The view of a game park is combined here with the myth of Orpheus, who enchanted wild beasts with his playing. The insets on either side are views of villa gardens. The juxtaposition of different motifs in one picture is characteristic of late Pompeian wall painting. Here again the aim was not so much to create a surprising illusion as to evoke many different associations in the mind of the viewer.

Plate 15   Fresco in the garden of the House of Venus (II 3.3). View of a park with a marble statue of Mars or a military hero.

their function: the cryptoporticus was not much more than three feet wide, and even before its completion the northeast wing had been subdivided to make storage space.

A Parlor Overlooking Diana's Sacred Grove

Another form of garden shrine was achieved at far less expense by a wine merchant at the edifice known as the House of the Moralist (III 4.2; figs. 86 and 87).[83] These premises housed both a dwelling and a shop and had been made by joining two older houses together; behind them the owner turned the courtyard of just over 3,000 square feet into a kind of grove sacred to Diana (*lucus* or *silva Dianae*). From the surviving roots of young trees all oriented around a central point we may deduce that the garden had been laid out not long before. Between the roots the excavators found a statuette of Diana and a bronze incense burner (see fig. 87).[84] Wall paintings and literary sources tell us that such "woods" *(silvae)* and "sacred groves" were often created on the grounds of large villas.[85] Our wine merchant also appears not to have been the only Pompeian to lay out a miniature woods for himself.[86] The rear of the house was opened toward the garden by means of large windows and balconies (fig. 88). The dining room on the ground floor where the wine merchant entertained his guests has been preserved. The familiar maxims and adages painted on the walls illuminate the moral principles and rules of conduct he wished to impress upon them.[87]

Each of the houses discussed above imitated villa style in a different way. Of course the selection of architectural components depended on the possibilities offered by the lot, the existing structure, and the owner's means. Both owners and "architects" may have been inspired by the great variety of models in the immediate vicinity. When one considers the limited space available, the amount of inventiveness they displayed seems astonishing. And while the majority of homeowners had too little space to add new architectural elements, this by no means forced them to forgo the aura of a villa altogether.

Porticos and peristyles both represented elements of a villa, and their

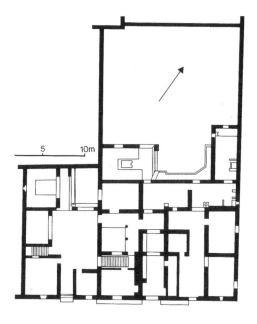

Figures 86–87 Ground plan of the House of the Moralist (III 4.3) and view of its garden after excavation. This building owned by a wine merchant combined a residence and a shop. Two originally separate atrium houses were combined, and a garden was added in the style of a sanctuary. The remains of tree roots suggest how it was once planted. The small shrine was presumably dedicated to Diana, for a statue of the goddess was found in the garden.

POMPEII

Figure 88 Reconstruction of the House of the Moralist (after Spinazzola). The reception rooms had large windows overlooking the garden. In most houses such a view did not exist in reality, and had to be supplied by a wall painting. The wine merchant who owned this house could at least offer his guests views of real trees, like the owner of a villa.

combination with the appropriate types of room brought out even more of the villa character in the later houses. In this connection a large and imposing dining room played a key role, and we find one in virtually all the houses discussed thus far.[88] Whenever possible, the dining room was placed so as to afford a view of the garden. In the grand houses these *triclinia* became real dining halls; the House of Menander possessed the largest in Pompeii, dating from the Augustan era (I 10.4; fig. 111c). After A.D. 62 formal dining rooms on this scale were created in the House of Pansa (VI 6.1), the House of Castor and Pollux (VI 9.6–7), the complex of dwellings joined together that is known as the House of the Citharist (I 4.5), and the House of the Golden Cupids (VI 16.7).[89]

But summer rooms and exedrae also had porticos added to them. The "truncated peristyle" added to the venerable House of Sallust in the late era is a particularly good example (VI 2.4; fig. 89).[90] The two porticos at the sides end in two small rooms that are open to the small peristyle garden through disproportionately large windows. In the room to the right two pictures of lovers from mythology of the type frequently found in bedrooms can still be made out, despite the damage incurred during the Second World War.[91] Clearly these little rooms represent imitations of the day room located on the grounds of large villas at points with especially fine views, of the type to which Pliny the Younger liked to withdraw (*Epistles* 2.17.20ff.). Two comparable rooms on the scale appropriate to a small suburban villa can be found in a Flavian house at the edge of Herculaneum overlooking the sea.[92] By contrast, the only view from the day room of the House of Sallust was of the flower beds in the little garden and a wall decorated with a mythical landscape (fig. 90 and plate 11.2). This visual opening is flanked by two pedestals with marble statues of nymphs.[93] In this manner a villa garden was created with an architectural element largely stripped of its function, for the little rooms hardly offered much accommodation. Perhaps they soon found a use as tool sheds or storerooms. A

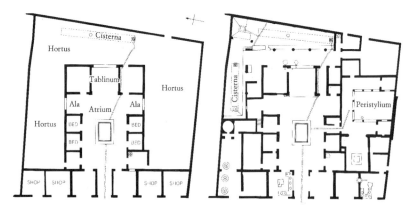

Figure 89 Ground plans of the House of Sallust before and after renovation (VI 2.4; after J. B. Ward-Perkins). This example shows how the orientation of the house was shifted away from the interior and toward the garden. The house was embellished with various elements of villa architecture.

Figure 90 View of the fresco on the garden wall in the "peristyle court" built on to the House of Sallust. The painted "marble" statues create an illusionist transition from the little garden to the mythical landscape in the large fresco, which depicts Actaeon being torn apart by hounds after surprising Artemis at her bath. In the wall to the right a window of one of the two small garden rooms *(diaetae)* is visible.

similarly placed room in the House of the Epigrams (V 1.18) shows that the arrangement was not unique.

Large windows were used to provide other rooms with a "vista" of a portico, or a tiny courtyard with a miniature garden or paintings of a garden.[94] We should also view in this same context the numerous *tablina* (main rooms) separated from garden courtyards only by a low wall, which thus turned them into "garden rooms" reminiscent of country villas.[95] This phenomenon, too, is most frequently associated with houses from the late period.

Gardens Filled with Sculptures

For the owner of a house with a sizable peristyle courtyard, the obvious next step was to plant a garden in it. Some of these gardens acquired an aura of luxury through the use of expensive plants and decorative objects such as fountains, sculptures, and other marble pieces. Once overloaded with such fixtures, they were intended more to be looked at than actually used. There can be little doubt that their design imitated the gardens and parks around villas, some notion of which is conveyed both by paintings and by literary sources. The rather strange fashion of filling in the spaces between columns with walls waist-high, which we encounter in a number of late houses, seems to be a feature of this imitation. The side of the wall facing the garden is always painted with more scenes of beautiful gardens, thereby expanding the associations suggested by the garden itself (fig. 91).[96] Since almost nothing remains of the original gardens at large villas, the imitations in Pompeii and Herculaneum represent modest but nevertheless useful sources of information about them.

The House of the Golden Cupids (VI 16.7; fig. 92), which has been described in detail in an excellent recent publication, offers a particularly important example of a lavish peristyle garden.[97] Despite its small size, it is reached by a broad staircase from the raised portico on its western side. The façade of the "Rhodian peristyle" (Vitruvius 6.7.3) is rendered even more impressive by the combination of a flight of steps and a gable (figs. 93 and 94).[98] It creates a grand front for the dining room behind it, but a front completely out of proportion to the small garden. In the middle of this

Figure 91   Peristyle in the House of Menander (I 10.4). In later houses the spaces between the columns were filled in with a low wall that was decorated with paintings on the side toward the garden. They were designed to heighten the effect of the garden as an independent element in the decor of the house. Such gardens were meant to be looked at rather than walked in.

garden there is a pool, as we so often find; this one is very large and once had a statue on its rim. It was encircled by a tiny path dotted with sculptures and marble pieces.

Dominating the borders of the garden is a series of tall pillars distributed more or less evenly, surmounted by heads and reliefs of Dionysiac masks (see fig. 94). Most of these herms are representations of Dionysus or one of the figures associated with him, including Eros; there is also one of Jupiter Ammon. The large and small masks *(oscilla)* hanging between the columns further emphasize the basic Dionysiac theme, but other types of decoration frequently found at villas are present as well. A tiny statue of Omphale next to the steps serves as a "reference" to Greek art and mythology. The reliefs set into the eastern wall, including a Hellenistic votive relief, are perhaps intended to imitate an art collection.[99] A herm with an almost unrecognizable portrait of Menander alludes to the gallery of great Greeks—statesmen, philosophers, and poets—so popular with villa owners.[100] The sculptures in the grass around the garden fountain included various animals and

The Domestic Arts in Pompeii   169

a group of hounds pursuing a boar; we may consider these "excerpts" from a "marble *paradeisos*," so to speak. There is even an allusion to the theme of the palaestra. Thus in addition to the dominant Dionysiac theme we find all the major categories of villa statuary represented, even if by only a single piece in some cases.[101] Smaller marble objects stood among all these statues as well, including tables, the fountain basin, the remains of a candelabrum, and a sundial.

Just like the architectural elements, this entire diversified inventory of objects had to be squeezed into an extremely small space; as a result, while the position of some could be chosen for effect, that of others was purely arbitrary.[102] In this instance, too, the ruling principle appears to have been simply to display a great quantity of objects, and discrepancies with regard both to size and to artistic quality were no more disturbing to the owner of the house than to the owner of the collection at the miniature villa in the Via dell'Abbondanza (see figs. 75 and 78). The owner of the House of the Golden Cupids apparently had no scruples about converting a Dionysus herm into a fountain with a water spout or taking some expensive tall

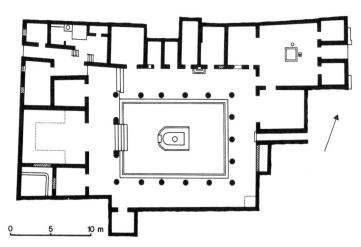

Figure 92   Ground plan of the House of the Golden Cupids (VI 16.7). After being "Hel-lenized," Roman houses ceased to be oriented around their central atrium, the heart of the inward-looking design. In many houses such as this one the atrium has been abandoned entirely in favor of a peristyle. All the reception rooms here are oriented toward the garden, which has been fitted out according to its new function as a central area of communication, in imitation of villa life.

POMPEII

Figures 93–94   Two views of the little villa garden at the House of the Golden Cupids. A broad set of steps leads down from the hall of the "Rhodian" peristyle into the garden. Marble herms, reliefs, and other sculptures were placed along the paths, and round masks *(oscilla)* hung between the columns. The garden decor was intended to evoke or even create a little sanctuary of Dionysus.

pilasters decorated with fine reliefs—clearly intended for a larger garden—and sawing them in half to make supports for two more reliefs.[103]

We observed a sculpture collection with a similar mixture of themes crammed into a tiny space along the watercourse of the miniature villa in the Via dell'Abbondanza. Whereas there the statues of the Muses along the little watercourse may have created a nice effect on their tall pedestals, the sphinx and the young "Heracles" with a goose look distinctly incongruous among the Dionysiac herms. Taken together they can be understood only as an attempt to imitate larger garden layouts with sculptures haphazardly assembled from a variety of the available thematic sets.[104] A statue that may have had a meaningful connection with its setting at a large villa could sink to the level of mere decoration when it was miniaturized and placed in the context of a small Pompeian peristyle, where its main function was simply to add a touch of class. Often enough the selection of objects for the collection may have been dictated by what local merchants happened to have on hand. I believe it would not be difficult to collect material demonstrating that, during the period just before the eruption, studios specializing in production for this market existed in Campania and elsewhere.[105] Yet, despite the random nature of much of the repertoire of imitation villa statuary in Pompeii, it appears that certain thematic preferences did exist. It is striking, for example, that, in contrast to villa decor, portraits of famous Greeks, including rulers, and statues related to themes from myth and the palaestra occur only rarely and in the most selective detail.[106] On the other hand, if a Pompeian house has any sculptures at all, one will almost certainly find groups of animals and works related to Dionysiac themes.

The most beautiful and unified collection of sculptures on these two themes so popular with Pompeians is to be found in the little garden in the house of M. Lucretius (IX 3.5; figs. 95–97), although it still contains a few inconsistencies.[107] The garden is located in a central courtyard and is visible from the main rooms of the house. Sculptures of all kinds of animals appear to be lying or ambling around a circular basin in the middle, including an Egyptian ibis; the basin itself also has two dolphins with cupids. Between the animals one finds a young satyr shading his eyes from the sun as if looking for something, while another is attempting to remove a thorn from the foot of his friend Pan. A goat standing on its hind legs sniffs at yet

Figures 95–96 Ground plan and view of the reconstructed garden at the House of M. Lucretius (IX 3.5; from an old photograph). In this instance the small garden area lies at the junction between the front portion of the house and the raised wing at the rear. All the main reception rooms had a view of the garden, which was filled with sculptures related to Dionysiac themes in a manner reminiscent of a nativity scene. The figures were placed around a cascade and a circular pool.

The Domestic Arts in Pompeii 173

Figure 97 View from the *tablinum* toward the elevated garden at the House of M. Lucretius (IX 3.5; from an old photograph).

another satyr, frozen in the form of a herm. The juxtaposition of "lifelike" and more stylized works, especially the herm, suggests that this must have been one of the chief charms of late Hellenistic garden sculpture in Roman villas.

The central position of the statuary garden in the house of M. Lucretius allowed for one further special effect. Thanks to the rising terrain, the garden behind the main room lay on a higher level than the street, so that to a guest arriving at the front door it must have appeared like a stage set. Thus the most expensive decorative feature of the house was made to serve the function of impressing visitors.[108]

Dining under the Stars

Even in smaller houses, especially ones with no peristyle, two features we have already encountered were extremely popular, namely, outdoor tables with two or three masonry couches (*bi-* or *triclinia*) shaded by a pergola, and

POMPEII

fountains. Both had the advantage of retaining their pleasure-giving function even in the smallest garden, and of evoking something of the aura of a villa even in the humblest surroundings, either alone or in combination.

Almost all of the many stone or brick couches (usually shaded by pergolas) that we find in Pompeian gardens seem to date from the last decades of the city's existence.[109] Although they are found in even the simplest houses, they are not a universal feature of life in a Mediterranean climate, as we might tend to assume. This is shown not only by their late appearance on the scene, but also by their close connection with other villa features, especially fountains and wall paintings alluding to villa life. The House of Sallust referred to above (VI 2.4; see figs. 89 and 90) shows how both fountains and frescos were used in a vacant area behind the main room and portico to give even a "left-over" corner of the property a touch of villa flair. The dining area was built at the narrowest point. A faded illusionist painting on the outer wall expanded the real architecture of the old portico into a kind of peristyle, where between painted pillars vistas of a park filled with rare birds can be glimpsed (figs. 98 and 99).[110] In three of these spaces fountain basins were depicted in niches surrounded by lattices. A fourth fountain beside the dining area contained real running water, creating a further link between reality and illusion.[111]

In region I a man by the name of Cornelius Tages, a member of a family of freedmen who probably made his money as a wine merchant, bought up no fewer than four separate houses and joined them into a single complex (I 7.11; figs. 100 and 101).[112] Since he had no grand atrium, he admitted visitors through a special door (no. 12) directly into the garden and the adjacent rooms, which constituted the showpiece of the house. A masonry base for two dining couches (p) stood in the center of his irregularly shaped garden, with four columns supporting a pergola above it. Behind this structure stood an aedicula containing a fountain with a cascade, adorned by a bronze nymph.[113] The water collected between the couches and may have given the occupants the feeling of reclining on a small island (see fig. 101)—a possibility that could actually be realized by owners of villas like the one at Sperlonga. The illusion was heightened by the paintings on the couches' bases, which depicted scenes along the Nile with the most varied inventory of architecture and actors and ran the thematic gamut from the

POMPEII

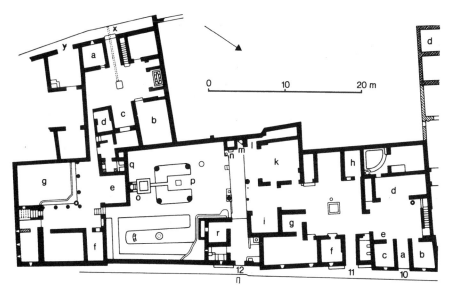

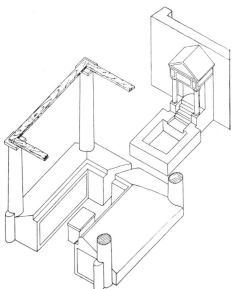

Figures 100–101 Ground plan and reconstruction of the garden architecture, fountain, and masonry couches at the House of the Ephebe (I 7.10–12). The presumed owner of the house, a freedman named Cornelius Tages, bought up several small houses and designed the garden to be the main reception area. The couches were connected with a fountain, and the desired illusion—that one was lying beside a little stream or on an island—was heightened by corresponding paintings.

Figures 98–99 Portico and garden behind the House of Sallust (VI 2.4). The drawings show them after excavation in the early nineteenth century (Gell) and in a reconstruction (Overbeck). The wall paintings and architecture complement one another in the effort to create the richest possible evocation of a villa atmosphere. The masonry couches were placed at the narrow end of the garden, in order to maximize the "vista" (compare fig. 90).

sacred to the erotic. Nearby stood the pride of the owner's art collection: the well-known classicizing bronze statue of a youth *(ephebos)* on a round base holding a candelabrum in the form of a vine (now in the Museo Nazionale in Naples; fig. 102).[114] A dinner guest might well have felt transported to the distant banks of the Nile or one of the luxurious retreats on the shores of the Euripus. In a manner of speaking, the valuable bronze statue anchored such reveries in the wealth of the present.

The "Egyptian" picnic spot was surrounded by imitations of villas and their parks. Immediately to the left, four small marble herms framed a corner of the garden[115] that probably contained three marble statuettes: a figure of Pan carrying a basket of flowers and treading on a krupezion (an instrument resembling a castanet, worked by the foot), a recumbent satyr, and a doe nursing her young.[116] Surely we would not go far wrong if we were to imagine the wall at the back to have been painted with a view of a park. Opposite this "mythological" garden populated by figures associated with Dionysus, and to one side of the fountain aedicula, stood a painting of a game park. In a moment I shall return to this motif and its connection with villas, but first it should be noted that once again we find the characteristic painted and gilded statues of heroes or Mars standing on tall pedestals in front of the picture frame.[117] We have already encountered similar painted statues at the House of Sallust (see fig. 90), and they are frequently found next to vistas of gardens or game parks. They replace real marble in the decoration of the garden and are typical of late wall frescos in garden environments (compare figs. 90 and 106).[118] In this case the painted statues

Figure 102 Bronze statue of a servant holding a candelabrum found in the garden at the House of the Ephebe (Naples, Museo Nazionale). It originally functioned as a "dumb waiter," standing on a round base next to the couches under a pergola in the garden and adding grace to the whole ensemble. The classic lines emphasized the artistic character of the work and recalled works of art in large villas. The statue was produced by an eclectic workshop in the Augustan era. For the body the sculptor used a classical statue of a boy in the style of Polyclitus, but he placed a girl's head of early classical type on top of it. The homoerotic charm of this "dumb waiter" may well have constituted no small part of the viewers' enjoyment of this quite valuable work of art, which probably belonged to the collection of a wealthy villa owner before its arrival at the rather modest home of Cornelius Tages.

POMPEII

connect the *paradeisos* image with a richly furnished villa interior. The dining room (k), which affords a view of the garden, represents at least an imitation of such an interior, with its costly paving of different kinds of marble known as *opus sectile* ("cut work"),[119] gilded decoration, and Alexandrian fittings.[120]

Steps lead down from the garden containing the fountain and dining area to the peristyle (g) of a small house (I 7.19) that was apparently a later acquisition joined to the owner's original property. Its entrance lies on the opposite side of the *insula*. Here the truncated peristyle is "completed" by painted Ionic columns, with a scene of a park between them, similar to the scene in the House of Sallust. This time the niches separated from the park by a lattice contain a statue of Venus in addition to a marble vase and a fountain basin.[121] Finally, from the tiny main room (c) of this extended house a large "window" looked out onto what may well have been the smallest *trompe l'oeil* garden in Pompeii: in the narrow light-well traces of the typical painted garden lattice and trees were found.

Two aspects of Cornelius Tages' house are of particular significance here: first, the direct juxtaposition of costly decorative objects and fittings (such as the bronze statue and the floor in *opus sectile*) on the one hand and the very limited living space on the other; and second, the characteristic framing of genuine villa elements with painted vistas and illusions. The *paradeisoi* and banks of the Nile, which remained out of reach in reality, lay probably no further away in the owners' imaginations than villa gardens, parts of which could be imported into their actual living space in the form of outdoor dining areas, fountains, and garden sculptures.

In both its technical design and its artistic decor the fountain dining room at the House of the Ephebe (or House of Cornelius Tages) is modeled after similar arrangements at villas or large gardens *(horti)* in Rome. Proof of this is offered by the far grander grotto dining room in the "clubhouse" of Julia Felix (II 4).[122] There water also collected in a pool between the couches after trickling over a set of steps. And like Cornelius Tages' guests, the diners looked at a Nilotic landscape. In the House of Julia Felix, the dining area is on a true villa scale. Rakob has pointed out the frequency with which this type is found, and its connection with fountains or grotto dining areas in the imperial Domus Aurea and Transitoria. In such a case as this it becomes apparent how we should picture the adoption of various villa elements as occurring in a number of steps. We have already encountered a similar example in the rooms with a view of the sea at the little terrace villa in Herculaneum.

If space was too limited to place free-standing masonry couches around a fountain, many Pompeians could at least manage to have a fountain, which might, for instance, be set into the back wall of the house. Along with permanent dining areas, this seems to have been a feature characteristic of late houses in particular.[123] The most impressive solution is found in connection with a "truncated portico" at the House of the Bull (V 1.7).[124] It appears to have been inspired by façades of imposing urban buildings. The "frames" of such fountains are usually decorated with mosaics and occur in a wide variety of sizes. But even the largest of them give the impression of miniature imitations of the great garden fountains in luxurious parks. Not too long ago the remains of one were found on the Quirinal.[125]

Two of the most beautiful mosaic fountains in Pompeii are located next door to each other, in the houses named after them: the House of the Large Fountain (VI 8.22; figs. 105, 113b, and plate 13) and the House of the Little Fountain (VI 8.23; fig. 104 and plate 12).[126] Each fountain is aligned with the axis of the front door, like a costly piece of furniture, so that the gaze of someone entering the house would fall on it immediately.

From their setting amid painted illusions of villas and landscapes symbolizing felicity we can deduce that these fountains also stood for everything implied by the word "villa." Another good example of this is provided by the tiny House of the Grand Duke (VII 4.56).[127] This dwelling stands on a narrow, poorly proportioned strip of land and consists of only a few rooms grouped around a cramped atrium. Here, too, the little fountain stands in the courtyard in the line of sight from the entrance. Three columns and one engaged column attempt to give the space at least the aura of a peristyle (fig. 103). The *tablinum* has been made into a "garden room" by widening the opening, and another room has been given a large window opening onto the same "villa area." The pool in front of the fountain is divided into

Figure 103 View of the fountain and a portion of the "colonnade" at the House of the Grand Duke (VII 4.56). If a small house offered scant space for an extensive garden, a fountain with elaborate mosaics surrounded by landscape paintings often provided the only reminiscence of villa life.

three parts; once again they must be ponds for different types of fish, as in the garden of the miniature villa. However, the most important aspect of the decor in determining the overall impression is the walls, which were covered with paintings of ornamental topiary gardens. Above a waist-high lattice-work fence are scenes of a park landscape. Here, too, a small marble table helps to bridge the transition between illusion and reality.

At another very small dwelling with a similarly irregular ground plan, the House of the Bear (VII 2.45; fig. 113f), the courtyard was designed in much the same way, with a room opening onto it.[128] No space remained for columns, but as if to make up for this the fountain was given broader proportions and the walls even richer decoration. A fountain supported by a nymph once stood in front of the garden vista (as at the House of Sallust), and the water spout was shaped like a sphinx. Farther up was a group of animals, and above the fountain Venus and her shell. These large-format wall paintings merit separate discussion.

POMPEII

Figure 104 Reconstruction of the portico with fountain and frescos at the House of the Small Fountain (VI 8.23–24; after Gell, 1832). During the last few decades before Pompeii's destruction, a fashion developed for large paintings that often covered the entire surface of the garden walls. Not unlike travel posters of exotic places in our own day, they suggested lush gardens, rare plants, birds, and costly marble sculptures, or game preserves such as actually existed on great estates. Such garden paintings became highly popular again in Europe in the neoclassical period. In the reconstructions of the early nineteenth century, the modest spaces take on a festive character.

Figure 105 Depiction of the garden, with fountain and paintings, at the House of the Large Fountain after excavation (VI 8.22; after Gell, 1832).

The Domestic Arts in Pompeii

Large Pictures for Small Dreams

Large frescos of the type we first encountered at the House of the Ephebe are common in Pompeii. Usually covering entire walls, they repeat the same motifs again and again, in apparently arbitrary combinations: gardens lavishly adorned with pergolas, fountains, and sculpture; landscape vistas containing seaside or country villas; *paradeisoi* and the type of scene known as a "sacred" or Nilotic landscape.[129] Particularly good examples are found at the House of the Small Fountain (see fig. 104, plate 12) and the House of the Large Fountain (see fig. 105, plate 13).[130]

Such large-format pictures have been found mainly in small houses where there were few or no architectural or other decorative villa elements. They served as the most inexpensive form of villa imitation. It is once again striking that they were used almost exclusively in the garden area, either alone or to decorate part of a peristyle.

In the medium-sized House of Romulus and Remus (VII 7.10) the wall at the end of the small "truncated peristyle" was covered with a fresco of a park filled with sculptures, including the already familiar fountains supported by nymphs, a statue of Silenus, and a large marble bowl (fig. 106).[131] In the adjoining portico the wall opens up with a view of a tranquil game park. At the tiny House of the Ceii (I 6.15; see fig. 113e), however, there was no room for even the most shrunken peristyle in the courtyard, so the walls were decorated with large frescos of a Nilotic landscape, an "Egyptianizing" sacred landscape, and a large *paradeisos* against a dark background.[132] In the foreground we once again find painted marble fountains, here in the form of shallow basins supported by sphinxes. The courtyard is surrounded by a narrow channel that was intended to catch and hold rainwater and was apparently treated as a miniature watercourse. One sees how directly the paintings were connected with the real, three-dimensional garden from the fact that a painted marble fountain nymph appears to be pouring painted water into the actual channel below. A tiny room in a corner of the courtyard was conceived as a garden room with a large window opening onto this miniature villa idyll, but in the last year of the town's history it served as a storeroom.

Figure 106   Paintings in the truncated peristyle at the House of Romulus and Remus (VIII 7.10): on the left a villa garden with a marble urn and rare animals; on the right a "game preserve" with a collection of exotic animals that could hardly have existed peaceably together in reality. The juxtaposition of the pictures shows that the aim was not to create a visual illusion, but rather to conjure up attractive scenes of prestigious and desirable ideals.

Large wall frescos first made their appearance in Pompeii during the reign of Vespasian, as Schefold has correctly observed. In the wall designs of the second to fourth styles, comparable subjects were depicted only in friezes or painted panels *(pinakes)*. Nevertheless, however well large-scale pictures fit our notions of Flavian style, they are not an innovation of this period. From Vitruvius we know that in his time and even earlier long promenades *(ambulationes)* were painted with scenes of harbors, hills, coastlines, rivers, springs, straits, shrines, woods, mountains, herds of animals, and shepherds (7.5.2); in the era of Augustus it was chiefly a certain Ludius (?), according to Pliny, who added to this Hellenistic repertoire new themes typically associated with villa life: "villas and porticos, gardens, groves, woods, hills, fish ponds, watercourses, rivers, shores, and whatever else one might wish, such as various ramblers or travelers, on sea or land, mounted on donkeys or riding in carriages to their country houses, also fishermen, bird catchers, hunters, and vintners" (*Natural History* 35.116).

The text reveals that Ludius painted not panel pictures but frescos.[133] Such depictions were first placed in actual villa porticos as "vistas," and later imitated in more modest villas and houses as replacements "for a very beautiful view at minimal cost" (ibid., 35.117). The fact that a contemporary of Pompeian householders mentions heightening the beauty of real living conditions, *qualia quis optaret,* is worth stressing. The late appearance of such pictures in Pompeii can be explained on the one hand by the unusually extensive building activity after the earthquake of A.D. 62, and on the other hand by the dominant style, which took its orientation from villa decor. It demonstrates once more how problematic it can be to deduce "stylistic developments" from derivative works of art.

In a number of cases the "vista" character of wall paintings becomes evident from the way they are framed. We have already encountered examples of this at the House of the Ephebe, the House of the Small Fountain, and the House of the Ceii. Another example is offered by a wall in the House of the Amazons (VI 2.14; plate 14.1).[134] Behind a marble balustrade, on which we once again find perched the birds that were such a popular motif, lie a park and in the distance the sea, with no fewer than three island villas. An aedicula with Egyptian divinities in the foreground recalls the character of gardens as sacred groves. The whole vista is framed by garlands of ivy.

The connection between depictions of *paradeisoi* and villa life is documented by accounts of game parks on great country estates.[135] Having originated in the Orient, they arrived in Italy by way of the royal game parks of Hellenistic potentates.[136] Polybius mentions that the young Scipio indulged his passion for hunting in the royal game preserves of Macedonia (32.15). A marble relief in the Vatican that may once have formed part of a balustrade gives an indication of what the transition between a Roman garden and a *paradeisos* may have looked like (fig. 107).[137] The wild animals' range is demarcated by a fence interrupted at intervals by overgrown niches that hold statues of cupids and are flanked on top by herms. Thanks to a

Figure 107 A marble relief in the Museo Chiaramonti at the Vatican. It shows a view of a game preserve from a villa garden. Herms with busts of famous Greeks numbered among the standard decorative objects in villa gardens and represented the values of classical education and culture. Such herms were a great rarity, however, in the middle-class houses of Pompeii.

passage in Varro, even the painting of a mythologically enhanced *paradeisos* in the House of Orpheus (VI 14.20; plate 14.2) can be directly linked with the villa life of great families; it is immaterial whether the Pompeian house-holder was himself aware of such a connection or not.[138] Varro reports that Q. Hortensius Hortalis was in the habit of entertaining guests in the game preserve at his villa at Ostia, where a slave dressed up as Orpheus would attract the animals with his music.[139] The huge fresco at Pompeii covers the entire rear wall of the little house and, like the fountains mentioned above, is visible to visitors arriving at the front door. Here, too, two garden vistas—from grotto *nymphaea*—cement links with the villa.

Clearly, a picture placed to catch the eye in this manner is more striking than a smaller one forming part of a series in a long *ambulatio*. The artistic quality of such large frescos, designed to awaken associations rather like a travel poster, is correspondingly crude. The same stereotyped animals occur repeatedly, obviously copied from models in the painters' pattern books and assembled *ad hoc,* with the result that their juxtaposition often appears senseless or absurd.[140] One finds, for instance, hunting scenes and groups of animals in combat next to assemblages of peaceful creatures, as in the rocky landscape at the House of the Ancient Hunt (VII 4.48; fig. 108).[141] It is likely that patrons' ideas of a *paradeisos* were not infrequently overlaid with associations from the world of gladiatorial and animal combat. Characteristically, the "Gladiators' Barracks" in Pompeii (V 5.3) contains a *paradeisos* fresco.[142]

The scenes painted on the bases of the masonry couches at the House of

Figure 108 Nineteenth-century sketch of a painting at the House of the Hunt (VII 4.48; by an anonymous artist). The idea of game preserves at great villas was frequently conflated with scenes of hunting and animal combat in the arena.

the Ephebe are an important clue to understanding the vistas of exotic landscapes, especially views of Egypt. We know this clue is accurate because the same theme occurs in large-format frescos almost exclusively in connection with fountains or watercourses. We saw that *euripi* were also included among the themes of villa paintings by Ludius, and at the miniature villa in the Via dell'Abbondanza we encountered a reflection or derivative of a villa watercourse in combination with a collection of Egyptian statuary. The main point of such Egyptian landscapes appears to be to increase the sense of well-being already created by reminiscences of villa life such as architecture, furnishings, and decor; to these cues suggesting felicity the paintings added allusions to famous landscapes associated with the good life. It is no accident that Seneca equates Baiae and Canopus in epitomizing the height of luxury—and decadence (*Epistles* 51.3).[143]

The large-format paintings of bucolic, mythological, and sacred landscapes must no doubt have served the same purpose. They would also provide inviting locales to which the owner's thoughts could stray as he enjoyed his little garden. Once again the world of royalty offers a comparison. After Nero had created a game park and acres of bucolic landscape around his Golden House (Domus Aurea), he said that he was "at last beginning to be housed like a human being."[144]

The Pompeians who renovated their houses after the earthquake typically attached little or no importance to creating a logical architectural context for the large-format vistas they had painted on their walls; indeed, they often dispensed with even the suggestion of a frame that would have brought the painting into some relation with the room in which it was located. The spatial relationships between paintings in a room was apparently also a matter of indifference: it did not matter whether they existed side by side, one above the other, or in any particular order. What counted was size—namely, as large and conspicuous as possible—and the quantity of associative motifs. The aim was to render as realistically as possible the objects and settings the owner wished to have conjured up.

A typical example of this can be found in the *nymphaeum* at the House of the Centenarian (IX 8.6; fig. 109).[145] The lower part of the wall, which has a stripe all the way around it, is presented as a garden balustrade hung with ivy; at its foot are various birds and lizards. Above it, however, one finds ponds containing a rich assortment of fish, while to the sides there are garden scenes with the now familiar fountain bases supported by sphinxes.[146] Finally, the wall at the entrance and the door at the end are covered with scenes of game parks, even though in the middle of the latter there is a real fountain, painted to look as if it were built of rare marble. The water runs down a flight of marble steps into a large basin. The link between architecture and painted decor in this room is once again the world of the luxury villa and its gardens. Each separate motif recalls a different aspect of this world, but as a whole the room is—to our modern eyes—a grotesque potpourri. Here it becomes obvious that the owners of such a retreat were interested first and foremost in having a great variety of images to help them pretend they had been transported to the world of their imagining. We can only conclude that they must have had mental

Figure 109 *Nymphaeum* in the garden at the House of the Centenary (IX 8.6). The paintings surrounding the fountain have no "realistic" association whatsoever. It is characteristic, for example, that the depiction of a fish pond is placed directly above a garden scene. This indicates that such paintings were "read" in quite arbitrary succession, corresponding to their function as evocations of a whole series of different associations.

powers of association that allowed them to overlook striking contradictions in their immediate surroundings!

We now come to the wall paintings in the principal reception rooms of important houses modernized in the town's final decades. Pompeians began borrowing their wall decor schemes from the homes of the aristocracy in Rome in the first century B.C. In both cities subdivision of space by means of architectural elements and landscape vistas remained very popular all the way down to the fourth style, at least in the more important rooms. But although later walls may have a more unified character, their vistas and glimpses of fancifully imagined architecture still lent them a dimension of unreality. The original inspiration behind them, namely, the grandiose architecture of royal palaces, continued to play a role here, too, even if the homeowners were no longer aware of the source.

In the very last houses, however, we find that one element has come to

the fore with a very specific connection to villa life: the designs that Schefold has so convincingly described as imitation *pinacothecae*.[147] As is well
known, impressive examples from the reign of Vespasian can be found in
the freedmen's dwelling at the House of the Vettii (VI 15.1; fig. 110)[148]—
which also contains an important example of villa imitation in the form of
a "sculpture garden"—and at the House of the Tragic Poet (VI 8.3).[149]
Comparative analysis has demonstrated the degree to which the selection
of "pictures" for these "galleries" was determined by the standard pattern
books available to the painters.[150] The Pompeians' overfondness for this
type of decor and their tendency to turn even the tiniest room into a
pinacotheca are familiar to every visitor to the site. Their increased ambitions
in this regard are accompanied by a decline in the quality of the older
architectural form of wall decoration. We can observe this in a number of

Figure 110   Reception room with wall paintings in the fourth style (ca. A.D. 60–70) at the
House of the Vettii (VI 15.1). The large-format mythological pictures were intended to
provide evidence of the owner's education and at the same time recall actual *pinacothecae*
containing original Greek paintings.

details in the very last wall paintings. A room in the House of the Vettii contains a good example: a frieze with a fish motif that is far too large in proportion to the other elements of the design.[151] The families that commissioned such work had a preference for realistic depictions of certain motifs, but they also liked regular "wallpaper" patterns in strong contrasting colors.[152] These qualities can be directly linked with the "framed" giant frescos in the gardens and understood as elements of the new style.

It is difficult to avoid overemphasizing the importance of Pompeian painting because it is so well preserved. This is true not only with respect to its quality—especially in the late houses and in connection with its figured compositions—and the information it provides on lost masterworks of Greek panel paintings, but also for what it reveals about the function and meaning of the world it depicts within the overall context of Neronian and Flavian culture and the Pompeians' daily lives. As in the case of the sculptures and decorated fountains in their gardens, the owners' principal aim in decorating their walls must have been to achieve as grand and impressive an effect as possible. The late wall paintings thus represent a phenomenon similar to the painted vistas in the second style at nearby villas. If we regard Pompeian wall paintings of the last two decades, at least, as one element of a derivative domestic taste acquired at second and third hand from aristocratic neighbors, then we will take a more skeptical view of claims for them as direct expressions of profound learning and piety. But this is a broad and complex field of inquiry better addressed elsewhere.

Domestic Taste and Cultural Identity

The examples of Pompeian architecture we have looked at thus far have ranged from the many-faceted miniature villa and houses incorporating one or more villa elements to architectural "garden furniture," collections of decorative statuary, and finally to large-scale wall paintings and *pinacothecae*. In this survey architecture has been treated more extensively than other elements because it made the greatest demands on owners in terms of expense, planning, and *engagement*. Here we can be sure it is not a question of decor adopted simply because it happened to be in fashion. Anyone undertaking the various forms of construction considered here must have had a particular set of ideas in mind. The fact that a close connection exists between the buildings themselves and the other decorative elements enabled me to include the latter in this analysis, thereby expanding its scope and increasing the amount of information to be drawn from the evidence.

The resulting picture is unambiguous: although the owners of these houses made use of different forms—and achieved differing degrees of success—they all shared the same aim, namely, to create the illusion of a villa. They all envisaged their ideal as a world of luxury. And everywhere we find the same characteristic taste, derived from models that have been heaped one upon the other and jumbled together until the sense of their original meaning and function is largely lost. It is the taste of a broad class of comfortable to well-to-do Pompeians who took their orientation entirely from the values and style of the very rich and imitated them as their pocketbooks allowed.

This becomes apparent when we compare the ground plans of the most important houses we have discussed. The most interesting and "original" architectural forms of villa imitation are to be found in houses of medium size (figs. 112a–e). They enclose much less space than the great Hellenistic houses of the Samnite elite and the largest houses of the first century B.C., such as the Insula Occidentalis or the House of Menander (fig. 111c). The miniature villa in the Via dell'Abbondanza (fig. 112a) falls into this category along with the Houses of Apolline, the Black Anchor, the Ephebe, the Moralist, and the Golden Cupids. Its sole advantage over similar houses lies in the large size of its garden—and in this connection we should not forget that perhaps prices for lots were lower in this less thickly populated quarter. The dimensions of the rooms in these medium-sized houses are quite comparable as well. Their owners clearly belonged to a well-to-do "middle class," which seems to have been particularly keen on adopting the kind of taste oriented toward villa imitation.

The same style also predominates in some smaller houses, however, including some of the very smallest, which frequently consist of not much more than several small rooms off a cramped atrium, with a courtyard only a few yards square. Sometimes, but not always, a few elements of a portico,

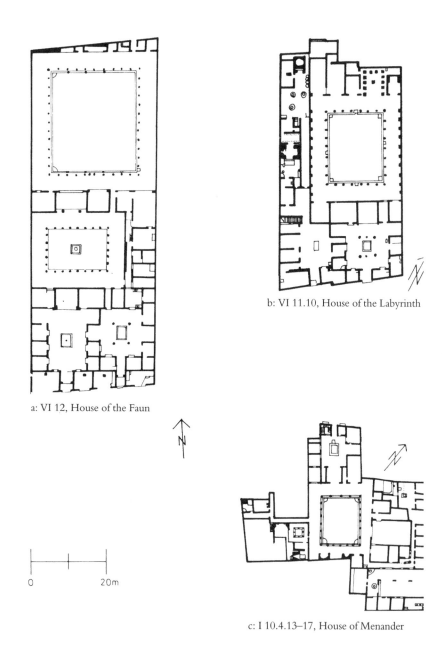

a: VI 12, House of the Faun

b: VI 11.10, House of the Labyrinth

c: I 10.4.13–17, House of Menander

0   20m

Figure 111a–c Comparative ground plans I

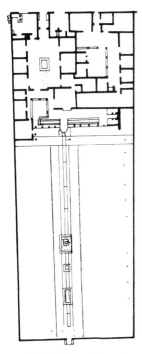

b: VI 7.23, House of Apolline

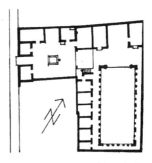

a: II 2.5, House of Loreius
Tiburtinus

c: VI 10.7, House of the Black
Anchor, upper story

d: III 4.3, House of the
Moralist

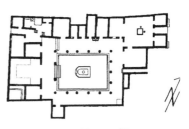

e: VI 16.7, House of the
Golden Cupids

Figure 112a–e   Comparative ground plans II

a: IX 3 + 24, House of M. Lucretius

b: VI 8.22, House of the Large
Fountain

c: I 7.10–12.19, House of
the Ephebe

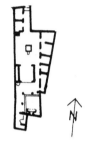

d: VII 4.56, House of
the Grand Duke
of Tuscany

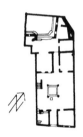

e: I 6.15, House of the Ceii

f: VII 2.45, House of the Bear

Figure 113a–f   Comparative ground plans III

reduced in size, can be found in such courtyards. We have encountered examples of this type in the houses of the Grand Duke, the Ceii, and the Bear (fig. 113a–f). Thanks to the characteristics described above, the new style could be realized in almost every type of space and could fit virtually every pocketbook. Since the owners of the smallest houses had to limit themselves to wall decoration for the most part, the manifestations of the new taste appear more stereotypical and less varied than in the houses that could accommodate villa elements in the architecture.

At the same time the new style spread even into the large older houses. We saw examples of this at the House of the Centenarian (see fig. 109) and the House of Sallust (see fig. 90). Yet here—apart from the occasional fountain, *piscina,* or large *triclinium*—the absence of larger elements is striking; we meet with the clearest manifestations of the new taste in the wall paintings in individual rooms.[153] Some of the old Samnite *domus* like the House of the Faun have virtually nothing in the new style, and here and there old paintings appear to have been carefully repaired. This does not invalidate the general argument, however, since we must take into account that as a rule the owners of small and medium-sized houses put much more effort into rebuilding after the earthquake than the great families did. This difference may well be due to the fact that the lesser property-holders earned their living in Pompeii and thus stayed on after the earthquake, whereas those few very rich families still in residence probably moved away (cf. Seneca *Nat. Quest.* VI 1.1).[154] Thus, unfortunately, we are not in a position to say much about their domestic taste.

The picture assembled here matches the results Castrén obtained from his study of the town council *(ordo)* in Pompeii. He concluded that the composition of the council and the social class of other office-holders showed signs of shifting in the Claudian period, shifts that became manifest in the years between the earthquake and the destruction of the city. In those years political influence was achieved by large numbers of Pompeians whose families had been either unknown earlier or not represented in the council for decades. Simultaneously, the names of those families who had been able to maintain their hold on both political and social leadership from the early Augustan period down to Claudian times disappear. Castrén observes, "The rise of the new families and of the descendants of freedmen is a proof of a gradual replacement of the landed aristocracy in the administration of the municipalities, a development that becomes visible already during the reign of Claudius."[155] In Pompeii (as in other Italic cities) many members of the new plutocracy were descended from freedmen. As the city gradually recovered, builders, brokers, traders, and craftsmen became the people in demand; the economic and social situation must have favored members of this group more in Pompeii than elsewhere, and no doubt some of the owners of the medium-sized, freshly renovated houses discussed here numbered among them.[156] We have come across several homes built or renovated by owners who apparently had made their money in commerce or a trade, some of them in a relatively short time. The best example was the House of Cornelius Tages, named after a man who appears to have bought up the properties next to his original small house one after the other and connected them (see figs. 100 and 101).[157]

Membership on the town council cannot be documented for any owners of the houses we have discussed. But even if they failed to advance to such a position, they surely numbered among the leaders in the town's economic life, and worked closely with council members, as the wax tablets of Caecilius Iucundus demonstrate.[158] And although these families may not have succeeded in placing one of their members on the council, they shared the same aspirations as the families who did; this is demonstrated by the grave of the young aedile Vestorius Priscus, who died while in office (probably in A.D. 75/76).[159] On his tomb his family placed depictions of the deceased that showed him in his role as an official and recalled the gladiatorial games he had sponsored, but—characteristically—they also added paintings of the grand entrance to his house, his fine collection of silverware, a luxurious garden, and a *paradeisos*.[160]

In a recent study Henrik Mouritsen, using a new method, has reached results different from Castrén's; Mouritsen believes that the old families continued to set the tone in the political order and social life of the town even in the late period. Such conclusions have in principle little effect on my thoughts concerning domestic taste. What I have been able to show with my examples is a specific way of creating private living space that is found above all in medium-sized houses. It would be entirely mistaken, however, to connect this taste with a particular social stratum definable in terms of legal or economic status. People with very small dwellings may have had the same taste as those with larger homes, but lacked the physical space in which to express it. Regarding the spread of the new style among the elite, Fausto Zevi suggests that, for the period following the founding of the colony, a group of families continued to reside in their old houses with walls decorated in the first style and rejected any notion of altering the style in which their forebears had lived. In fact it is striking how many owners of relatively large old houses, including those with paintings in the second style, did *not* introduce miniaturized elements from villa architecture or large, poster-like landscape paintings into their homes.[161]

We see many inhabitants of late Pompeii captivated by thoughts of the luxury in which the Roman upper classes lived, however, and full of desires to imitate it. The garden architecture, "sacred" groves, fountains and picnic spots, *pinacothecae,* painted sculptures, landscape vistas and *paradeisoi,* the costly materials and imitations of them—all these testify to a need to participate in some form of luxurious villa life. The residential sphere is dominated by architectural or artistic imitations of a world with which, as a rule, the occupants had no direct links at all through their own traditions or experience. And very few of them could have gained access to this world of Greek culture and literature through education. Almost nothing in their homes reflects their own everyday world or religious ties and beliefs, apart from the household shrines to the Lares, and these tend to seem unconnected to the rest of their surroundings. On all sides we find the same elements repeated in the decor; the choice of fresco motifs is so limited and repetitious as to be depressing.

All the same, the architectural elements in particular reflect the love and attention people lavished on their little imitation villas, and the importance of this decorative vocabulary in their daily lives. It is significant that the Pompeians were not satisfied with imaginary painted scenes; they needed to come into contact with some three-dimensional, *physical* re-creation of a villa. There can be no doubt that this reflected splendor somehow made them happier, enhancing their lives. This heightened quality of life was not internalized but designed to impress visitors and passers-by. The aim was to demonstrate that one had arrived, that one could afford the very best—or at least a picture of it.

If these considerations point in the right direction, then they must of necessity affect our understanding of late Pompeian culture. It becomes impossible to interpret the gardens and tiny courtyards of Pompeii as touching reflections of the old Italic sense of nature; nor could one conclude from the architecture and painting that the last inhabitants were imbued with religious piety and a deep appreciation for Greek education and culture.[162] On the contrary, the late houses must be seen as evidence of the materialistic values that dominated Roman society in the early Empire.

We lack firm archeological evidence that would tell us how widespread this domestic style was in Italy. Pompeii itself happened to lie in a landscape dotted with villas that could provide direct inspiration. The house lots also tended to be larger than in many other towns, giving the Pompeians more room to renovate and add on to their dwellings as fashions changed. Property owners at Pompeii were familiar with the world of villas not only from the surrounding district, but also from the town itself, where owners of the great houses in the center and terrace houses on the periphery adopted elements of villa style early on. The villa character of the corresponding houses in Herculaneum is particularly striking (and indeed many of the phenomena we have observed in Pompeii can also be found there in even more lavish variations).[163] These imposing "town villas" and the lesser villas just outside the walls doubtless played an important role in mediating local development of the new taste. The towns on the Bay of Naples and near other centers of villa culture certainly occupy a special position in this respect.

Nevertheless, social and economic conditions in other romanized parts of the Empire cannot have been very different, at least in the essentials. Scattered archeological findings in the area of ornate garden tombs and tomb paintings reflecting visions of earthly happiness suggest that similar forms of expression also occurred elsewhere.[164]

P. Veyne has shown that Trimalchio's lifestyle, outlook, and values make Petronius' grandiose, overblown character the prototype of a figure common in the early Empire, namely, the independent freedman *(libertus)*.[165] The guests at his feast are freedmen of the same stamp as the host. Like him, they had a chance to try their luck as independent craftsmen or merchants, unhampered by obligations to a patron. Trimalchio differs from them only in his immense degree of success, which Petronius used as the basis for a caricature, portraying the fatal consequences of such a lifestyle and outlook.

Although freedmen of this kind could quickly achieve a measure of affluence and occasionally even great wealth, they could not aspire to a career in public life or social recognition. The resulting tensions found expression in the unregulated area of self-display, which offered many possibilities. Trimalchio is sharp and lucky enough to have made a fortune, and with it he buys an enormous country estate. Withdrawing from business affairs, he sets out to imitate the leisurely life of a landed aristocrat, although without the same opportunities to serve as a magistrate or participate in politics. Within the sharply defined social categories of the day, he has arrived at the top of his particular heap, and he must try to enjoy his good fortune with the assistance of others in the same position.

Material wealth and possibilities for displaying it offered some compensation in the face of a rigidly inflexible social order. The extent to which these rules governed life in Pompeii, even in the circle of freedmen, has been demonstrated by Andreau in his analysis of Caecilius Iucundus' wax tablets and the way in which the names on them are listed.[166]

The Pompeians whose houses we have examined were well off; they had no enormous wealth like Trimalchio, but they could have been his guests. They, too, were engaged in imitating the world of the Roman aristocracy—with the means at their disposal. While they were perhaps convinced that they had achieved a degree of real upper-class living in at least one little corner of their homes, Trimalchio's success appears to have given him full access to its glory. Petronius' satire reveals this "good for-tune" as a great illusion, however. Like the Pompeian homeowners, Tri-malchio cannot alter who he is. His habits, thoughts, feelings, and intellec-tual horizons appear thoroughly out of place in the domestic setting and lifestyle he is intent on copying.

Trimalchio's friends are ideal representatives of Pompeians who adopted the style we have encountered at the "House of Trimalchio" and in late Pompeii in general. And while it must be stressed that this taste was by no means limited to freedmen's circles, a good deal of evidence suggests that the freedmen families who were engaged in crafts and trade took the lead in spreading it, especially in provincial Italian towns.[167]

As we have seen, this style derives from the desire not just to imitate the decor of aristocrats' houses, but also to share their world, to participate in the good life and the happiness it brings—through the creation of illusions, if need be. The Flavian emperors, aware of the existence of these desires and aspirations in broad segments of the population, seem to have taken them into account in their policies, with highly effective public projects and entertainment programs. It is instructive to read certain passages in the *Silvae* in this connection, for example, passages in which the poet Statius depicts ordinary people (I.6), or the emperor's invited guests with the emperor as a new Jupiter (IV.2), in a heaven eclipsing everything they have experienced before, a heaven that manifests itself in material form. In these instances the illusion is intentionally staged.[168]

The villa culture of the Roman aristocracy in the late Republic was well suited to serve as a model for the domestic taste of a broad "middle class," since this culture was itself composed of many disparate, loosely associated elements borrowed from other cultures. Even before the villa style began to spread it was marked by striking disjunction between, for example, the design of particular rooms and the way they were actually used, or between old and new forms of decorative elements and furnishings. But although the general domestic taste in late Pompeii retained many of the basic elements that had constituted upper-class style in the late Republic, one decisive difference existed: the aristocratic exponents of villa culture in the second and first centuries B.C. had a first-hand knowledge of Greek civilization through their education, and were thus able to create new meanings for the formal elements they adopted.

It remains for future investigators to study Pompeian domestic taste within the broader context of the Neronian-Flavian period and its prevailing styles. In Pompeii itself there seems to be a connection between shifts occurring in the social structure of the population and new forms of domestic architecture and decor. This link points the way toward further interesting questions, such as the causes behind the profound changes in style observable in all genres of art and architecture after the Julio-Claudian era, causes which are far from self-evident.[169]

Abbreviations

Notes

Illustration Credits

Index

Abbreviations

AA	*Archäologischer Anzeiger*
ADelt	*Archaiologikon Deltion*
AJA	*American Journal of Archaeology*
AM	*Mitteilungen des Deutschen Archäologischen Instituts. Athenische Abteilung*
ANRW	*Aufstieg und Niedergang der Römischen Welt* (Berlin: 1972)
AttiPalermo	*Atti dell'Accademia di scienze, lettere e arti di Palermo*
BdA	*Bollettino d'arte*
BJb	*Bonner Jahrbücher des Rheinischen Landesmuseums in Bonn und des Vereins von Altertumsfreunden im Rheinlande*
BullCom	*Bulletino della Commissione archeologica comunale di Roma*
CIL	*Corpus Inscriptionum Latinarum*
DArch	*Dialoghi di Archeologia*
EAA	*Enciclopedia dell'Arte Antica* (Rome: 1958–)
JdI	*Jahrbuch des Deutschen Archäologischen Instituts*
JRA	*Journal of Roman Archaeology*
JRS	*Journal of Roman Studies*
MarbWPr	*Marburger Winckelmannsprogramm*
MEFRA	*Mélanges de l'École française de Rome, Antiquité*
MemAccLinc	*Memorie. Atti dell'Accademia nazionale dei Lincei, Classe di scienze morali, storiche e filologiche*
MemAmAc	*Memoirs of the American Academy in Rome*
MonPitt	*Monumenti della pittura antica scoperta in Italia* (Rome: 1937)
NSc	*Notizie degli Scavi di antichità*
ÖJh	*Jahreshefte des Österreichischen Archäologischen Institute in Wien*

OpRom	*Opuscula Romana*
PBSR	*Papers of the British School at Rome*
PP	*La Parola del Passato*
PPM	*Pompei. Pitture e mosaici* (Enciclopedia Italiana, Rome: 1990)
RAC	*Reallexikon für Antike und Christentum* (Stuttgart: 1950)
RE	*Pauly's Realencyclopädie der classischen Altertumswissenschaft,,* rev. ed. (Stuttgart: 1894)
RenAccNap	*Rendiconti dell'Accademia di Archeologia, Lettere e Belle arti di Napoli*
RM	*Mitteilungen des Deutschen Archäologischen Instituts. Römische Abteilung*
YaleClSt	*Yale Classical Studies*

Notes

Townscape and Domestic Taste

1. Compare, however, Y. Thébert, "Private Life and Domestic Architecture in Roman Africa," in Paul Veyne, ed., *History of Private Life* (Cambridge, Mass.: 1987); J.-A. Dickmann, "Strukturen des Raumes und repräsentatives Wohnen am Beispiel pompejanischer Stadthäuser" (Ph.D. diss., University of Munich, 1992).

2. This concept is discussed at greater length in Walter Trillmich and Paul Zanker, eds., *Stadtbild und Ideologie: Die Monumentalisierung hispanischer Städte zwischen Republik und Kaiserzeit. Kolloquium Madrid 1987, Abhandlungen der Bayerischen Akademie der Wissenschaften,* vol. 103 (Munich: 1990), pp. 9ff., and in the section on the Pompeian townscape in this book.

3. W. Hoepfner and E. L. Schwandner, *Haus und Stadt im klassischen Griechenland* (Munich: 1986); W. Schuller et al., eds., *Demokratie und Architektur* (Munich: 1989); T. Hölscher, "The City of Athens: Space, Symbol, Structure," in A. Molho et al., *City-States in Classical Antiquity and Medieval Italy* (Ann Arbor: 1991), pp. 355–380.

4. See P. Gros and M. Torelli, *Storia dell'urbanistica: Il mondo romano* (Rome: 1988), which contains a copious bibliography.

5. P. Zanker, *The Power of Images in the Age of Augustus* (Ann Arbor: 1988), trans. Alan Shapiro, pp. 316–333; M. Pfanner, "Modelle römischer Stadtentwicklung am Beispiel Hispaniens und der westlichen Provinzen," in Trillmich and Zanker, *Stadtbild und Ideologie,* pp. 59ff.

6. These aspects are discussed more fully in P. Zanker, "Veränderungen im öffentlichen Raum der italischen Städte der Kaiserzeit," in *L'Italie d'Auguste à Dioclétien: Colloque internationale Rome 1992* (Rome: 1994), pp. 259–284.

7. For more on this subject see R. Neudecker, *Die Pracht der Latrine: Zum Wandel öffentlicher Bedürfnisanstalten in der kaiserzeitlichen Stadt* (Munich: 1994). For "street activity and public interaction," compare the new approach by R. Laurence, *Roman Pompeii: Space and Society* (London: 1994).

8. R. Förtsch, *Archäologischer Kommentar zu den Villenbriefen des jüngeren Plinius* (Mainz: 1993).

9. S. T. A. M. Mols, *Houten Meubels in Herculaneum* (Nijmegen: 1994).

10. A. Wallace-Hadrill, "The Social Structure of the Roman House," *PBSR*, 56 (1988): 43–97; "Elites and Trade in the Roman Town," in J. Rich and Wallace-Hadrill, eds., *City and Country in the Ancient World* (London: 1991); and *Houses and Society in Pompeii and Herculaneum* (Princeton: 1994). For a recent discussion on the problem of the "private" and "public" spheres, see M. Grahame, "Public and Private in the Roman House: Investigating the Social Order of the *Casa del Fauno*," in R. Laurence and A. Wallace-Hadrill, eds., *Domestic Space in the Roman World: Pompeii and Beyond, JRA* Supplement 22 (1997): 137–164. In this essay Grahame applies a theory developed by Hillier and Hanson in order to determine the degree of "privacy" existing between friends or visitors on the one hand and inhabitants of the house on the other. See also Annapaola Zaccaria Ruggiu, *Spazio privato e spazio pubblico nella città Romana,* Collection de l'École Française de Rome 210 (Rome: 1995).

11. T. Veblen, *The Theory of the Leisure Class* (New York: 1899).

12. J.-A. Dickmann, "Strukturen des Raumes und repräsentatives Wohnen am Beispiel pompejanischer Stadthäuser" (unpublished dissertation, University of Munich, 1992); "The Peristyle and the Transformation of Domestic Space in Hellenistic Pompeii," in Laurence and Wallace-Hadrill, eds., *Domestic Space,* pp. 121–136.

13. Raeder, "Vitruv, *De Architectura* VI 7 *(aedificia Graecorum)* und die hellenistischen Wohnhaus- und Palastarchitekturen," *Gymnasium,* 95 (1988): 316–368.

14. R. Förtsch, *Archäologischer Kommentar zu den Villenbriefen.*

15. J. Overbeck and A. Mau, *Pompeji,* 4th ed. (Leipzig: 1884).

16. P. M. Allison, *The Distribution of Pompeian House Contents and Its Significance* (Ph.D. diss., University of Sydney, 1992); "Artefact Distribution and Spatial Function in Pompeian Houses," in B. Rawson and P. Weaver, eds., *The Roman Family in Italy* (Canberra and Oxford: 1997); J. Berry, "Household Artefacts: Towards a Re-interpretation of Roman Domestic Space," in Laurence and Wallace-Hadrill, eds., *Domestic Space,* pp. 183–195.

17. Summary in H. Mielsch, *Die römische Villa: Architektur und Lebensform* (Munich: 1987); R. Neudecker, *Die Skulpturenausstattung römischer Villen in Italien* (Munich: 1988), with review by R. Förtsch, *Gnomon,* 64 (1992): 520–534.

18. The so-called four styles of Pompeian wall painting are categories determined by scholars on the basis of developments perceptible in extant paintings: down to the early first century B.C., painting is characterized by molded plaster relief imitating masonry and marble, sometimes with pictures inserted in a frieze at eye level (first style, an Italian version of a Hellenistic style; also known as the masonry style); from the early first century B.C. until c. 15 B.C., plausible architectural forms were reproduced by purely pictorial means, and sometimes these architectural motifs were used to "frame" figured paintings (second style); from c. 15 B.C. until A.D. 50, architectural forms became increasingly insubstantial and imaginative, and the wall reverted to a flat plane surrounding a central pictorial motif, sometimes very large (third style); after A.D. 50, the central panels became smaller and were combined with unreal architecture, while borders were added to contribute a sense of depth (fourth style).

19. In this respect my essay in 1979 did not lay sufficient emphasis on the phenomenon as part of an overarching cultural program.

20. Wallace-Hadrill, "Elites and Trade in the Roman Town."

21. See L. Friedländer, *Darstellungen aus der Sittengeschichte Roms,* 10th ed. (Leipzig: 1923), vol. 2, pp. 191ff., especially p. 228.

Urban Space as a Reflection of Society

1. As it would be impossible to list the vast literature on traditional urban studies here, I will mention only a few studies that stimulated my own thinking: K. Lynch, *The Image of the City* (1960); G. Cullen, *The Concise Townscape* (1961); L. Mumford, *The City in History: Its Origins, Its Transformations, and Its Prospects* (1961); L. Benevolo, *Storia della città* (1975); W. Braunfels, *Abendländische Stadt-baukunst: Herrschaftsform und Baugestalt* (1976), and *Mittelalterliche Stadtbaukunst in der Toskana,* 4th ed. (1979); Mark Girouard, *Cities and People: A Social and Architectural History* (1985).

2. Jean Andreau, "Histoire des séismes et histoire économique. Le tremblement de terre de Pompéi (62 ap. J.-C.)," *Annales: Economies, sociétés, civilisations,* 28 (1973): 369–395. Since the postulation of a second earthquake, principally by K. Schefold, *RM,* 64 (1957): 152–153, new observations have been made by the research group associated with V. M. Strocka; see V. Kockel, "Archäologische Funde und Forschungen in den Vesuvstädten II," *AA* (1986): 543. See also *Archäologie und Seismologie. La regione vesuviana dal 62 al 79 d.C. Problemi archeologici e sismologici. Colloquium Boscoreale 1993* (Munich: 1995).

3. S. De Caro, "Saggi nell'area dell' tempio di Apollo a Pompei," *Annali dell'Istituto Orientale di Napoli,* 3 (1986): 19ff. For a survey see De Caro, "La città sannitica,"

in Zevi, ed., *Pompei,* vol. 1, pp. 23–46, and M. Cristofani, "La fase 'etrusca' di Pompei," in Zevi, ed., *Pompei,* vol. 1, pp. 9–22.

4. For this epoch of the town's history see S. C. Nappo, "Urban Transformation at Pompeii in the Late Third and Early Second Centuries B.C.," in Laurence and Wallace-Hadrill, eds., *Domestic Space,* pp. 91–120.

5. P. Castrén, *Ordo populusque Pompeianorum: Polity and Society in Roman Pompeii (Acta Instituti Romani Finlandiae,* 8) (Rome: 1975), pp. 38 ff.; F. Coarelli, D. Musti, and H. Solin, eds., *Delo e l'Italia (Opuscula Instituti Romani Finlandiae,* 2) (Rome: 1982).

6. See P. Zanker, *The Power of Images in the Age of Augustus* (Ann Arbor: 1988), pp. 5–8. Since 1988 much has been published on this topic; E. S. Gruen offers a survey in *Culture and Identity in Rome* (Ithaca, N.Y.: 1992).

7. For the tufa block façades, see A. Hoffmann, "Elemente bürgerlicher Repräsentation: Eine späthellenistische Hausfassade in Pompeji," in *Akten des XII. Internationalen Kongresses für Klassische Archäologie in Berlin 1988* (Berlin: 1990), pp. 490ff.; B. Gesemann, *Die Straßen der antiken Stadt Pompeji: Entwicklung und Gestaltung* (Frankfurt a.M.: 1996); F. Pirson, *Mietwohnungen in Pompeji und Herkulaneum: Untersuchungen zur Architektur, zum Wohnen und zur Sozial- und Wirtschaftsgeschichte der Vesuvstädte* (Ph.D. diss., University of Munich, 1996); and F. Pirson, "Rented Accommodation at Pompeii: The Evidence of the *Insula Arriana Polliana* VI 6," in Laurence and Wallace-Hadrill, eds., *Domestic Space,* pp. 165–181. For the House of the Faun, see A. Mau, *Pompeji in Leben und Kunst,* 2nd ed. (Leipzig: 1908), pp. 300ff.; J. Overbeck and A. Mau, *Pompeji,* 4th ed. (Leipzig: 1884), pp. 346ff. See also A. Hoffmann, "Elemente bürgerlicher Repräsentation," and review of P. Zanker, *Pompeji: Stadtbilder als Spiegel von Gesellschaft und Herrschaftsform* in *Gnomon,* 64 (1992): 426–433. Recent publications by Fausto Zevi have revealed the central importance of the House of the Faun and its owner for the history of Pompeii: see F. Zevi, "La città sannitica. L'edilizia privata e la Casa del Fauno," in Zevi, ed., *Pompei,* vol. 1, pp. 47–76; "Sul tempio di Iside a Pompei," *PP,* 49 (1994): 40ff.; "La Casa del Fauno," in *Pompei. Abitare sotto il Vesuvio* (exhibition catalogue; Ferrara: 1996), pp. 36ff. Some of the artefacts found in the house are shown in the catalogue, pp. 207–214. For the double atrium and the porticos, including their use as *ambulationes,* see Dickmann, "The Peristyle and the Transformation of Domestic Space." Dickmann correctly stresses the function of public buildings in Hellenistic cities as models for the introduction of peristyles into Pompeian domestic architecture. For the history and decoration of the House of the Faun, see also the works cited in note 30 of chapter 3 below.

8. Hoepfner and Schwandner, *Haus und Stadt,* pp. 50, 108, 169.

9. H. Lauter in B. Andreae and H. Kyrieleis, eds., *Neue Forschungen in Pompeji*

(Recklinghausen: 1975), p. 148. For Pella, see C. Makaronas, *ADelt*, 16 (1960), Meletes 74, fig. 1 and plates 48–49, 67ff.

10. J. H. D'Arms, *Romans on the Bay of Naples: A Social and Cultural Study of the Villas and Their Owners from 150 B.C. to A.D. 400* (Cambridge, Mass.: 1970); H. Mielsch, *Die römische Villa*, pp. 37ff.

11. See E. von Mercklin, *Antike Figuralkapitelle* (Berlin: 1962), pp. 70ff., for the House of the Figured Capitals (VII 4.57), no. 188, a and b, figs. 351–357. Compare also Margareta Staub-Gierow, *Casa del Granduca VII 4, 56. Casa dei Capitelli figurate VII 4, 57* (Munich: 1994).

12. Compare the diagram of the wall in the exhibition catalogue *Pompei. Abitare sotto il Vesuvio*, following page 47.

13. E. Pernice, *Pavimente und figürliche Mosaiken: Die Hellenistische Kunst in Pompeji*, vol. 6 (Berlin: 1938); M. E. Blake, "The Pavements of the Roman Buildings of the Republic and Early Empire," *MemAmAc*, 8 (1930): 7ff.; M. de Vos, in F. Zevi, ed., *Pompei 79: Raccolta di studi per il decimonono centenario dell'eruzione Vesuviana*, 2nd ed. (Naples: 1984), 161–179.

14. B. Andreae, *Das Alexandermosaik aus Pompeji* (Recklinghausen: 1977); T. Hölscher, *Griechische Historienbilder* (Würzburg: 1973), pp. 122–162. For a recent interpretation of the Alexander mosaic, see F. Zevi, "La Casa del Fauno," in the exhibition catalogue *Pompei. Abitare sotto il Vesuvio*.

15. H. Lauter, in Andreae and Kyrieleis, eds., *Neue Forschungen*, p. 148.

16. For habitation in *tabernae* and the social and economic use of real estate in the town, see Pirson, *Mietwohnungen in Pompeji und Herkulaneum* and "Rented Accommodation at Pompeii."

17. H. Lauter, in Zanker, ed., *Hellenismus in Mittelitalien*, pp. 415ff.; W. Johannowsky, ibid., p. 272; Kockel, "Vesuvstädte II," pp. 465–466.

18. M. Bieber, *The History of the Greek and Roman Theater* (Princeton: 1961), pp. 108ff.

19. See E. Rawson, "Theatrical Life in Republican Rome and Italy," *PBSR*, 53 (1985): 97–113, later published in *Roman Culture and Society* (Oxford: 1991), pp. 468–487.

20. J. Delorme, *Gymnasion: Étude sur les monuments consacrés à l'éducation en Grèce* (Paris: 1960); see also the entry under "Gymnasium" by Delorme in *RAC*, 13 (1986): 155ff.

21. The "theater peristyle" is discussed by Overbeck and Mau, *Pompeji*, pp. 193ff.; Mau, *Pompeji in Leben und Kunst*, pp. 164ff.; La Rocca, M. de Vos, and A. de Vos, *Pompei*, 2nd revised ed. (Milan: 1994), pp. 158–161; and A. de Vos and M. de Vos, *Pompei, Ercolano, Stabia: Guida archeologica Laterza* (Rome: 1982), pp. 67ff.

22. The suggestion had previously been advanced by Petersen, *RM*, 14 (1899): 103–

104. Recently, Dickmann has taken a critical view, "The Peristyle and the Transformation of Domestic Space," p. 125.

23. The palaestra is discussed by Overbeck and Mau, *Pompeji*, pp. 150ff.; Mau, *Pompeji in Leben und Kunst*, pp. 171ff.; La Rocca et al., *Pompei*, pp. 165–166; de Vos, *Guida archeologica*, pp. 71ff.; Kockel, "Vesuvstädte II," p. 464. An Oscan inscription found at the site mentions that the building was constructed for the *vereiia*, the young people. This was originally a military institution of the aristocracy, which is also documented in other Samnite communities. See S. De Caro, "La città sannitica," in Zevi, ed., *Pompei*, vol. 2, p. 37; F. Zevi, "Sul tempio di Iside a Pompei," *PP*, 49 (1994): 45.

24. *RAC*, 13 (1986): 163ff. See the entry under "Gymnasium" (J. Delorme).

25. See H. Eschebach, *Die Stabianer Thermen in Pompeji* (Berlin: 1979), and the review by V. Kockel in *Gnomon*, 54 (1982): 178–179; and most recently Kockel, "Vesuvstädte II," p. 467.

26. A. S. Hunt and C. C. Edgar, eds., *Select Papyri*, vol. 2 (1934), pp. 234ff., no. 269.

27. The Triangular Forum is discussed by Overbeck and Mau, *Pompeji*, pp. 75ff.; Mau, *Pompeji in Leben und Kunst*, pp. 133ff.; La Rocca et al., *Pompei*, pp. 146–151; de Vos, *Guida archeologica*, pp. 60ff.; and Kockel, "Vesuvstädte II," p. 462.

28. See Kockel, "Vesuvstädte II," pp. 462–463.

29. See the most recent remarks by H. Lauter, *Die Architektur des Hellenismus* (Darmstadt: 1986), pp. 64ff.

30. A. Maiuri, *Bicentenario degli scavi di Pompei* (Naples: 1948), p. 28; D. Elia and G. Pugliese, "Caratelli, Il santuario dionisiaco di Pompei," *PP*, 34 (1979): 442–481; Kockel, *AA* (1985): 568–569.

31. Temple of Isis: Tran Tam Tinh, *Essai sur le culte d'Isis à Pompéi* (Paris: 1964), pp. 30ff.; Kockel, "Vesuvstädte II," pp. 464ff. On the dating of the Hellenistic structure see H. Lauter-Bufé, *Die Geschichte des sikeliotisch-korinthischen Kapitells* (Heidelberg: 1987), pp. 36–37, plate 26 (soon after 150 B.C.), and *Alla Ricerca di Iside: Analisi, Studi e Restauri dell'Iseo pompeiano nel Museo di Napoli* (Naples: 1992); also various contributions in *PP*, 49 (1994).

32. See Overbeck and Mau, *Pompeji*, pp. 110ff.; Mau, *Pompeji in Leben und Kunst*, pp. 188ff.; La Rocca et al., *Pompei*, pp. 171–173; de Vos, *Guida archeologica*, pp. 78–79. Compare the recent monograph by D. Russo, *Il tempio di Giove Melichio a Pompei* (Naples: 1991). For the cult statue see H. Von Rohden, *Die Terracotten von Pompeji* (Stuttgart: 1880), pp. 20–21, 42–43; A. Levi, *Le terrecotte figurate del Museo Nazionale di Napoli* (Florence: 1925), p. 186, plate 11; W. Johannowsky, in Zanker, ed., *Hellenismus in Mittelitalien*, p. 287. The walls around the precinct of Zeus Meilichios may have come later. It is possible that the shrine was originally wider, and the altar not placed at an angle until later. For the identification with Asclepius, see S. De Caro, in *PP*, 49 (1994): 9–10.

33. H. Lauter, *JdI*, 94 (1979): 416ff. For the extension of the forum see the soundings taken from the area between the Temple of Apollo and the basilica, discussed by P. Arthur in the *Antiquarian Journal*, 66 (1986), pp. 29ff., and Hoffmann, *Gnomon*, 64 (1992): 428.

34. The date of the temple's renovation is a matter of controversy. Lauter assigns the more elaborate structure to pre-Roman times, but I do not find his arguments entirely convincing. Also skeptical are Kockel, "Vesuvstädte II," pp. 454ff.; and F. Zevi, "Pompei della città sannitica alla colonia sillana: per una interpretazione dei dati archeologici," in *Les Élites municipales de l'Italie péninsulaire des Gracques à Néron. Colloquium Clermont-Ferrand 1991* (Naples and Rome: 1996), pp. 125–138. For a recent discussion of the statue of Jupiter, see H. G. Martin, *Römische Tempelkultbilder* (Rome: 1987), pp. 142ff. and 222ff.

35. For discussion of the *macellum* see H. Lauter, *AA* (1971): 59–60, and *JdI*, 94 (1979): 429 and 434; Kockel, "Vesuvstädte II," p. 456.

36. K. F. Ohr and J. J. Rausch, *Die Basilika in Pompeji* (Berlin: 1991); H. Lauter, *JdI*, 94 (1979): 430; Kockel, "Vesuvstädte II," pp. 459–460; Lauter-Bufé, *Die Geschichte des Kapitells*, p. 38.

37. Lauter, *JdI*, 94 (1979): 435–436.

38. A. Maiuri, *NSc* (1941): 371ff.

39. M. Schede, *Die Ruinen von Priene*, 2nd ed. (Berlin: 1964); Hoepfner and Schwandner, *Haus und Stadt*, pp. 141ff.

40. For a discussion of the Temple of Apollo in the Hellenistic period see De Caro, "La città sannitica," pp. 25–26. The capitals (circa 110–100 B.C.) are discussed by Lauter-Bufé, *Die Geschichte des Kapitells*, p. 39; for the dating see also Lauter, *JdI*, 94 (1979): 427, and Kockel, "Vesuvstädte II," pp. 454–455.

41. F. Zevi in Zanker, ed., *Hellenismus in Mittelitalien*, pp. 84ff.; A. Degrassi, *Inscriptiones Latinae Liberae Rei Publicae*, vol. 2 (Rome: 1963; reprinted 1972), pp. 56–57, no. 528.

42. F. E. Brown, *Cosa: The Making of a Roman Town* (Ann Arbor: 1980).

43. P. Gros, *Architecture et Société* (Brussels: 1978), pp. 51 and 88; F. Coarelli, in *Les "Bourgeoisies" municipales aux IIe et Ier siècles av. J.-C. Colloque 1981* (Paris: 1983), pp. 217ff.

44. For recent discussions of the founding of the Roman *colonia* at Pompeii and its constitution, with citations of the earlier literature, see E. Lo Cascio, in *Les Élites municipales. Colloquium Clermont-Ferrand*, pp. 111–124; H. Mouritsen, *Elections, Magistrates and Municipal Elite: Studies in Pompeian Epigraphy*, Analaecta Romana Supplement 15 (Rome: 1988), pp. 87–88, 116–117; H.-J. Gerke, *Hermes*, 111 (1983): 471–490. The question of the Sullan colonists and their importance for the cultural life of the town is discussed by V. Kockel in H. von Hesberg and P. Zanker, eds., *Römische Gräberstraßen: Selbstdarstellung, Status, Standard. Kolloquium*

1985 (Munich: 1987), pp. 185ff. For the economic consequences of the transformation, see J. Andreau, *Revue des Études Anciennes,* 82 (1980): 183ff. See also S. Adamo Muscettola, "La trasformazione della città tra Silla e Augusto," in Zevi, ed., *Pompei,* pp. 75–114; Zevi, "Pompei della città sannitica alla colonia sillana."

45. For the *capitoleum,* see Zevi, "Pompei della città sannitica alla colonia sillana," p. 126; Lauter, *JdI,* 94 (1979): 430ff.; La Rocca et al., *Pompei,* pp. 132–135. For the cult statue, see Martin, *Römische Tempelkultbilder,* pp. 142–143 and plates 21 and 22; Kockel, "Vesuvstädte II," pp. 455ff.

46. For discussions of the Temple of Venus see Mau, *Pompeji in Leben und Kunst,* pp. 120–121, and *RM,* 15 (1900): 270–308 and plates 7 and 8; A. Maiuri, *Saggi di varia antichità* (Naples: 1954), pp. 241ff., and *BdA,* 45 (1960): 173–174; A. Hoffmann, "L'Architettura," in Zevi, ed., *Pompei 79,* pp. 102–103; de Vos, *Guida archeologica,* pp. 26–27; Kockel, "Vesuvstädte II," pp. 461–462; Adamo Muscettola, "La trasformazione della città tra Silla e Augusto," pp. 77–78; Zevi, "Pompei della città sannitica alla colonia sillana," pp. 128–129. For the role of the goddess Venus in election propaganda soon after the founding of the colony, see Castrén, *Ordo populusque Pompeianorum,* p. 86.

47. For the Temple of Apollo see Zevi, "Pompei della città sannitica alla colonia sillana," p. 128; De Caro, "La città sannitica," p. 25; *CIL* X 800; Degrassi, *Inscriptiones Latinae Liberae Rei Publicae,* vol. 2, p. 107, no. 644.

48. For discussions of the *theatrum tectum* see Overbeck and Mau, *Pompeji,* pp. 171ff.; Mau, *Pompeji in Leben und Kunst,* pp. 160ff.; de Vos, *Guida archeologica,* pp. 69–70; R. Meinel, *Das Odeion* (Frankfurt: 1980), pp. 36ff., 180ff., 205ff; Kockel, "Vesuvstädte II," p. 466; M. Fuchs, *Untersuchungen zur Ausstattung römischer Theater* (Mainz: 1987), pp. 46–47. For inscriptions, see J. Bauer, "Munificentia Privata Pompeiana," unpublished master's thesis (University of Munich, 1988), pp. 15–16 and 40–41. Compare the discussion of the construction under the aspect of two *genera civium* in Zevi, "Personaggi della Pompei sillana," *PBSR,* 63 (1995): 1–24; and "Pompei della città sannitica alla colonia sillana," p. 130.

49. Compare F. Kolb, *Agora und Theater: Volks- und Festversammlung* (Berlin: 1979). My interpretation does not exclude use of the new building as a theater; compare Zevi, "Personaggi della Pompei sillana."

50. For more on the two donors, see Castrén, *Ordo populusque,* pp. 209–210 and 212.

51. Compare H. Lauter, *Die Architektur des Hellenismus,* p. 173.

52. For the forum baths see Overbeck and Mau, *Pompeji,* pp. 200ff.; Mau, *Pompeji in Leben und Kunst,* pp. 20ff.; de Vos, *Guida archeologica,* pp. 49ff.; Kockel, *AA* (1986): 467, and in von Hesberg and Zanker, eds., *Römische Gräberstraßen,* p. 185; L. Eschebach, *Antike Welt,* 22 (1991): 257–287.

53. *CIL* X 819; Degrassi, *Inscriptiones Latinae,* vol. 2, pp. 105–106, no. 641.

54. *CIL* X 829; Degrassi, *Inscriptiones Latinae,* vol. 2, pp. 108–109, no. 648; H. Esche-bach et al., *Die Stabianer Thermen in Pompeji* (Berlin: 1979); H. Eschebach, *RM,* 80 (1973): 235ff. Compare Zevi, "Pompei della città sannitica alla colonia sil-lana," p. 129.

55. For discussions of the amphitheater see Overbeck and Mau, *Pompeji,* pp. 176ff.; Mau, *Pompeji in Leben und Kunst,* pp. 216ff.; de Vos, *Guida archeologica,* pp. 150–151 and 362; R. Graefe, *Vela erunt* (Mainz: 1976), pp. 67ff., 104ff., and plates 77ff.; Kockel, *AA* (1986): 466, and in von Hesberg and Zanker, eds., *Römische Gräberstraßen,* p. 185; Zevi, "Pompei della città sannitica alla colonia sillana," pp. 131–132.

56. H. Dessau, *Inscriptiones Latinae Selectae* (1892–1916), no. 5318.

57. Castrén, *Ordo populusque,* pp. 88–89; Gehrke, *Hermes,* 111 (1983): 488, note 87; Bauer, *Munificentia Privata,* pp. 59–60. For Aeclanum see Degrassi, *Inscriptiones Latinae,* vol. 2, pp. 54–55, no. 523 with commentary.

58. V. Kockel, *Die Grabbauten vor dem Herkulaner Tor in Pompeji* (Mainz: 1983), pp. 53ff.

59. For the founding of other Sullan colonies see E. Gabba, *Athenaeum Pavia,* 29 (1951): 270–271.

60. Degrassi, *Inscriptiones Latinae,* vol. 2, pp. 107–108, no. 645. For the inscription see Gehrke, *Hermes,* 111 (1983): 488; Mouritsen, *Elections, Magistrates and Municipal Elite,* p. 88.

61. A. Hoffmann in *Wohnungsbau im Altertum: Bericht über ein Kolloquium, Diskussionen zur archäologischen Bauforschung,* vol. 3 (Berlin: 1978), p. 162; A. Hoffmann, *Architectura,* 10 (1980): 1–14; and "L'Architettura," in Zevi, ed., *Pompei 79,* pp. 97ff.; and most recently his review in *Gnomon,* 64 (1992): 430.

62. Compare Nappo, "Urban Transformation at Pompeii."

63. H. Lauter in Andreae and Kyrieleis, eds., *Neue Forschungen,* p. 121. Lauter has kindly communicated to me his belief that the dating of house IX 1.20 needs to be reconsidered.

64. See the section "Two Forms of Living Space" below.

65. For information on new excavations in the *Insula Occidentalis,* see Kockel, "Vesuvstädte II," pp. 507ff.

66. Ibid., pp. 508ff.

67. V. Spinazzola, *Pompei alla luce degli scavi nuovi di via dell'Abbondanza,* 3 vols. (Rome: 1954), vol. 1, pp. 437ff.; vol. 2, pp. 869ff.; *PPM,* vol. 1, pp. 193ff. (with a good analysis of the houses); Dickmann, "The Peristyle and the Transformation of Domestic Space," p. 134.

68. Kockel, *Die Grabbauten vor dem Herkulaner Tor,* pp. 9–10, notes 77 and 11, and in von Hesberg and Zanker, eds., *Römische Gräberstraßen,* pp. 187–188.

69. For the most recent discussion see Kockel, "Vesuvstädte II," pp. 556–557, and in von Hesberg and Zanker, eds., *Römische Gräberstraßen*, p. 192.

70. Compare H. von Hesberg and P. Zanker in *Römische Gräberstraßen*, pp. 9ff.

71. Kockel's survey of the colonists' construction (ibid., pp. 183ff.) emphasizes different points, in particular the new residents' highly interesting adoption of specific burial forms so far documented only in Pompeii.

72. For an earlier discussion of the issues in the section that follows, compare Zanker, *The Power of Images*, especially Chapter 8; on public buildings in Pompeii see also De Caro, "La città in età imperiale," in Zevi, ed., *Pompei*, vol. 2, pp. 11–38.

73. De Caro, "La città sannitica," p. 25; R. Etienne, *La vie quotidienne à Pompei*, 2nd ed. (Paris: Hachette, 1977), p. 333.

74. Compare S. R. F. Price, *Rituals and Power* (Cambridge: 1984); M. Wörrle, *Stadt und Fest im kaiserzeitlichen Kleinasien* (Munich: 1988).

75. For the Temple of Fortuna Augusta see Overbeck and Mau, *Pompeji*, pp. 114ff.; Mau, *Pompeji in Leben und Kunst*, pp. 129ff.; La Rocca et al., *Pompei*, pp. 141–143; de Vos, *Guida archeologica*, pp. 52–53. A more recent discussion with citations of further literature can be found in H. Hänlein-Schäfer, *Veneratio Augusti: Eine Studie zu den Tempeln des ersten römischen Kaisers* (Rome: 1985), pp. 105–106; De Caro, "La città in età imperiale," pp. 20ff. For the inscription, see *CIL* X 820. For *Ministri Fortunae Augustae*, see Castrén, *Ordo populusque*, pp. 76–77.

76. For more on M. Tullius M. F., see Castrén, *Ordo populusque*, pp. 96–97, and p. 231, no. 420, 4.

77. H. Heinrich comes to this conclusion in his unpublished dissertation on series of capitals in Campania (Munich).

78. P. Gros, *Aurea Templa* (Rome: 1976), with review by H. von Hesberg, *Göttingsche Gelehrte Anzeigen*, 223 (1981): 218ff.

79. For the statues in the Temple of Fortuna, see G. Fiorelli, *Pompeianarum Antiquitatum Historia*, vol. 3 (Naples: 1864), pp. 48–49; A. Ruesch, *Guida illustrata del Museo Nazionale di Napoli* (Naples: 1908), p. 260, no. 1095; A. De Franciscis, *Il ritratto romano a Pompei* (Naples: 1951), p. 34, fig. 21; P. Cain, *Männerbildnisse neronisch-flavischer Zeit* (Munich: 1993), p. 175, where the statue is dated after A.D. 62.

80. For the *macellum* see Mau, *Pompeji in Leben und Kunst*, pp. 90ff.; Overbeck and Mau, *Pompeji*, pp. 128ff.; La Rocca et al., *Pompei*, pp. 128–132; de Vos, *Guida archeologica*, pp. 43ff.; Kockel, "Vesuvstädte II," p. 456; J. J. Dobbins, "Problems of Chronology, Decoration, and Urban Design in the Forum of Pompeii," *AJA*, 98 (1994): 629–694.

81. For the two statues from the *macellum* (nos. 6044 and 6041 in the inventory of the Museo Archeologico Nazionale, Naples), see De Franciscis, *Il ritratto romano*,

pp. 70–73, and Zanker in Zevi, ed., *Pompei 79,* p. 194.

82. For the Sanctuary of the Lares, see Mau, *Pompeji in Leben und Kunst,* pp. 98ff.; Overbeck and Mau, *Pompeji,* pp. 128ff.; La Rocca et al., *Pompei,* pp. 127–128; de Vos, *Guida archeologica,* pp. 43ff.; Kockel, "Vesuvstädte II," p. 456; De Caro, "La città in età imperiale," pp. 15–16. For the galleries of statues of the imperial family see C. B. Rose, *Dynastic Commemoration and Imperial Portraiture in the Julio-Claudian Period* (Cambridge: 1997). For the dating see J. J. Dobbins, "The Imperial Cult Building on the Forum of Pompeii," in *Subject and Ruler,* ed. A. Small, *JRA* Supplement 17 (1996), 96–114.

83. For the Temple of Vespasian, see Mau, *Pompeji in Leben und Kunst,* pp. 102ff.; Overbeck and Mau, *Pompeji,* pp. 117–118; La Rocca et al., *Pompei,* pp. 125–127; de Vos, *Guida archeologica,* pp. 41ff.; Kockel, "Vesuvstädte II," p. 457 (who argues for dating it in the Augustan period); De Caro, "La città in età imperiale," pp. 14–15. Recently J. J. Dobbins has argued that the present form of the temple dates from the Augustan period, but he assumes that much of it was rebuilt after the earthquake of A.D. 62; see "Problems of Chronology in the Forum of Pompeii," pp. 661–668.

84. B. M. Felletti Maj, *La tradizione italica nell'arte Romana* (Rome: 1977), pp. 337ff.; J. J. Dobbins, "The Altar of the Genius of Augustus in the Forum of Pompeii," *RM,* 99 (1992): 251–263.

85. *CIL* X 816; Hänlein-Schäfer, *Veneratio Augusti,* pp. 133ff., plate 9a (with citation of earlier literature). Compare also I. Gradel, "Mammia's Dedication, Emperor and Genius: The Imperial Cult in Italy and the *Genius Coloniae* in Pompeii," *Analecta Romana,* 20 (1992): 43–58, whose divergent interpretation is correctly rejected by Dobbins, "Problems of Chronology in the Forum of Pompeii," pp. 662–663.

86. Castrén, *Ordo populusque,* pp. 71, 96, and 188, no. 237; Kockel, *Die Grabbauten vor dem Herkulaner Tor,* p. 59. Compare Mouritsen, *Elections, Magistrates and Municipal Elite.*

87. For the Eumachia Building, see Mau, *Pompeji in Leben und Kunst,* pp. 106–107; Overbeck and Mau, *Pompeji,* pp. 131–132; La Rocca et al., *Pompei,* pp. 121–125; de Vos, *Guida archeologica,* pp. 39–40; Kockel, "Vesuvstädte II," pp. 457–458; Zanker, *The Power of Images,* pp. 320–323; Bauer, *Munificentia Privata,* pp. 47ff. and 63ff.; De Caro, "La città in età imperiale," p. 16; Dobbins, "Problems of Chronology in the Forum of Pompeii," pp. 647ff. K. Wallat, in *AA* (1995): 345–373, has recently identified the marble door frame with the temple for the imperial cult.

88. For laudatory inscriptions, see *CIL* X 808, 809; for the most recent discussion of the Forum of Augustus, see J. Ganzert and V. Kockel, in *Kaiser Augustus und die*

verlorene Republik (exhibition catalogue, Berlin: 1988), pp. 149ff. For more on the links between the Forum of Augustus and the decor of the *chalcidicum*, see H. Döhl, in Zevi, ed., *Pompei 79*, pp. 185–186.

89. Compare Zanker, *The Power of Images*, pp. 135–139, and H. von Hesberg in *Kaiser Augustus und die verlorene Republik*, pp. 93ff.

90. This was observed by Kockel, "Vesuvstädte II," p. 458.

91. De Franciscis, *Il ritratto romano*, p. 53, figs. 52–54. There is a good photograph of a detail of the statue in T. Kraus and L. von Matt, *Lebendiges Pompeji: Pompeji und Herculaneum* (Cologne: 1973), pp. 40–41.

92. Zanker, *The Power of Images*, pp. 239–245.

93. Compare Hänlein-Schäfer, *Veneratio Augusti*, passim, and Zanker, *The Power of Images*, p. 307.

94. H. Döhl, in Zevi, ed., *Pompei 79*, pp. 185ff.; J. Bergemann, *Römische Reiterstatuen* (Mainz: 1990), pp. 17, 19, 37.

95. A. Mau, *RM,* 11 (1896): 150–156.

96. Maiuri offers a detailed interpretation, *L'ultima fase edilizia di Pompei* (Rome: 1942), pp. 10ff.

97. Ibid., pp. 27–28.

98. Kockel, "Vesuvstädte II," pp. 465–466; Graefe, *Vela erunt,* pp. 36ff.; Fuchs, *Untersuchungen zur Ausstattung römischer Theater,* pp. 44ff.; De Caro, "La città in età imperiale," pp. 25–26.

99. See Fuchs, *Untersuchungen zur Ausstattung römischer Theater,* passim.

100. Castrén, *Ordo populusque,* p. 176, nos. 197, 9, and 15; D'Arms, *Romans on the Bay of Naples.* There are good observations on the *cursus honorum* in Bauer, *Munificentia Privata,* pp. 66ff. Compare Mouritsen, *Elections, Magistrates and Municipal Elite.* On the title *tribunus militum a populo,* cf. C. Nicolet in *MEFRA* 79 (1967), pp. 29–76.

101. Bauer presents a convincing argument for this interpretation, *Munificentia Privata,* pp. 52–53.

102. Zanker, *AA* (1981): 349ff.

103. Zanker, *The Power of Images*, pp. 147–153.

104. E. Rawson, "*Discrimina ordinum:* The *lex Julia theatralis,*" *PBSR*, 55 (1987): 83–114, republished in *Roman Culture and Society*, pp. 508–545.

105. For more on the *campus,* see A. Maiuri, *NSc* (1939): 165–238; Etienne, *La vie quotidienne,* pp. 361–363; La Rocca et al., *Pompei*, pp. 254ff.; de Vos, *Guida archeologica,* pp. 147ff.; Wilhelmina F. Jashemski, *The Gardens of Pompeii, Herculaneum and the Villas Destroyed by Vesuvius,* vol. 2 (New Rochelle, N.Y.: 1993), pp. 91–92; De Caro, "La Città in età imperiale," p. 27.

106. For literature on the training of youth and fitness in the Augustan era, see

D. Kienast, *Augustus* (Darmstadt: 1982), pp. 153–154. For the architecture and functions of the *campus,* see H. Devijver and F. van Wousterghem, *Acta Archaeologica Lovaniensia,* 20 (1981): 33–68; and 21 (1982): 93ff.

107. W. F. Jashemski, *The Gardens of Pompeii,* vol. 1 (New Rochelle, N.Y.: 1979), pp. 160–161.

108. For inscriptions relating to the sundials, see *CIL* X 802 (Temple of Apollo) and 831 (archaic temple and bench).

109. For the marble floor in the odeon see *CIL* X 845. Another gift of the same magistrate is mentioned in *CIL* X 955. See further O. Puchstein, *AA* (1906): 302–303; Bauer, *Munificentia Privata,* p. 41.

110. *CIL* X 853–857d; Bauer, *Munificentia Privata,* pp. 30ff.

111. *CIL* X 817; compare Castrén, *Ordo populusque,* p. 102.

112. *CIL* X 1064; Bauer, *Munificentia Privata,* p. 34. Compare Gesemann, *Die Straßen der antiken Stadt Pompeji.*

113. For more on the water supply, see the article by van Buren in *RE,* vol. 21, part 2 (1952), under "Pompeji"; H. Eschebach, *Cronache Pompeiane,* 5 (1979): 24–60, and *Antike Welt,* 10, part 2 (1979): 3ff.; Kockel, "Vesuvstädte II," pp. 551–552; De Caro, "La città in età imperiale," p. 29. For the most recent research results see *Cura Aquarum in Campania. Proceedings of the Ninth International Congress on Water Management and Hydraulic Engineering in the Mediterranean Region 1994,* ed. Nathalie de Haan and Gemma C. M. Jansen, *Bulletin Antieke Beschaving* Supplement 4, 1996.

114. J. Dybkjaer Larsen, *Analecta Romana Instituti Danici,* 11 (1982): 41ff.

115. H. Eschebach and T. Schäfer, *Pompeii Herculaneum Stabiae: Bolletino,* 1 (1983): 11–40; Laurence, *Roman Pompeii: Space and Society;* Gesemann, *Die Straßen der antiken Stadt Pompeji.*

116. For more on the construction of aqueducts in the Augustan era see W. Eck in *Die Wasserversorgung antiker Städte: Pergamon, Geschichte der Wasserversorgung,* vol. 2 (Mainz: 1987), p. 72.

117. Kockel, *Die Grabbauten vor dem Herkulaner Tor,* pp. 18ff, and in von Hesberg and Zanker, eds., *Römische Gräberstraßen,* p. 188.

118. Compare Trillmich and Zanker, eds., *Stadtbild und Ideologie,* passim.

119. The fundamental accounts of this period are Maiuri, *L'ultima fase di Pompei,* and Castrén, *Ordo populusque,* pp. 108ff. See Dobbins, "Problems of Chronology in the Forum of Pompeii."

120. Zanker, *JdI,* 94 (1979): 460ff.

121. See Maiuri, *L'ultima fase di Pompei,* pp. 68ff. For the inscription: *CIL* X 846; Zevi, ed., *Pompei 79,* p. 43 (illustration). For the temple statuary: H. Döhl in Zevi, ed., *Pompei 79,* pp. 183–184. For the benefactor: Castrén, *Ordo populusque,*

pp. 114 and 209, nos. 318, 11, and 12. Compare *Alla ricerca di Iside;* Zevi, "Sul tempio di Iside a Pompei"; P. Hoffmann, *Der Isistempel in Pompeji* (Münster: 1993).

122. H. Döhl in Zevi, ed., *Pompei 79,* p. 182; S. De Caro in *PP,* 49 (1994): 9–10.

123. *CIL* X 858 and 859; Maiuri, *L'ultima fase di Pompei,* p. 86.

124. For more on the new baths, see Mau, *Pompeji in Leben und Kunst,* pp. 212ff.; Overbeck and Mau, *Pompeji,* pp. 233ff.; La Rocca et al., *Pompei,* pp. 318–320; de Vos, *Guida archeologica,* pp. 206–207. Compare also I. Nielsen, *Thermae et Balnea: The Architecture and Cultural History of Roman Public Baths,* II (Copenhagen: 1991), p. 8, no. C47, fig. 79; P. Bargellini, "Le terme centrali di Pompei," *Les thermes romains,* proceedings of a conference held in Rome in 1988 (Rome: 1991). Two more small baths dating from the same period have recently been excavated or investigated: L. Jacobelli, *Le pitture erotiche delle terme suburbane a Pompei* (Rome: 1995); A. Koloski Ostrow, *The Sarno Bath Complex* (Rome: 1990).

125. J. L. Franklin, Jr., *Pompeii: The Electoral Programmata Campaigns and Politics,* A.D. 71–79 (Rome: 1980), with reviews by T. Pekary, H.-J. Gehrke, and H. Galsterer (see Kockel, "Vesuvstädte II," p. 537). Compare Mouritsen, *Elections, Magistrates and Municipal Elite.*

126. For the excavation and recovery efforts after the eruption in A.D. 79, see Zevi, "Sul tempio di Iside a Pompei," pp. 51ff.; Zevi, "Il terremotò del 62 e l'edilizia privata," in *Pompei,* vol. 2, pp. 44–45.

127. See Dobbins, "The Altar of the Genius of Augustus," "Problems of Chronology in the Forum of Pompeii," and "The Imperial Cult Building on the Forum of Pompeii"; K. Wallat, "Der Zustand des Forums von Pompeji am Vorabend des Vesuvausbruchs 79 n. Chr.," in *Archäologie und Seismologie,* pp. 75–92, and the other contributions to that volume.

The Domestic Arts in Pompeii

Note. Andrew Wallace-Hadrill offers a good overview of the issues connected with domestic environments as indicators of identity and social status in his essays "The Social Structure of the Roman House" and "The Social Spread of Roman Luxury" (*PBSR,* 56 [1988]: 43–97, and 58 [1990]: 145–192, respectively). The situation in Pompeii in the early imperial period is discussed by H. Mouritsen in *Elections, Magistrates and Municipal Elite,* where he revises some of Castrén's conclusions in *Ordo Populusque,* on which I draw here. This and other recent evidence, including J.-A. Dickmann's unpublished dissertation from 1992, "Strukturen des Raumes und repräsentatives Wohnen am Beispiel pompejanischer Stadthäuser," suggest that late Pompeian taste in domestic interiors should be seen as a general phenomenon and not be linked quite so directly with the specific outlook of freedmen, as I conclude in the present work. Compare also the section "Social Identification and Cultural Self-Definition" in chapter 1.

1. Older works on the subject of the Pompeian house include, in addition to the works cited below in note 3, Overbeck and Mau's *Pompeji,* 4th ed. (Leipzig: 1884), and Crema, *L'architettura romana* (Torino: 1959). Compare T. Kraus and L. von Matt, *Lebendiges Pompeji: Pompeji und Herculaneum* (Cologne: 1973); Robert Etienne, *La vie quotidienne à Pompéi,* 2nd ed. (Paris: Hachette, 1977); E. La Rocca, M. and A. de Vos, and F. Coarelli, *Guida archeologica di Pompei,* 2nd ed. (Rome: 1976); J. B. Ward-Perkins, *Pompeii A.D. 79* (New York: 1978); B. Tamm, *OpRom,* 9 (1973): 53ff.; J. R. Clarke, *The Houses of Roman Italy, 100 B.C.–A.D. 250* (Berkeley: 1991); E. de Albentiis, *La casa dei Romani* (Milan: 1990); and the extensive bibliography on house decoration in the exhibition catalogue *Pompei. Abitare sotto il Vesuvio* (Ferrara: 1996), pp. 291–298.

2. Valuable observations of some of these phenomena were made for the first time by K. Schefold, however, to whose work I am indebted despite our differences in interpretation and evaluation of the material. See especially *Neue Beiträge zur klassischen Altertumswissenschaft: Festschrift B. Schweitzer* (Stuttgart: 1954), pp. 297ff.; *Pompejanische Malerei: Sinn und Ideengeschichte* (Basel: 1952); *RM,* 60/61 (1953–54): 107ff.; and his essay in Andreae and Kyrieleis, eds., *Neue Forschungen in Pompeji* (Recklinghausen: 1975), pp. 53ff.; *ANRW,* I, 4 (1974), pp. 945ff.

3. Compare the observations of H. Drerup in *MarbWPr* (1959), 1ff. Later discussions include D'Arms, *Romans on the Bay of Naples;* A. Boethius and J. B. Ward-Perkins, *Etruscan and Roman Architecture* (Harmondsworth: 1970); P. Grimal, *Les jardins romains,* 2nd ed. (Paris: 1969); A. G. McKay, *Houses, Villas and Palaces in the Roman World* (London: 1975); H. Mielsch, *Die römische Villa: Architektur und Lebensform* (Munich: 1987); and S. De Caro in the exhibition catalogue *Pompei. Abitare sotto il Vesuvio,* p. 21.

4. A fragment by Cato mentions luxurious villas as early as 152 B.C.: E. Malcovati, *Oratorum Romanorum Fragmenta,* 2nd ed. (Torino: 1955), no. 185. Compare D'Arms, *Romans on the Bay of Naples,* pp. 10–11.

5. Compare the ancient sources and the archeological evidence in F. Noack and K. Lehmann-Hartleben, *Baugeschichtliche Untersuchungen am Stadtrand von Pompeji* (Berlin and Leipzig: 1936).

6. For more on this consult the guidebook, *The J. Paul Getty Museum* (Malibu: 1975).

7. A. de Franciscis, in Andreae and Kyrieleis, eds., *Neue Forschungen,* pp. 9ff., and *The Pompeian Wall Paintings in the Roman Villa of Oplontis,* trans. Rosemary Kunisch (Recklinghausen: 1975). For the decoration (with new literature), see the exhibition catalogue *Pompei. Abitare sotto il Vesuvio,* pp. 135ff. and 266ff.

8. M. Rostowzew, *JdI,* 19 (1904): 103ff., and *RM,* 26 (1911): 1ff.; G. D'Anneo, *AttiPalermo,* 18 (1940): 236ff.; W. J. P. Peters, *Landscape in Romano-Campanian Mural Painting* (Assen: 1963); B. Förtsch, *Archäologischer Kommentar zu den Villenbriefen des jüngeren Plinius* (Mainz: 1993), p. 201 (catalogue of the descriptions of villas).

9. B. Fehr, *MarbWPr* (1969), pp. 31ff.

10. D. Pandermalis, in P. Zanker, ed., *Hellenismus in Mittelitalien, Abhandlungen Göttingen,* series 3, no. 97 (Göttingen: 1986), vol. 2, pp. 387ff.

11. Compare M. Leppert's unpublished dissertation on imperial Roman villas (University of Freiburg, 1974); Zanker, in Zanker, ed., *Hellenismus in Mittelitalien,* pp. 377–378. For the current state of Demetrias see V. Milojcic and D. Theocharis, *Demetrias,* vol. 1 (Bonn: 1976), pp. 75ff.

12. Vitruvius VI 3.8–10; F. Mazois, *Le palais de Scaurus,* 3rd ed. (Paris: 1859); Crema, *L'architettura Romana,* pp. 115–116 and figs. 106–109; Boethius and Ward-Perkins, *Etruscan and Roman Architecture,* p. 156; Förtsch, *Archäologischer Kommentar zu den Villenbriefen,* passim.

13. For more on the second style, see Roger Ling, *Roman Painting* (Cambridge: 1991), pp. 23–51; for the view expounded here, see K. Fittschen in Zanker, ed., *Hellenismus in Mittelitalien,* pp. 539ff.; P. Williams-Lehmann, *Roman Wall Paintings from Boscoreale in the Metropolitan Museum* (New York: 1953), pp. 82ff. Compare also R. A. Tybout, *Aedificiorum figurae: Untersuchungen zu den Architekturdarstellungen des frühen zweiten Stils* (Amsterdam: 1989), with review by B. Wesenberg, *Gnomon,* 64 (1992): 433–438; Clarke, *The Houses of Roman Italy,* pp. 78–123.

14. Associated with the relatively modest palace at Pergamum was the precinct of Athena with its colonnades, library, and works of art. The actual residence of the ruler formed only the smaller part of a typical Hellenistic "palace"; the larger part was composed of different sacred precincts. Compare K. Schefold, *Pompejanische Malerei,* p. 21, and A. Boethius, *The Golden House of Nero* (Ann Arbor: 1960), pp. 96ff. For Hellenistic palace gardens, compare Grimal, *Les jardins romains,* pp. 76–77; V. M. Caroll-Spillecke, *Kepos. Der antike griechische Garten* (Munich: 1989), especially pp. 51ff.

15. G. Zimmer, *Gymnasium,* 96 (1989): 493–520.

16. For more on villa life in this period, compare G. Hahn, "Der Villenbesitz der römischen Großen in Italien zur Zeit der Republik" (Ph.D. diss., University of Bonn, 1922); W. Kroll, *Die Kultur der ciceronischen Zeit* (Leipzig: 1933). For later discussions, compare J. H. D'Arms, in *I Campi Flegrei nell'archeologia e nella storia. Acc. Linc. Atti Convegni,* 33 (1977), pp. 347ff.; R. Neudecker, *Die Skulpturenausstattung römischer Villen;* Mielsch, *Die römische Villa.*

17. Lucretius sketches a nice picture of the villa owners restlessly traveling back and forth in *De Rerum Natura,* III 1060ff.

18. O. E. Schmidt, *Neue Jahrbücher für Antike und deutsche Bildung,* 2 (1899): 328ff. and 466ff. (Cicero's villas), reprinted and edited by H. G. Niemeyer and E. Thomas in the series of the Wissenschaftliche Buchgesellschaft: *Libelli,* vol. 324 (Darmstadt: 1972). Compare M. A. Sollmann in *Studies D. M. Robinson,* 2 (1953), pp. 1238ff., and Wallace-Hadrill, "The Social Structure of the Roman House."

19. Compare, for instance, the group that Cornelia, the mother of the Gracchi, gathered around her at her villa; Plutarch, *C. Gracch.* 19.1.2.

20. E. S. Gruen, *Culture and National Identity in Republican Rome* (Ithaca, N.Y.: 1992). For the archeological aspect of the subject, compare especially H. Jucker, *Vom Verhältnis der Römer zur bildenden Kunst der Griechen* (Frankfurt a.M.: 1950); J. M. André, *L'Otium dans la vie morale et intellectuelle romaine* (Paris: 1966); and most recently Mielsch, *Die römische Villa.*

21. Compare Hahn, *Der Villenbesitz der römischen Großen,* p. 12. One of the first libraries was probably that of Perseus V of Macedonia, which Aemilius Paullus gave to his sons: Plutarch, *Aemilius Paullus* 28. For libraries in villas, see R. Neudecker, *Die Skulpturenausstattung römischer Villen in Italien* (Munich: 1988), p. 70.

22. See Cicero's Letters to Atticus I 1.5, 4.3, 5.6, 6.2, 7.1, 8.2, 9.2, 10.3, 11.3, 16.15 and 18; Letters to Friends VII 23.2–3. Compare also Neudecker, *Die Skulpturenausstattung römischer Villen,* and the relevant contributions (especially those of H. Galsterer, G. Zimmer, and T. Hölscher) in *Das Wrack. Der antike Schatzfund von Mahdia. Katalog Ausstellung Bonn* (Cologne: 1994), vol. 2.

23. S. H. A. (Spartianus), *Vita Hadriani* 26. Compare Jucker, *Vom Verhältnis der Römer zur bildenden Kunst,* pp. 37–38; B. Kapossy, *Gymnasium,* 74 (1967): 38ff.; Zanker, in W. Helbig, *Führer durch die öffentlichen Sammlungen klassischer Altertümer in Rom,* 4th ed., H. Speier, ed., vol. 4, pp. 155–156; C. S. Sweet, *AJA,* 77 (1973): 229; J. Raeder, *Die statuarische Ausstattung der Villa Hadriana bei Tivoli* (Frankfurt and Bern: 1983). For a recent discussion of the Greek terms, see R. Förtsch, *Archäologischer Kommentar zu den Villenbriefen des jüngeren Plinius* (Mainz: 1993).

24. Compare F. Coarelli, *DArch,* 4/5 (1970/71): 476ff.

25. See the entry under *"hortus"* by Lugli in De Ruggiero, *Dizionario epigrafico di antichità romane,* rpt. (Rome: 1961); S. Platner-Ashby, *A Topographical Dictionary of Ancient Rome* (Oxford: 1929), pp. 264ff. Compare also Noack and Lehmann-Hartleben, *Baugeschichtliche Untersuchungen,* pp. 202ff., and Grimal, *Les jardins romains,* pp. 107ff. For discussions of *domus* and *horti* at Rome in the recent literature, see C. Häubler, in *Das Wrack,* vol. 2, pp. 911–926.

26. Neudecker, *Die Skulpturenausstattung römischer Villen,* pp. 147ff.; M. R. Wojcik, *La villa dei Papiri ad Ercolano* (Rome: 1986); D. Pandermalis, *AM,* 86 (1971): 173ff.; W. Trillmich, *JdI,* 88 (1973): 256ff.

27. For the sources of their wealth, see Castrén, *Ordus populusque,* pp. 37ff.

28. For more on the problems discussed here, see Zanker, ed., *Hellenismus in Mitteli-talien*, pp. 14ff. and passim. Compare also K. Schefold, in *Neue Beiträge: Festschrift B. Schweitzer*, pp. 297ff.

29. H. Lauter, in Andreae and Kyrieleis, eds., *Neue Forschungen*, p. 148. Compare also H. Gabelmann, *BJb*, 176 (1976): 468–469, where he notes correctly that the width of *insulae* already assumes houses will be of the expanded atrium type.

30. For the House of the Faun, compare Kockel's summary of Hoffmann's research in "Vesuvstädte II"; unfortunately, Hoffmann's manuscript remains unpublished, although it was completed years ago. Compare A. Hoffmann, "Ein Rekonstruktionsproblem der Casa del Fauno in Pompeji," *Bericht über die 30. Tagung für Ausgrabungswissenschaft und Bauforschung. Colmar 1978* (Bonn: 1980): 35–41; "Elemente bürgerlicher Repräsentation"; and review in *Gnomon*, 64 (1992): 433–438; Zevi, "Pompei della città sannitica alla colonia sillana"; Zevi, "Sul tempio di Iside a Pompei," *PP* 49 (1994): 37–56.

31. These gardens were also taken over from Hellenistic models; see H. Lauter-Bufé, in Andreae and Kyrieleis, eds., *Neue Forschungen*, p. 169, and Fittschen, in Zanker, ed., *Hellenismus in Mittelitalien*, p. 547.

32. Fittschen, in Zanker, ed., *Hellenismus in Mittelitalien*, pp. 545ff. See also the discussion there on the problems connected with dating vista paintings in the second style (p. 543). Even if the later dates apply to the paintings in Pompeii, this style may have been popular in Italy before the Sullan era. Compare Tybout, *Aedificiorum figurae*, and the review by B. Wesenberg, *Gnomon*, 64 (1992): 433–438; Ling, *Roman Painting*, pp. 23ff.

33. See K. Schefold, *Vergessenes Pompeji* (Bern: 1962), which also has a color plate of this painting, pp. 36–37, 41ff., plates 3.2 and 20.

34. F. Studniczka, *Das Symposion Ptolemaios' II, Abhandlungen der philologisch-historischen Klasse der Königl. Sächsischen Gesellschaft der Wissenschaften*, vol. 30, no. 2 (Leipzig: 1914): 31–32; F. Caspari, *JdI*, 31 (1916): 42ff.

35. The structure known as the Palazzo delle Colonne in Ptolemais (Roman Cyrenaica) comes to mind: H. Lauter, *JdI*, 86 (1971): 149ff. For the connection with palace architecture (Nile ships of the Ptolemies), see M. Nowicka, *Bibliotheca Antiqua*, 9 (1969): 154ff.

36. Eschebach, *Die städtebauliche Entwicklung des antiken Pompeji, RM*, Ergänzungsheft 17 (Heidelberg: 1970), foldouts 2 and 3; La Rocca et al., *Guida archeologica di Pompei*, p. 326. Sadly, there is to date no publication available on the complex of buildings.

37. Noack and Lehmann-Hartleben, *Baugeschichtliche Untersuchungen*.

38. Compare Boethius and Ward-Perkins, *Etruscan and Roman Architecture*, p. 157 and fig. 82.

39. Back in the 1930s Noack and Lehmann-Hartleben noted the resemblance of these small villas to hillside houses in Rome, *Baugeschichtliche Untersuchungen*, pp. 202ff.

40. V. Spinazzola, *Pompei alla luce degli scavi nuovi di via dell'Abbondanza* (Rome: 1953), vol. 1, pp. 435ff.; K. Schefold, *Die Wände Pompejis* (Berlin: 1957), pp. 17ff.; La Rocca et al., *Guida archeologica di Pompei*, pp. 199ff. See the section "Display and Self-Promotion in Houses and Tombs," chapter 2.

41. A. Maiuri, *La casa del Menandro* (Rome: 1933); Schefold, *Die Wände Pompejis*, pp. 38ff.; La Rocca et al., *Guida archeologica di Pompei*, pp. 175ff.; Roger Ling, *The Insula of the Menander at Pompeii*, vol. 1 (Oxford: 1997). The phenomenon can be documented elsewhere in the later first century B.C. Compare the well-excavated house (*domus* III) in Bolsena, as shown in A. Balland et al., *Bolsena II: Les architectures* (Rome and Paris: 1971), pp. 234–235 and plate 9; and the loggia in the SUNY house in Cosa, as described by V. J. Bruno, *Archeology*, 23 (1970): 233ff. Compare also R. Ling, "The Insula of Menander at Pompeii: Interim Report," *Antiquarian Journal*, 63 (1983): 34–57.

42. I have based the dating principally on Maiuri, *L'ultima fase edilizia di Pompei* (Rome: 1942), passim, but his conclusions must now be considered outdated in part. Compare the critique by J. Andreau, "Le tremblement de terre de Pompéi," pp. 369ff.; and F. Zevi, "Il terremotò del 62 e l'edilizia privata," in Zevi, ed., *Pompei*, vol. 2 (Naples: 1992).

43. For recent studies on the dating of the earthquake, see Étienne, *La vie quotidienne*, pp. 15–16; J. P. Adam in F. Guidoboni, ed., *I terremoti prima del Mille in Italia e nell'area mediterranea* (Bologna: 1989), pp. 460–474; *Archäologie und Seismologie: La regione vesuviana dal 62 al 79 d.C. Problemi archeologici e sismologici. Colloquium Boscoreale 1993* (Munich: 1995).

44. For more on the subject see Spinazzola, *Pompei alla luce degli scavi nuovi*, vol. 1, pp. 369ff; A. Maiuri, *La casa di Loreio Tiburtino e la villa di Diomede in Pompei*, I *monumenti italiani*, ser. 2, fasc. 1 (Rome: 1947). The voluminous literature includes E. D. van Buren, *MemAmAc*, 12 (1935): 151–152; Jucker, *Vom Verhältnis der Römer zur bildenden Kunst*, pp. 28ff.; Schefold, *Die Wände Pompejis*, pp. 50ff.; H. Drerup, *RM*, 66 (1959): 164–165, and *MarbWPr* (1959), p. 14; H. Kähler, *Rom und seine Welt* (Munich: 1960), pp. 217ff.; F. Rakob in T. Kraus, ed., *Das römische Weltreich* (Berlin: 1967), pp. 184–185 and no. 85; Boethius and Ward-Perkins, *Etruscan and Roman Architecture*, pp. 315–316; McKay, *Houses, Villas and Palaces*, pp. 44–45; Castrén, *Ordo populusque*, p. 184; La Rocca et al., *Guida archeologica di Pompei*, pp. 240–241. Compare Jashemski's detailed discussion (with good documentation of the sculptures), *The Gardens of Pompeii*, vol. 1 (New Rochelle, N.Y.: 1979), p. 45; vol. 2 (New Rochelle, N.Y.: 1993), pp. 78–83. If the seal found in the first *cubiculum* to the left of the entrance (Spinazzola, *Pompei*

alla luce degli scavi nuovi, vol. 1, p. 369 and fig. 414) is any indication, the house could have belonged to a D. Octavius Quartio, of whom nothing else is known (Della Corte, *Case e abitanti di Pompei*, 3rd ed. [Rome: 1965], pp. 370–371, no. 800, with fantastic combinations based on the inscriptions on the walls; Castrén, *Ordo populusque*, p. 199, no. 285); F. B. Sear, *Roman Wall and Vault Mosaics, RM*, Ergänzungsheft 23 (Heidelberg: 1977), p. 93. F. Jung, "Gebaute Bilder," *Antike Kunst*, 27 (1984): 106ff.

45. Maiuri, *L'ultima fase di Pompei*, pp. 152ff.

46. Paintings of villas suggest that such miniature bridges were extremely popular on the grounds. A watercourse *(euripus)* almost large enough for a villa is found at the Praedia of Julia Felix (II 4.3). Schefold, *Die Wände Pompejis*, pp. 53–54; La Rocca et al., *Guida archeologica di Pompei*, p. 244, with ground plan; H. Döhl, *Plastik aus Pompeji* (unpublished *Habilitation*, University of Göttingen, 1976), p. 101.

47. Cicero, *Ad Quintum fratrem* 3.7.7 and *De Legibus* 2.2. Grimal, *Les jardins romains*, pp. 296ff. The Villa of the Pisones in Herculaneum offers two examples; see Crema, *L'architettura Romana*, p. 232, fig. 251; D. Mustilli, *RenAccNap*, new series, 31 (1956): 77ff.; Drerup, *MarbWPr* (1959), p. 3. Further examples can be found in Rakob, *RM*, 71 (1964): 182ff., especially fig. 9.

48. S. Aurigemma, *Villa Adriana* (Rome: 1961), pp. 100ff.; Rakob in Kraus, ed., *Das römische Weltreich*, pp. 190ff. on fig. 30. Compare W. L. Macdonald, *Hadrian's Villa and Its Legacy* (New York and London: 1995), pp. 108ff.

49. Noack and Lehmann-Hartleben, *Baugeschichtliche Untersuchungen*, pp. 205–206; D. Mustilli, *RenAccNap*, 31 (1956): 91ff.; Drerup, *MarbWPr* (1959), p. 9, where the typological "development," however, is in my view given too much emphasis. Clarke, *The Houses of Roman Italy*, p. 19; Mielsch, *Die römische Villa*, pp. 49ff.

50. Pliny, *Epistulae* 2.17 and 5.6; Förtsch, *Archäologischer Kommentar zu den Villenbriefen*. Compare K. Lehmann-Hartleben's edition with commentary, *Lettere scelte con commento archeologico* (Florence: 1936), pp. 42ff.

51. Spinazzola, *Pompei alla luce degli scavi nuovi*, vol. 1, p. 390, fig. 443; vol. 2, pp. 973ff., plates 90–96. Compare Jucker, *Vom Verhältnis der Römer zur bildenden Kunst*, p. 28.

52. Spinazzola, *Pompei alla luce degli scavi nuovi*, vol. 1, p. 383, figs. 432ff.

53. Cicero, *Att.* 1.16.15 and 17; 1.13.1; *De Legibus* 2.3.7. Compare the shrine to Hercules in the villa of Pollus Felix near Sorrento: Statius, *Silvae*, 3.1. For excavated villas, such as the villa on Brioni, see A. Gnirs, *ÖJh*, 18 (1915): insert, 99ff. For the use of a shrine as a day room *(diaeta)* compare P. Williams-Lehmann, *Roman Wall Paintings from Boscoreale* (New York: 1953), p. 107, with further examples of "shrines" at villas on p. 123.

54. Spinazzola, *Pompei alla luce degli scavi nuovi*, vol. 1, pp. 396ff., figs. 454–457, and

461; Döhl, *Plastik aus Pompeji,* pp. 149–150. The "boy with a goose" that has been turned into a *herakliskos,* or "little Hercules," is an interesting example of a change of taste on the part of the owner. The simple and familiar myth made the content of the Hellenistic masterpiece accessible. The bronze head between the claws of the Sphinx, which serves as a water spout, also creates a mythological link. Compare *Aquileia e Milano: Antichità Altoadriatiche,* vol. 4 (Udine: 1973), pp. 105ff., fig. 7; *Arte e civiltà nell'Italia settentrionale,* vol. 1 (Bologna: 1964), plate 28, no. 62; vol. 2 (Bologna: 1965), p. 146, no. 224 (I am indebted to H. Pflug for this reference).

55. Compare the "museum" in the park of Varro's villa near Casinum, which one should probably imagine as no more than a porticus decorated with the appropriate statues: Varro, *Res rusticae* 3.5.8. Compare also K. Schefold, *Pompejanische Malerei* (Basel: 1952), where the term is, however, understood in a very broad sense. I am indebted to R. Neudecker for pointing out to me a small poem found on the shaft of a herm that announces the equipping of such a garden "museum" at a villa on the Via Appia: see R. Paribeni, *NSc* (1926): 284.

56. Spinazzola, *Pompei alla luce degli scavi nuovi,* vol. 1, pp. 402ff., figs. 458ff.

57. Ibid., p. 391, figs. 444, 445; Schefold, *Die Wände Pompejis,* p. 53, no. 1. Compare also the section "Large Pictures for Small Dreams" below.

58. Spinazzola, *Pompei alla luce degli scavi nuovi,* vol. 1, p. 411, figs. 470 and 478. (Figure 80 of this book shows the sculpture as placed by the excavators in a decorative but false position.) This is reminiscent of the ivy-covered statues that resemble gardeners at the villa of Cicero's brother (Cicero, *Ad Quintum fratrem* 3.1.5). Compare Jucker, *Vom Verhältnis der Römer zur bildenden Kunst,* p. 43, and M. Kunze, "Griechische Einflüsse auf Kunst und Gesellschaft im Rom der späten Republik und der frühen Kaiserzeit," in E. C. Weiskopf, ed., *Hellenistische Poleis,* vol. 3 (Berlin: 1974), p. 1611.

59. Spinazzola, *Pompei alla luce degli scavi nuovi,* vol. 1, p. 409, figs. 467–468.

60. For the fountain figures compare B. Kapossy, *Brunnenfiguren der hellenistischen und römischen Zeit* (Zurich: 1969), pp. 40 and 60. For more on the popularity of *nymphaea* at villas, see Grimal, *Les jardins romains,* pp. 304ff.

61. Noack and Lehmann-Hartleben, *Baugeschichtliche Untersuchungen,* pp. 70ff., 186, and 221ff.; N. Neuerburg, "L'architettura delle fontane e dei ninfei nell'Italia antica," *RenAccNap,* 5 (1965): 31, no. 35 and fig. 49.

62. Spinazzola, *Pompei alla luce degli scavi nuovi,* vol. 1, pp. 410ff.

63. Ibid., p. 412, fig. 472.

64. Compare the basin painted with fish in the House of Epidius Sabinus discussed by Schefold, *Die Wände Pompejis,* p. 237.

65. See the entry under "piscina" in *RE,* vol. 20, part 2 (1950). Archeological exam-

ples are cited by G. Schmidt, *Il livello antico del Mar Tirreno* (Rome: 1972); Mielsch, *Die römische Villa*, pp. 23ff.

66. D'Arms, *Romans on the Bay of Naples*, p. 41.

67. In my view Drerup and Rakob overestimate the aesthetic component by interpreting the rigid perspectival arrangement as a stylistic phenomenon. If one imagines the aedicula filled by a statue or even a statuette similar in size to the two muses, then it would surely have blocked the view of the more distant elements in the series. And the fact that the lower part of the garden *euripus* is angled makes one even more skeptical: Drerup, *RM*, 66 (1959) and *MarbWPr* (1959); Rakob, in T. Kraus, ed., *Das römische Weltreich* (Berlin: 1967).

68. The only detailed description of the house is found in an unpublished manuscript by T. Warscher in the library of the German Archeological Institute in Rome: "A Key to the 'Topographischer Index für Pompeji' of Helbig," vol. 1 (1954), 63–83 (reference number: Ib Pompeji 5269). Warscher cites the most important earlier descriptions, including E. Breton, *Pompeia décrite et dessiné*, 2nd ed. (Naples: 1855), p. 271; G. Fiorelli, *Descrizione di Pompei* (Naples: 1875), pp. 115–116; Mau, *Pompeji in Leben und Kunst*, 2nd ed. (Leipzig: 1908), p. 368; Schefold, *Die Wände Pompejis*, pp. 102ff.; E. La Rocca et al., *Guida archeologica di Pompei*, pp. 287–288; Döhl, *Plastik aus Pompeji*, pp. 104ff. (with an evaluation of the finds relating to the marble decoration); Jashemski, *The Gardens of Pompeii*, vol. 2, pp. 130ff.; E. B. Andersson, "Fountains and the Roman Dwelling: Casa del Torello in Pompeii," *JdI*, 105 (1990): 234. Compare also the extensive documentation in *PPM*, vol. 4., pp. 470ff. The old identification of the house's owner (first proposed by Fiorelli) as a certain A. Herennuleius Communis, whose name also appears on the wax tablets of Caecilius Iucundus (Castrén, *Ordo populusque*, p. 175, no. 192; J. Andreau, *Les affaires de Monsieur Jucundus* [Rome: 1974], pp. 191 and 217), has been shown by Döhl to be erroneous. Surgical instruments were found in the house.

69. A picture of the fountain, now in a state of extreme disrepair, can be found in A. Ippel, *Pompeji* (Leipzig: 1925), p. 100, fig. 103.

70. W. Helbig, *Die Wandgemälde der vom Vesuv verschütteten Städte Campaniens* (Leipzig: 1868), p. 68, no. 240.

71. "Les murailles de la terrasse étaient couvertes de peintures peu soignées représentant des arbustes, des oiseaux et plusieurs figures qui semblent être des esclaves apportant des plats," Breton, *Pompeia décrite*, p. 272. Compare Döhl, *Plastik aus Pompeji*, pp. 111–112.

72. Compare the distribution of space at the rear wall of house III 2.1 ("House of Trebius Valens"), Spinazzola, *Pompei alla luce degli scavi nuovi*, vol. 1, pp. 281ff.; Schefold, *Die Wände Pompejis*, pp. 56–57; Rakob, *RM*, 71 (1964): 183. The fountain and *piscina* also correspond to the distribution at the House of Apolline: see Sear, *Roman Wall and Vault Mosaics*, pp. 68–69.

Notes to Pages 155–159

73. Döhl (*Plastik aus Pompeji*, p. 109) correctly points out the affinity with the House of the Mosaic of Neptune and Amphitrite in Herculaneum (V 6.7; Maiuri, *Ercolano*, vol. 1 [Rome: 1958], pp. 393ff.). Such artificial grotto elements can be found quite frequently in the later period of Pompeii's history. For their connection with villas, see Rakob, *RM*, 71 (1964): 185.

74. For further references to villa *diaetae*, see Förtsch, *Archäologischer Kommentar zu den Villenbriefen*, pp. 48ff.

75. P. Hermann, *Denkmäler der Malerei des Altertums* (Munich: 1904–1950), plates 224–228; further literature is cited by Schefold, *Die Wände Pompejis*, p. 103. Compare the good documentation in L. Caso, *Rivista di Studi Pompeiani*, 3 (1989): 111–130.

76. G. Fiorelli, in *Pompeianarum Antiquitatum Historia* (Naples: 1860–64), vol. 2, pp. 237ff., and *Descrizione di Pompei*, pp. 142–143; Mau, *Pompeji in Leben und Kunst*, pp. 368–369, and "Anhang" (1913), p. 49; T. Warscher, "Codex top. Reg. VI 10.1" (1936), nos. 90–120a, and "A Key to Helbig," vol. 4, nos. 409–418 (both works are unpublished manuscripts in the German Archeological Institute in Rome); Schefold, *RM*, 60/61 (1953–54): 111–112 ("Konkretisierung der Illusionsarchitektur"), and *Die Wände Pompejis*, p. 123; Grimal, *Les jardins romains*, p. 227; Sear, *Roman Wall and Vault Mosaics*, pp. 56–57; Jashemski, *The Gardens of Pompeii*, vol. 1, p. 45; vol. 2, p. 141. Compare also *PPM*, vol. 4, pp. 1050ff.

77. A reliable assessment of the various phases of construction is not possible without further detailed study. But for our purposes it is immaterial whether the house already possessed a simple garden arcade in the first century B.C.; the decisive final phase of remodeling dates without doubt from the last decade of the town's existence. See Sear, *Roman Wall and Vault Mosaics*, p. 58.

78. Grimal, *Les jardins romains*, p. 241, plate 16.2; Neuerburg, "L'architettura delle fontane," pp. 62, 75, 125–126, and plate 132; H. Lauter-Bufé, in Andreae and Kyrieleis, eds., *Neue Forschungen*, p. 171.

79. For depictions of Venus Pompeiana with a rudder, compare Spinazzola, *Pompei alla luce degli scavi nuovi*, vol. 1, pp. 191, fig. 222, and p. 215, fig. 243.

80. Compare the "sacred precinct" in the frescos at Oplontis; A. de Franciscis, in Andreae and Kyrieleis, eds., *Neue Forschungen*, figs. 23ff., and *Die pompejanischen Wandmalereien in der Villa von Oplontis* (Recklinghausen: 1975).

81. Noack and Lehmann-Hartleben, *Baugeschichtliche Untersuchungen*, p. 198.

82. Overbeck and Mau, *Pompeji*, pp. 369ff.; Mau, *Pompeji in Leben und Kunst*, pp. 376ff.; Sogliano, *RenAccNap*, 8 (1924): 136ff.; A. Maiuri, "La casa di Loreio Tiburtino"; Maiuri, *L'ultima fase di Pompei*, p. 157; Drerup, *MarbWPr* (1959): 12–13; Jashemski, *The Gardens of Pompeii*, vol. 1, p. 110; vol. 2, pp. 280ff. Compare also Williams-Lehmann, *Roman Wall Paintings*, pp. 104–105.

83. Spinazzola, *Pompei alla luce degli scavi nuovi*, vol. 2, pp. 727ff.; Schefold, *Die Wände*

Pompejis, p. 58; Jashemski, *The Gardens of Pompeii*, vol. 2, p. 102; *PPM*, vol. 3, pp. 406ff. For more on the owner, see Della Corte, *Case e abitanti di Pompei*, p. 358; Andreau, *Les affaires de Monsieur Jucundus*, pp. 244–245, and p. 268; Castrén, *Ordo populusque*, p. 165; La Rocca et al., *Guida archeologica di Pompei*, pp. 236ff.

84. Spinazzola, *Pompei alla luce degli scavi nuovi*, vol. 2, pp. 759–760, figs. 740 and 741.

85. Vitruvius 6.5.2ff.; Cicero, *Ad Quintum fratrem* 3.1.3; Horace, *Carmina* 3.22; *Epistulae* 1.10.12; Pliny the Elder, *Naturalis Historia* 31.6. Compare Förtsch, *Archäologischer Kommentar zu den Villenbriefen*, p. 77; Williams-Lehmann, *Roman Wall Paintings*, pp. 98ff.; F.-M. Pairault, *MEFRA*, 81 (1969): 425ff.

86. House I 2.17–19 has a small garden with an aedicula containing a statue of Aphrodite (Döhl, *Plastik aus Pompeji*, pp. 68ff.). House II 8.6 has a structure honoring Hercules in a large flower garden used for commercial purposes (W. F. Jashemski, *Antike Welt*, 8, part 4 [1977]: 7ff.). House VII 6.28 has a tree and altar in the peristyle, and fine paintings of gardens on the north wall of the peristyle (*NSc* [1910], p. 467, figs. 9 and 9a). House VIII 3.14 has what Fiorelli describes as "una statua di Diana ed innanzi un thymiaterion entrambi di marmo," *Descrizione di Pompei*, p. 326.

87. *CIL* IV suppl. 3, no. 6798; Spinazzola, *Pompei alla luce degli scavi nuovi*, vol. 2, pp. 754ff.

88. Förtsch, *Archäologischer Kommentar zu den Villenbriefen*, pp. 100ff.; Noack and Lehmann-Hartleben, *Baugeschichtliche Untersuchungen*, p. 222.

89. Étienne, *La vie quotidienne*, p. 255.

90. Mau, *Pompeji in Leben und Kunst*, pp. 294ff., with literature cited in the appendix of the second edition of 1913, p. 46; Maiuri, *L'ultima fase di Pompei*, pp. 98–99, and *MemAccLinc*, 8, 5 (1954): 450–451; Schefold, *Die Wände Pompejis*, pp. 93–94; La Rocca et al., *Guida archeologica di Pompei*, pp. 326–327; J. B. Ward-Perkins, *Pompeii A.D. 79* (New York: 1978), p. 46, with the plan reproduced here; Jashemski, *The Gardens of Pompeii*, vol. 1, p. 168; vol. 2, p. 121. See also *PPM*, vol. 4, pp. 87ff.

91. *PPM*, vol. 4, pp. 136ff. Schefold describes these paintings as "probably from the reign of Vespasian," *Die Wände Pompejis*, pp. 93–94.

92. A. Maiuri, *Ercolano*, vol. 1, pp. 302ff. See also Rakob in Kraus, ed., *Das römische Weltreich*, p. 185, no. 86.

93. C. M. Dawson, *Yale ClSt*, 9 (1944): 96–97, no. 35 and plate 13; Schefold, *RM*, 60/61 (1953–54): 117–118, and *Die Wände Pompejis*, p. 93.

94. Compare, for example, Spinazzola, *Pompei alla luce degli scavi nuovi*, vol. 2, p. 688.

95. Compare the House of M. Lucretius discussed in the section below, and the House of the Ephebe in the section "Dining under the Stars"; Spinazzola, *Pompei alla luce degli scavi nuovi*, vol. 1, pp. 281ff.

Notes to Pages 163–168

96. Maiuri discusses the good examples in the House of Menander, *La Casa del Menandro* (Rome: 1933). These small garden scenes, usually on dark backgrounds, are also freqently found on lower wall panels in other rooms. There is a particularly beautiful example in the *tablinum* of the House of Lucretius Fronto (V 4.11: see Jashemski, *The Gardens of Pompeii*, vol. 1, p. 35; vol. 2, pp. 153–156); see Schefold, *Die Wände Pompejis*, p. 85; A. Sogliano, *NSc* (1901), p. 153; *PPM*, vol. 3, pp. 1011, 1016.

97. Sogliano, *NSc* (1907), pp. 549ff.; Mau, *Pompeji in Leben und Kunst*, pp. 371–372; Maiuri, *L'ultima fase di Pompei*, pp. 113–114; Schefold, *Die Wände Pompejis*, pp. 153–154; La Rocca et al., *Guida archeologica di Pompei*, pp. 282ff.; Döhl, *Plastik aus Pompeji*, catalogue 26ff.; *PPM*, vol. 5, pp. 714–864. The arguments for a connection between the house and the family of the empress Poppaea are insufficient, and Della Corte's even more far-ranging interpretations are pure speculation, *Case e abitanti di Pompei*, pp. 76ff.; compare Castrén, *Ordo populusque*, p. 209. Compare also the extensive documentation of the entire sculpture collection in F. Seiler, *La Casa degli Amorini Dorati* (Munich: 1992), figs. 529ff.

98. Schefold, *RM,* 60/61 (1953–54): 111.

99. Seiler, *La Casa degli Amorini Dorati*, catalogue p. 38, fig. 614. Compare the classical Greek votive relief in house V 3.10, illustrated in Kraus and von Matt, *Lebendiges Pompeji*, p. 193, no. 266.

100. Seiler, *La Casa degli Amorini Dorati,* catalogue p. 29, figs. 590–593; G. Richter, *The Portraits of the Greeks*, vol. 2 (Oxford: 1965), p. 230, no. 14, figs. 1561 and 1563. Compare also the more recent studies by Neudecker, *Die Skulpturenausstattung römischer Villen,* and E. Bartman in E. K. Gazda, ed., *Roman Art in the Private Sphere: New Perspectives in the Architecture and Decor of the* Domus, Villa, *and* Insula (Ann Arbor: 1991), pp. 71ff.

101. Neudecker, *Die Skulpturenausstattung römischer Villen.*

102. Thus a fountain stood at each end of the south portico, for example, while a herm with a child (Eros?) stood at each end of the north portico.

103. *NSc* (1907), pp. 568ff.

104. Compare Döhl, *Plastik aus Pompeji*, p. 150.

105. Interesting in this context, for instance, are the corresponding statuettes from the *Isola sacra* found in Ostia, which are, however, of superior craftsmanship; R. Calza and M. F. Squarciapino, *Museo Ostiense* (Rome: 1962), p. 38, figs. 21 and 22; Helbig, *Führer durch die öffentlichen Sammlungen*, vol. 4, pp. 3037–3038. Part of the material has been assembled in Kapossy, *Brunnenfiguren.*

106. House VI 14.43. Döhl, *Plastik aus Pompeji*, catalogue 71.

107. Overbeck and Mau, *Pompeji*, p. 314; Mau, *Pompeji in Leben und Kunst*, pp. 372–373 (see also appendix to second edition of 1913 with list of earlier literature); Maiuri, *L'ultima fase di Pompei*, p. 128; Schefold, *Die Wände Pompejis*, pp. 246ff.;

Jashemski, *The Gardens of Pompeii,* vol. 1, pp. 42–43; vol. 2, pp. 231–233. For more on the garden, see Neuerburg, "L'architettura delle fontane," p. 131, no. 36; Kapossy, *Brunnenfiguren,* pp. 59 and 77–78; Döhl, *Plastik aus Pompeji,* pp. 141ff., catalogue 52–53. For the owner, see J. Day, *YaleClSt,* 3 (1932): 206ff.; M. Della Corte, *RM,* 57 (1942): 33–34, and *Case e abitanti di Pompei,* pp. 161–162. Andreau correctly argues that the case for identifying the owner as a wine merchant cannot be proved, *Les affaires de Monsieur Jucundus,* pp. 226 and 230. Unfortunately, it is equally impossible to prove whether M. Lucretius, "priest of Mars" *(flamen Martis),* who appears as the recipient of a letter in a fresco with an *instrumentum scriptorium,* is the name of the owner of the house. This priesthood is not otherwise documented in Pompeii: Sear, *Roman Wall and Vault Mosaics,* p. 93. Compare also the more recent essay by E. Dwyer, in Gazda, ed., *Roman Art in the Private Sphere,* pp. 71ff.

108. We previously encountered the same phenomenon of "staging" part of a domestic environment's decor at the miniature villa in the Via dell'Abbondanza. We will find it again in the mosaic fountains and dining couches discussed below in the section "Large Pictures for Small Dreams," and in large wall frescos.

109. P. Soprano, "I triclini all'aperto di Pompei," in *Pompeiana: Raccolta di studi per il secondo centenario degli scavi di Pompei* (Naples: 1950), pp. 288–310.

110. For sketches of the garden paintings see F. Mazois, *Les ruines de Pompei* (Paris: 1824), vol. 2, plate 37; and W. Gell, *Pompeiana* (London: 1832), plate 32; *PPM,* vol. 4, p. 120. For this type of painting compare the frescos in the "auditorium" of Maecenas, *BullComm,* 2 (1874): plates 14–16. One should not, however, deduce an early date from this. In many houses in Pompeii the context reveals that such large garden scenes on walls in the peristyle or courtyard were painted almost without exception during the very last period of the town's history, when the houses were being remodeled and fitted out as miniature villas.

111. Compare Overbeck and Mau, *Pompeji,* p. 301, fig. 165 (plan), and p. 304, fig. 167 (reconstruction); Rakob, *RM,* 71 (1964): 182 and plate 51.2.

112. See A. Maiuri, *NSc* (1927): 52ff. and (1929): 365ff.; *MonPitt Pompei,* vol. 2 (1938), pp. 13ff.; *MemAccLinc,* 8, 5 (1954): 459–460. See further Schefold, *Die Wände Pompejis,* pp. 31–32; Rakob, *RM,* 71 (1964): 182–183; Neuerburg, "L'architettura delle fontane," p. 117, no. 18; Grimal, *Les jardins romains,* pp. 444–445; La Rocca et al., *Guida archeologica,* pp. 212ff. (with the ground plan reproduced here). Compare *PPM,* vol. 1, pp. 619ff. For more on the owner, his business, and his social status, see Della Corte, *Case e abitanti di Pompei,* pp. 325ff. and no. 647. For a more recent discussion see Andreau, *Les Affaires de Monsieur Jucundus,* especially pp. 259 and 158, and nos. 129 and 41.

113. For this type, which was used in several places in conjunction with fountains, see Kapossy, *Brunnenfiguren,* pp. 12–13.

114. For a recent discussion of this work see H. Sichtermann, in Kraus, *Das römische Weltreich,* p. 246, no. 261; compare P. Zanker, *Klassizistische Statuen* (Mainz: 1974), pp. 77 and 87.

115. For the "fence" of herms, see H. Wrede, *Die spätantike Hermengalerie von Welschbillig* (Berlin: 1972), p. 126, no. 3.

116. Döhl, *Plastik aus Pompeji,* catalogue, 4–5.

117. Maiuri, in *MonPitt Pompei,* vol. 1, fig. 20.

118. Compare Schefold, *RM,* 60/61 (1953–54): 122.

119. E. La Rocca et al., *Guida archeologica di Pompei,* p. 214 with color illustration.

120. See *NSc* (1927): 75ff.

121. *MonPitt Pompei,* vol. 1, fig. 27; *NSc* (1929): 354ff., plate 20; Schefold, *Die Wände Pompejis,* p. 36 (where his dating of the picture as "early third style," however, is in my view incorrect). For more on such "truncated peristyles" with garden paintings, see Grimal, *Les jardins romains,* p. 209 and appendix I, p. 457.

122. *PPM,* vol. 3, pp. 184–309. On the grotto *triclinium* see F. Rakob, *RM,* 71 (1964): 182–183. Proof of the popularity of *triclinia* surrounded by flowing water is also offered by the clubhouse of the *pagus maritimus:* O. Elia, *BdA,* 46 (1931): 200ff., and K. Schauenburg, *Gymnasium,* 69 (1962): 521ff.

123. For a recent discussion of the dating, see H. Lauter-Bufé in Andreae and Kyrieleis, eds., *Neue Forschungen,* p. 170. I believe, however, that the argument made there for a "developing" fountain architecture does not hold up, at least not in the case of Pompeii. The existence of imitation in a second-rate town of this period seems to me largely accidental; the various "types" were probably all available in merchants' stock simultaneously. See also E. B. Anderson, "Fountains and the Roman Dwelling: Casa del Torello in Pompeii," *JdI,* 105 (1990): 207–236.

124. *PPM,* vol. 3, pp. 481ff.; Lauter-Bufé, in Andreae and Kyrieleis, eds., *Neue Forschungen,* p. 171, with illustration in Maiuri, *L'ultima fase di Pompei,* p. 45; Neuerburg, "L'architettura delle fontane," pp. 121–122, no. 23, fig. 153; Sear, *Roman Wall and Vault Mosaics,* pp. 60–61. See also Anderson, "Fountains and the Roman Dwelling," pp. 208–209.

125. Rome, Region VI, on the Via 22 Settembre under the Caserna dei Corazzieri: *EAA,* Supplement (1970), p. 662, see under "Roma, Reg. VI" (Coarelli); W. von Sydow, *AA* (1973): 554–555. Compare also the remains of a *nymphaeum* found under the Bibliotheca Hertziana in Rome: W. von Sydow, ibid., pp. 557ff.; Sear, *Roman Wall and Vault Mosaics,* pp. 79 and 81.

126. *PPM,* vol. 4, pp. 613ff., 621ff.; Neuerburg, "L'architettura delle fontane," pp. 121ff., nos. 25 and 16; Sear, *Roman Wall and Vault Mosaics,* pp. 73 and 75. For a recent study of the House of the Small Fountain see Thomas Fröhlich, *Casa della Fontana piccola VI 8, 23.24* (Munich: 1996).

127. Staub-Gierow, *Casa del Granduca VII 4, 56. Casa dei Capitelli figurati VII 4, 57* (Munich: 1994); Neuerburg, "L'architettura delle fontane," pp. 129–130, no. 32 and fig. 115; Schefold, *Die Wände Pompejis*, pp. 185–186; Sear, *Roman Wall and Vault Mosaics*, p. 67.

128. W. Erhardt, *La Casa dell'Orso VII 2, 44–46* (Munich: 1988); Neuerburg, "L'architettura delle fontane," pp. 128–129, no. 31 and fig. 117; Schefold, *Die Wände Pompejis*, pp. 174–175; Maiuri, *L'ultima fase di Pompei*, p. 126; Sear, *Roman Wall and Vault Mosaics*, p. 77.

129. Schefold, *RM*, 60/61 (1953–54): 117–118, and *Vergessenes Pompeji*, pp. 146–147. There is a list of *paradeisoi* and Nilotic scenes in the index of Schefold, *Die Wände Pompejis*, and a list of "topia" paintings in Grimal, *Les jardins romains*, pp. 457ff. Compare further D. Michel, *La Casa dei Cei* (Munich: 1990), and M. T. Andreae, "Tiermegalographien in pompeianischen Gärten," *Rivista di Studi Pompeiani*, 4 (1990): 45–124.

130. Compare note 126. The two engravings reproduced in figs. 104 and 105 are taken from W. Gell, *Pompeiana* (London: 1832), vol. 1, p. 194, plate 53, and vol. 2, p. 4, plate 56. Concerning the House of the Large Fountain Gell observes, "The high wall was, at the time of its excavation, perfect; and this drawing is probably now the only record of its existence, the author having been fortunate enough to copy it before the painting fell," p. 125.

131. Schefold, *Die Wände Pompejis*, pp. 194–195, and *Vergessenes Pompeji*, fig. 151.2.

132. D. Michel, *La Casa dei Cei* (Munich: 1990); Spinazzola, *Pompei alla luce degli scavi nuovi*, vol. 1, pp. 257ff.; Schefold, *Die Wände Pompejis*, pp. 26ff.; La Rocca et al., *Guida archeologica di Pompei*, pp. 189ff., with a ground plan and color plate of the *paradeisos*.

133. For a recent interpretation of this much discussed passage, see Grimal, *Les jardins romains*, pp. 92–93; R. Ling, *JRS*, 67 (1977): 1ff.

134. *PPM*, vol. 4, p. 168; Grimal, *Les jardins romains*, p. 485, plate 3.2; Tran Tam Tinh, *Essai sur le culte d'Isis a Pompéi* (Paris: 1964), p. 51.

135. See, for example, Varro, *Res rusticae* 3.13.2–3; Appian, *Bell. civ.* 1.104 (Sulla).

136. *RE*, vol. 7 (1912), col. 838, see under "Gartenbau" (Olek); *EAA*, vol. 3 (1960), p. 883, see under "giardino" (L. Guerrini); Grimal, *Les jardins romains*, pp. 79ff.; J. Borchhardt, *Istanbuler Mitteilungen*, 18 (1968): 166ff.; J. Aymard, *Essai sur les chasses romaines des origines à la fin du siècle des Antonins (Cynegetica)* (Paris: 1951).

137. Vatican, Museo Chiaramonti. Amelung, *Vat. Cat.*, vol. 1, pp. 679–680, no. 550 and plate 73; Helbig, *Führer durch die öffentlichen Sammlungen*, vol. 1, p. 252, no. 327 (E. Simon); H. Wrede, *Die spätantike Hermengalerie von Welschbillig*, p. 139, plate 78.1.

138. *PPM*, vol. 5, pp. 264–307. The fresco of Orpheus has suffered considerable dam-

age since its discovery. See E. Presuhn, *Die pompejanischen Wanddekorationen* (Leipzig: 1882), plate 23 (the same fresco appears here in plate 14, with contemporary tints!); P. Hermann, *Denkmäler der Malerei des Altertums,* vol. 2, pp. 61ff., fig 21, and plate 240; Schefold, *Die Wände Pompejis,* p. 132. The same theme together with a large painting of a hunt (*PPM,* vol. 5, p. 106) is depicted on the terrace wall at the miniature villa (II 2.2–5). Schefold, ibid., p. 53.

139. "At Quintus Hortensius's place near Laurentum . . . there was a forest which covered, he said, more than fifty *iugera;* it was enclosed with a wall and he called it, not a warren, but a game-preserve. In it was a high spot where was spread the table at which we were dining, to which he bade Orpheus be called. When he appeared with his robe and harp, and was bidden to sing, he blew a horn; whereupon there poured around us such a crowd of stags, boars, and other animals that it seemed to me to be no less attractive a sight than when the hunts of the aediles take place in the Circus Maximus," Varro, *Res rusticae* 3.13.2–3, trans. W. D. Hooper, Loeb Classical Library.

140. Andreae, "Tiermegalographien." The individual animal types are perhaps derived in the last analysis from Hellenistic models, presumably small in format *(pinakes?).* The well-known mosaics from Hadrian's Villa could represent a modest reflection of them (compare Helbig, *Führer durch die öffentlichen Sammlungen,* vol. 1, pp. 106 and 203 [Parlasca]).

141. Schefold, *Die Wände Pompejis,* pp. 180ff.; La Rocca et al., *Guida archeologica di Pompei,* p. 268.

142. *PPM,* vol. 5, pp. 1069–1098; Schefold, *Die Wände Pompejis,* p. 89.

143. For more on the popularity of travel to Egypt and the opulent lifestyle of Alexandria and its surroundings, see L. Friedländer, *Darstellungen aus der Sittengeschichte Roms,* 10th ed. (1922), pp. 423ff.

144. Suet. *Nero* 31, quoted from *Lives of the Caesars,* trans. J. C. Rolfe, Loeb Classical Library, vol. 2, p. 137: "in the grounds of the Golden House there was also a pond, surrounded with buildings representing cities, as well as fields, vineyards, meadows with livestock, and woods with wild animals of all kinds"; compare Tacitus, *Annales* XV 42.

145. Overbeck and Mau, *Pompeji,* p. 355; Mau, *Pompeji in Leben und Kunst,* p. 39, fig. 6; Schefold, *RM,* 60/61 (1953–54): 117–118, plate 50.2, and *Die Wände Pompejis,* p. 277 (in the style of the Vespasianic era); Neuerburg, "L'architettura delle fontane," pp. 133–134 (with bibliography) and fig. 116; Sear, *Roman Wall and Vault Mosaics,* p. 84.

146. A similar frieze, also unrelated to the rest of the wall decoration scheme, can even be found at the House of the Vettii: see Schefold, *Vergessenes Pompeji,* fig. 138.

147. K. Schefold, *Pompejanische Malerei,* pp. 32ff. (with earlier literature and ancient

sources listed on p. 180, note 32), and *La peinture pompéienne,* Coll. Latomus, vol. 108 (1972), pp. 50ff.; H. Jucker, *Vom Verhältnis der Römer zur bildenden Kunst,* pp. 29 and 35–36.

148. Hermann, *Denkmäler der Malerei,* vol. 1, pp. 29ff. and plates 20–48. The earlier literature is cited by Schefold, *Die Wände Pompejis,* p. 139; Kraus and von Matt, *Lebendiges Pompeji,* pp. 70ff.; La Rocca et al., *Guida archeologica di Pompei,* pp. 269ff.; *PPM,* vol. 5, pp. 468–572. For more on the man presumed to be the last owner, A. Vettius Conviva, see Andreau, *Les Affaires de Monsieur Jucundus,* pp. 172, 190, 194, 205, 267, 277, and Castrén, *Ordo populusque,* pp. 239–240. Given all that has been learned about the Augustales, it can be viewed as certain that the Augustalis A. Vettius Conviva came from a family of freedmen. As we know, they were at the top of the "second" local oligarchy. For the "program" of the *pinacothecae* see T. Wirth, "Zum Bildprogramm der Räume n und p in der Casa dei Vettii," *RM,* 90 (1983): 449–455; for the sculpture garden see Döhl, *Plastik aus Pompeji.*

149. *PPM,* vol. 4, pp. 527–608. Compare N. Wood, *The House of the Tragic Poet: A Reconstruction* (London: 1996); B. Bergmann, in *Art Bulletin,* 76 (1994): 225–256.

150. Schefold, *Vergessenes Pompeji,* pp. 186ff.

151. Ibid., plate 138.

152. For more on these symptoms of "decay," see O. Elia, *NSc* (1934): 278ff.; Schefold, *RM,* 60/61 (1953–54): 113ff.

153. Compare the House of Meleager (VI 9.2), in La Rocca et al., *Guida archeologica di Pompei,* pp. 268–269; the House of the Citharist (I 4.5.25.28), ibid., p. 167, and Döhl, *Plastik aus Pompeji,* pp. 77ff.; and some of the terrace houses in the theater quarter, Noack and Lehmann-Hartleben, *Baugeschichtliche Untersuchungen,* pp. 224–225.

154. Compare Seneca, *Naturales Quaestiones* VI 1.1. For the economic consequences of the earthquake, see J. Andreau, "Le tremblement de terre de Pompéi," pp. 369ff.

155. Castrén, *Ordo populusque,* p. 121. Castrén's conclusions, to which I refer here, must now be revised in part as proposed by Mouritsen in *Elections, Magistrates and Municipal Elite,* and "Order and Disorder in Late Pompeian Politics," in *Les Élites municipales de l'Italie péninsulaire des Gracques à Néron. Colloquium Clermont-Ferrand 1991* (Naples and Rome: 1996), pp.139–144; and also by W. Jongman, *The Economy and Society of Pompeii,* Dutch Monographs on Ancient History and Archaeology, 4 (Amsterdam: 1988).

156. See Andreau, "Le tremblement de terre de Pompéi," and *Les affaires de Monsieur Jucundus,* pp. 163ff.

157. Consider also the case of the wine merchant who owned the House of the Moralist and the tavern in the "miniature villa." See Andreau, *Les affaires de*

Monsieur Jucundus, pp. 223ff., for more on the social and economic situation of this group in Pompeii.

158. See Andreau, ibid., passim.

159. G. Spano, *NSc* (1910): 400, fig. 11 (plan), and 402 (inscription); M. Della Corte, *Memoire dell'Accademia di archeologia di Napoli,* 2, 2 (1913): 185–188 (dated to the reign of Vespasian); G. Spano, *MemAccLinc,* 7, series 3 (1943): 237–315; J.-M. Dentzer, *MEFRA,* 74 (1962): 533–594; V. Weber, *Historia,* 18 (1969): 377–380 (before 62, but after Claudius [coins]); Castrén, *Ordo populusque,* p. 239, no. 453.1 (aedile 75/76, dies in office [?]); H. Mielsch, *RM,* Ergänzungsheft 21 (1975), pp. 55–56, and p. 139, cat. no. 50, plates 44–45 (from the reign of Vespasian).

All the archeological evidence clearly suggests an earlier date, as Weber surmises. V. Kockel assumes the construction occurred in two phases, a phenomenon he has observed at graves outside the Herculaneum Gate. In my view, the tomb's affinity with the late domestic taste comprehensively excludes any allegorical interpretation with supposed allusions to the afterlife.

160. There is a color plate of the silverware in R. Bianchi-Bandinelli, *Roma: L'arte romana nel centro del potere* (Rome: 1969), p. 42.

161. Mouritsen, *Elections, Magistrates and Municipal Elite;* "A Note on Pompeian Epigraphy and Social Structure," *Classica et Mediaevalia,* 41 (1990): 131–149; and "Order and Disorder in Late Pompeian Politics." See also Zevi, "Pompei della città sannitica alla colonia sillana."

162. Such conclusions are frequently drawn, and are supposedly based on the conclusions of Grimal in *Les jardins romains.* However, Grimal himself takes a quite different view and has attached great importance to the influence of Hellenism.

163. A. Maiuri, *I nuovi scavi di Ercolano,* vol. 1 (Rome: 1958).

164. For cepotaphs see the entry under "cepotaphium" by Samter in *RE,* vol. 3 (Rome: 1899), col. 1966; J. M. C. Toynbee, *Death and Burial in the Roman World* (London: 1971), with a bibliography; H. Wrede, *RM,* 78 (1971): 127. Compare also H. Wrede, *Consecratio in formam deorum* (Mainz: 1981); W. F. Jashemski, *Classical Journal,* 66 (1970): 97ff. Compare further the statuettes mentioned in note 105 above from the cemeteries in Ostia. A collection of bucolic statues also belonged to the tomb of the Haterii: see A. Giuliano, *MemAccLinc,* 8, series 13, 6 (1968): plate 1 and fig. 21. Vistas of luxurious gardens continued to play a role in later tombs as well: see H. Wrede, *Die spätantike Hermengalerie von Welschbillig,* pp. 132–133, plates 76 and 77.

The continued use of elements from villas in later domestic architecture would be worth investigating; one only has to think of the well-preserved houses at Bulla Regia with their peristyles and fountains and corresponding *triclinia* and spots for rest and recreation: see A. Beschaouch, *Les ruines de Bulla Regia* (Rome:

1977). For the small *piscina* at the villa belonging to the Venantii family, with the inscription *Venantiorum Baiae,* see ibid., 78, fig. 74.

165. P. Veyne, *Annales: Économies, sociétés, civilisations,* 16 (1961): 213ff. See also the section "The Villa and Domestic Taste in the Empire" in chapter 1. I now believe that my description in this section tends to interpret the phenomenon too narrowly as the taste of freedmen.

166. Andreau, *Les affaires de Monsieur Jucundus,* pp. 170ff.

167. The need to distinguish between Rome and the provinces, and especially between imperial freedmen and others, is well known. For more on the view taken of themselves by the imperial *liberti,* who served as officials in the administration of the Empire, see the thoughtful essay by G. Lotito, *DArch,* 8 (1974/75): 275ff. That the taste and values of the Pompeians were not unknown to broad segments of the population of Rome is in my view demonstrated by the iconography of numerous Flavian marble urns: F. Sinn, *Stadtrömische Marmorurnen* (Mainz: 1987).

168. Cf. K. M. Coleman, ed., *Statius Silvae IV* (Oxford: 1988); H. Cancik, *Untersuchungen zur lyrischen Kunst des P. Papinius Statius,* Spudasmata, 13 (1965): 65ff. and 100ff.

169. Compare V. M. Strocka, ed., *Die Regierungszeit des Kaisers Claudius (41–54 n. Chr.): Umbruch oder Episode?* (Mainz: 1994).

Illustration
Credits

Figures

Alinari: 1, 9, 14, 34, 44, 76, 80, 91, 96

Anderson: 20, 83, 90, 94, 109

B. Andreae and H. Kyrieleis, eds., *Neue Forschungen in Pompeji* (Recklinghausen: 1975): 2

O. Brendel, *Introduzione all'arte romana* (Turin: 1982): 110

A. Degrassi, *Imagines* (Berlin: 1965): 26

H. Eschebach, *Antike Welt,* 10 (1979): 62

H. Eschebach, *Pompeji* (Leipzig: 1978): 27, 29, 58

H. Eschebach, *Die Stabianer Thermen* (Berlin: 1979): 16

H. Eschebach, *Die städtebauliche Entwicklung des antiken Pompeji, RM,* Ergänzungsheft 21: 11, 12, 25, 92

L. Eschebach: 17

Fotocielo: 28

W. Gell, *Pompejana* (London: 1832): 98, 104, 105

German Archeological Institute, Rome; InstNegRom: 3, 6, 7, 35, 39, 40, 50, 54, 93, 102, 106, 108

R. Graefe, *Vela Erunt* (Mainz: 1979): 56

H. Heinrich: 47

A. Hoffmann: 5, 8

Istituto Centrale per il Catalogo e la Documentazione: 31, 85

V. Kockel, *Die Grabbauten vor dem Herculaner Tor* (Mainz: 1983): 64, 65, 111, 112, 113

F. Krischen, *Die griechische Stadt* (Berlin: 1938): 4

E. La Rocca and M. and A. de Vos, *Pompeji* (Bergisch Gladbach: 1979): 35, 55, 73, 100

A. Maiuri, *NSc*, 17 (1939): 59, 60

A. Maiuri, *Pompei* (Naples: 1956): 46, 49, 61

A. Maiuri, *L'ultima fase edilizia di Pompei* (Rome: 1942): 68

Mau, *Pompeji in Leben und Kunst*, 2nd ed. (Leipzig: 1908): 42

Mau, *RM*, 11 (1896): 51, 67

F. Mazois, *Les ruines de Pompéi dessinées et mésurées*, vol. 3 (Paris: 1838): 18, 41, 45, 63; vol. 4: 10, 32

MemAmAc, 5 (1925): 23

Museum für Abgüsse Klassischer Bildwerke, Munich: 38, 43, 97

I. Nielsen, *Thermae et Balnea*, vol. 2 (Copenhagen: 1991): 70

F. Noack and K. Lehmann-Hartleben, *Baugeschichtliche Untersuchungen am Stadtrand von Pompeji* (Berlin and Leipzig: 1936): 71, 72

K. Ohr, *Die Basilika in Pompeji* (Berlin: 1991): 21

J. Overbeck and A. Mau, *Pompeji*, 4th ed. (Leipzig: 1884): 13, 99

Real Museo Borbonico (Naples: 1824–1857): 81, 95

D. Scagliarini Corlaita, *Studi sull'arco onorario romano* (Rimini: 1977): 52

M. Schede, *Die Ruinen von Priene* (Berlin: 1960): 22

R. Senff: 57

P. Soprano, *Pompeiana* (Naples: 1950): 101

V. Spinazzola, *Pompei alla luce degli scavi nuovi di via dell'Abbondanza* (Rome: 1953): 69, 74, 77, 79, 86, 87, 88

K. Stemmer: 103

V. Tran Tam Tinh, *Le culte d'Isis à Pompei* (Paris: 1964): 75, 78

Vatican, Museo Chiaramonti: 107

J. B. Ward-Perkins, in *Pompei AD 79*, exhibition catalogue (London: 1976): 89

C. Weichhardt, *Pompei vor der Zerstörung* (Munich-Leipzig: 1896): 15, 36, 53

W. Zahn, *Die schönsten Ornamente* (Berlin: 1828): 84

P. Zanker, *The Power of Images* (Ann Arbor: 1988): 48

P. Zanker and M. Pfanner: 19, 37

P. Zanker and von Harsdorf: 24, 30, 66

F. Zevi, ed., *Pompei 79: Raccolta di studi per il decimonono centenario dell'eruzione Vesuviana*, 2nd ed. (Naples: 1984): 40, 54a

Color plates

B. and D. R. Brothwell, *Manna und Hirse* (Mainz: 1994): 2

M. Carroll-Spillecke, *Der Garten von der antike bis zum Mittelalter* (Mainz: 1992): 9

V. Kockel: 3.1, 4, 5, 8.1, 12, 15, 16

F. P. Maulucci, *Pompei* (Naples: 1987): 3.2

PPM, 4, 1: 11.2, 14.1

E. Preshuhn, *Pompeji: Die neuesten Ausgrabungen von 1874–1881* (Leipzig: 1882): 14.2

P. Quignard, *Le sexe et l'effroi* (1994): 1

P. Zanker: 7, 8.2, 10.1 and 2, 11.1, 13

F. Zevi, ed., *Pompei* (Naples: 1991), vol. 1: 6

Index

Greek influence. See Hellenistic influence

Gymnasium, 5, 18, 44–49; peristyle, 47–48; Stabian baths and, 49–51

Hadrian's Villa, 147, 161

Hellenistic influence: democratic equality and townscapes, 5–6; social function of houses, 13–14; reception rooms, 14; villas and, 16–17, 136–141; Oscans and, 32; public structures and, 32; size of houses, 35; gymnasium and, 46, 47; landscapes and, 137, 143

Herculaneum, 30, 109, 166, 200

Herculaneum Gate, 74, 76, 93, 122, 123, 143, 162

Herms, 156, 169, 178

Hoffmann, A., 72

Holconius Celer, M., 107, 109

Holconius Rufus, M., 79, 82, 107, 109–113, 118

Hortensius, 152

Hortensius Hortalis, Q., 187

House of the Amazons, 186

House of the Ancient Hunt, 187, 188

House of Apolline, 156–160, 193, 195

House of the Bear, 182, 196, 197

House of the Black Anchor, 160, 193, 195

House of the Bull, 181

House of Caecilius Iucundus, 105, 106

House of Castor and Pollux, 165

House of the Ceii, 184, 186, 196, 197

House of the Centenarian, 189, 190, 197

House of the Citharist, 165

House of Cornelius Tages (Ephebe), 177–180, 198

House of the Cryptoporticus, 74, 145

House of the Ephebe, 177–180, 186, 187–188

House of the Epigrams, 168

House of Fabius Rufus, 74, 75

House of the Faun, 34–37, 59, 60, 74, 75, 194, 197; peristyle courtyards, 34, 41, 142–143; additions to, 37–38; mosaics, 39–40; atrium, 40, 41; villas, influence on, 142–143

House of the Figured Capitals, 37, 38, 39

House of the Golden Cupids, 165, 168–172, 193, 195

House of the Grand Duke, 181–182, 196, 197

House of Julia Felix, 180

House of the Labyrinth, 143, 194

House of the Large Fountain, 181, 184, 186, 196

House of the Little Fountain, 181, 183, 184

House of Loreius Tiburtinus, 170, 171, 188, 193, 195; floor plan, 145–147; dining areas, 146, 147; peristyle, 146–147; aediculae, 147, 148, 152, 153; *euripus,* 147, 150–156; proportions, 147–148, 154–156, 162; friezes, 148–149; shrine, 149–150; statuary, 150–152

House of M. Lucretius, 172–174, 196

House of Menander, 145, 165, 193, 194

House of the Moralist, 163–166, 193, 195

House of Orpheus, 187

House of Pansa, 165

House of Romulus and Remus, 184, 185

House of Sallust, 166–168, 175, 177, 178, 180, 197

House of the Tragic Poet, 191

House of the Trojan Shrine, 74

House of the Vetii, 191, 192

Houses: Greek, 5, 13–14; social status and, 10, 12–14, 19; decoration, 10–11; ground plans, 10–12, 193–197; residents and visitors, 10–12; values and, 14–15; size of, 34–35, 43; of Roman colonists, 72; self-promotion in, 72–77; terrace houses, 73, 74. *See also* Identity; Villas; *individual houses*

Identity, 9–10, 14–15; social status and, 10, 12–14, 19; visitors and, 10–12; villa imitation and, 19–20, 140; cultural self-definition and, 21–24, 74–75, 150, 192–203; architecture and, 192–193

Insula, 34, 41

Insula Occidentalis, 74, 75, 143, 193

Interior decor, 13; discourse of, 14–15; associational function, 140, 190. *See also* Pictorial decoration; Statues

Juventus (della Corte), 46–47

Kockel, V., 122

Kydias, 152

Index

Self-Romanization, 59–60

Senate, 7, 24

Seneca, 188

Shops, 41–42

Shrines, 8, 162; private, 52–53; in theater quarter, 52–53; reproductions, 146, 147; miniature, 147, 149–150

Silvaea (Statius), 202

Slaves, 32, 76

Social life: baths and, 8; villas and, 11, 18–19, 138–139; spatial arrangement and, 12–14; privacy and, 18–19

Social status, 10, 12–14, 19

Social War, 61, 140

Sorrento Peninsula, 143

Spectacula. See Amphitheater

Sperlonga, 175

Stabian baths. See Baths: Stabian

Statius, 202

Statues, 127–129; self-promotion and, 4, 7, 75–77, 122–124; to imperial family, 9, 85, 102–104, 109; Hellenistic influence on, 17, 18, 151–152, 169–172; in Priene, 58; in Temple of Fortuna Augusta, 84–85; in *macellum,* 85, 88–89, 105; in forum, 86; in Sanctuary of the Lares, 87, 88; in Eumachia Building, 94–95; self-promotion and, 97–101; equestrian, 102–103; in forum, 102–106; honorific monuments, 102–107, 110–112; in villas, 139; miniature, 150–152, 169, 172; painted, 167, 178–179; in gardens, 168–174; *ephebos,* 178

Streets, 126

Sulla, Publius Cornelius, 61–62, 64, 66, 68, 70, 79

Summer rooms, 159–160, 166

Summi viri, 93–95, 104

Sundials, 79–80, 117

Surdinus, 104

Symbolism: in Greek cities, 5–6; in Roman villas, 17–19, 20

Tabernae, 57

Tablina, 146, 168, 181

Taste, strategies for research, 15–16

Tempietto, 52

Temple of Apollo, 53, 59, 65, 66, 78–81, 117, 126

Temple of Apollo (Rome), 78–79

Temple of Athena (Priene), 58–59

Temple of Fortuna Augusta, 82–85, 103, 106

Temple of Isis, 52–53, 126–127

Temple of Venus, 64–65, 78–79, 126

Temple of Vespasian, 87–91, 96, 130, 132

Temple of Zeus Meilichios (Asclepius), 45, 52–53, 127–128

Temples: Greek, 5, 6–7; Roman, 6–7; Doric temple, 31, 44, 45, 51; roof tiles, 52; to Jupiter, 53–55, 59; Augustan age and, 78–79

Terrace houses, 73, 74, 141, 144–145, 147, 148

Theater, 4, 5, 7, 8; performances, 44, 110; roofed, 65–68, 117; crypta and, 107–108, 113; seating by rank in, 107–114; elaborateness of, 112–113

Theater quarter: Delos, 35; performances, 44; gymnasium, 44–47; peristyles, 47–48, 51; baths, 49–51; propylon, 51–52; shrines, 52–53; terrace houses in, 141, 144–145

Tivoli, 60, 138

Tombs, benches at, 122–124. *See also* Funerary monuments

Town council, 197–198

Townscapes, 3; successive, 3–5; Greek, 5–6; Roman, 6–8; spatial arrangements, 7; subdivisions, 8; meeting spots, 9; effect on inhabitants, 28

Triangular Forum, 31, 45, 48

Triclinia, 146–148, 150, 161, 165, 174–181

Trimalchio, 201–202

Troy Games, 114

Tryphe, 18

Tullius, M., 82–84, 118

Tusculum, 152

Urban space. See Public space; Townscapes

Values, 14–15, 200; abstraction and, 22; *luxuria* and, 23, 37; marble and, 117

Varro, 152, 154, 187

REVEALING ANTIQUITY

G. W. Bowersock, General Editor